Pilots to Presidents

BRITISH COLUMBIA AVIATION LEADERS AND PIONEERS

1930-1960

Peter Corley-Smith

D1737848

Sono Nis Press • Victoria, BC • 2001

Canadian Cataloguing in Publication Data

Corley-Smith, Peter, 1923-
  Pilots to presidents

  Includes bibliographical references.
  ISBN 1-55039-116-X

  1. Aeronautics—British Columbia—Biography. 2. Aeronautics—
British Columbia—History. I. Title.
TL523.C676 2001   629.13'092'2711   C2001-910113-9

Sono Nis Press gratefully acknowledges the support of the Canada
Council for the Arts and the Province of British Columbia, through the
British Columbia Arts Council.

Cover design by Jim Brennan

Published by
Sono Nis Press
PO Box 5550, Stn. B
Victoria, BC V8R 6S4

Telephone: (250) 598-7807
Toll Free: 1-800-370-5228

sononis@islandnet.com
http://www.islandnet.com/sononis/

Printed and bound in Canada by Morriss Printing Company Ltd.

*In memory of
Martin Lynch,
who was not only a superb editor
but a human encyclopedia;
consequently, every manuscript
sent for his insightful review
came back generously enhanced.*

*Those who were
fortunate enough to receive his
help
will not soon forget him.*

Five distinguished aviation leaders photographed in their tuxedos after an International Air Transport Association dinner at Government House in Victoria, *c.* 1956. *Left to right*: Russ Baker, President, Pacific Western Airlines; Carl Agar, Director and co-founder of Okanagan Helicopters Limited; Grant McConachie, President, Canadian Pacific Air Lines; Don MacLaren, Trans-Canada Airlines; Hon. F. M. Ross, Lieutenant-Governor of British Columbia; Gordon MacGregor, President, Trans-Canada Airlines.

Acknowledgements

As ALWAYS, the research for this book has involved much tedious and time-consuming grubbing for documents, articles, newspaper reports and photographs. Fortunately, this drudgery is more than compensated for by the many interesting people one meets and talks to. Most seem a little bemused that they are considered worthy of mention as historical figures; some, on the other hand, clearly regard it as long overdue. In either case, I have found to my relief that nearly all hold approximately the same opinions—though with differing emphasis—about the leaders I have attempted to portray here.

So many people have helped me over the past several years that it is difficult to come up with a list short enough to be acceptable, but not so short as to omit people deserving acknowledgement. If it turns out that I have done so, it is purely through inadvertence. A sincere thank you to the following, who have helped me along the way:

Jack Baker, Madge Baker, Gordon Ballentine, Mansell Barron, Eleanore Begg, Roy Begg, Helen Bekering-Vinkers, Barney Bent, Stan Bridcut, Gordon Cameron, Robert Cameron, Eric Cowden, the late Ted Cressy, Tim Dubé, Charles Estlin, Dick Fisher, Bruce Gowans, Eric Hallam, Ross Herrington, Sheldon Luck, Fred Hotson, the late Maurice McGregor, Bill and Joan McLeod, the late Ken Molson, Nina Morrison, Curly Nairn, Doris and Herman Peterson, Robert Petite, Jack Petley, Hazel Poole, Lloyd Ryder, Lyman Sands, Jack Schofield, Howard Smiley, Jim Spilsbury, Lynne Stonier-Newman and George Williamson.

Among the many institutions that have helped me find my way through its collections, I am first of all grateful to the one in which I have the privilege to be a Research Associate: the Royal British Columbia Museum, Victoria (RBCM). As well, I have been helped by the following institutions: Canadian Broadcasting Corporation; British Columbia Archives and Records Service, Victoria (which changes its name so often it is difficult to keep abreast of the latest one); British Columbia Legislative Library, Victoria; British Columbia Ministry of Forests Library, Victoria; City of Vancouver Archives; Maritime Museum, Vancouver; City of Victoria Archives; Maritime Museum of British Columbia, Victoria; Vancouver Public Library; University of Victoria Library;

National Museums of Canada, Ottawa; National Archives of Canada, Ottawa; Canada's Aviation Hall of Fame, Wetaskiwin, Alberta; Manitoba Archives, Winnipeg; Canadian Pacific Railway Corporate Archives, Montreal; Yukon Archives, Whitehorse; Science Museum, London, UK; Richmond Museum-Archives; David Thompson Library, Nelson; Nelson Museum; Nicola Valley Museum-Archives, Merritt; Kootenay Lake Historical Society Archives, Kaslo; Nakusp Museum; Creston Valley Museum; R. N. (Reg) Atkinson Museum, Penticton; Kelowna Centennial Museum; Orchard Industry Museum, Kelowna; Greater Vernon Museum-Archives; Atlin Historical Museum; Boundary Museum, Grand Forks; Revelstoke Museum; Cowichan Lake Museum, Duncan; Railway Museum, Cranbrook; Rossland Mining Museum; Consolidated Mining and Smelting (COMINCO), Trail; Fraser-Fort George Regional Museum, Prince George; Kitimat Centennial Museum; Dawson Creek Station Museum; Hudson's Hope Museum; Bulkley Valley Museum, Smithers; North Peace Museum, Fort St. John; Whistler Museum; Zeballos Museum; Pemberton Museum; the US Air Force Historical Research Agency, Maxwell AFB, Alabama—all have been generous with their help. Particular thanks to archivists Andrew Geider, Canadian Airlines International Archives; Tim Dubé and Peter Robertson, National Archives of Canada; and Jennifer Romanko, curator of Canada's Aviation Hall of Fame.

I owe much to my friends and colleagues: Bob Turner for years of help with all aspects from research to perceptive editing advice; to Dave Parker, Bob Griffin, Jim Wardrop, Robin Patterson, Terry Eade, Phil Nott and Tina Strange for consistent help and support when needed—which in my case is frequently.

As well, just a phone call away, I have had access to the most user-friendly encyclopedia I have come across. It resides in the mind of Martin Lynch, long-time editor of the editorial page and business columnist for the Toronto *Globe and Mail*. He can usually answer my question from memory; if not, he turns to his own enviable reference library; on the rare occasions when that fails, he always knows someone with the answer. In addition, he is a superbly competent editor when it comes, not only to content, but to style, spelling, grammar, consistency and ambiguity. What more could one ask?

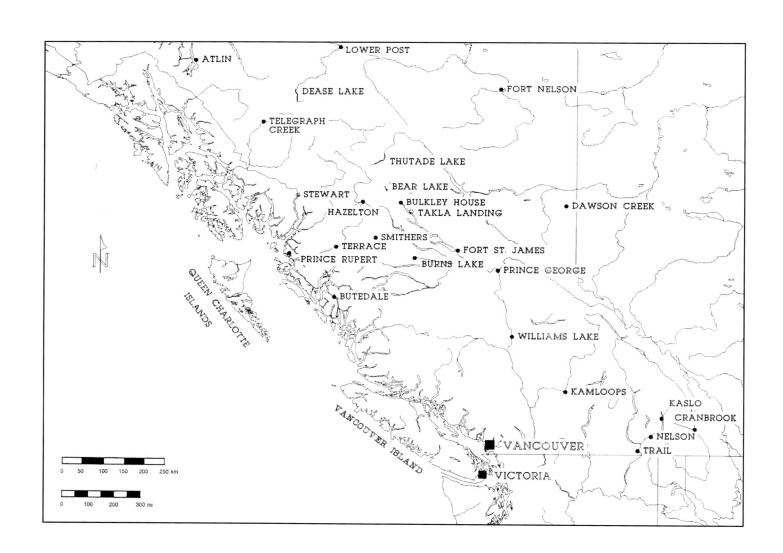

ATLIN

LOWER POST

DEASE LAKE

FORT NELSON

TELEGRAPH
CREEK

THUTADE LAKE

BEAR LAKE

STEWART

BULKLEY HOUSE

DAWSON CREEK

HAZELTON

TAKLA LANDING

SMITHERS

TERRACE

FORT ST. JAMES

PRINCE RUPERT

BURNS LAKE

PRINCE GEORGE

BUTEDALE

QUEEN CHARLOTTE
ISLANDS

WILLIAMS LAKE

KAMLOOPS

KASLO
CRANBROOK

VANCOUVER ISLAND

NELSON

VANCOUVER

TRAIL

VICTORIA

0   50   100   150   200   250 km

0   100   200   300 mi

Contents

Preface

COMMERCIAL AVIATION in British Columbia was a well-established and critically important industry by the Depression years of the 1930s. Bush pilots had expanded services to nearly all parts of the province and scheduled services, although still limited, were running in the Victoria-Vancouver-Seattle region along with some airmail operations. Moreover, aircraft were being used increasingly in fisheries and forestry for patrols, inventory and survey.

But by the mid-1930s many changes were occurring in the industry. Aircraft were greatly improved in range and speed, commercial possibilities were expanding and larger companies and governments were becoming more and more involved in shaping the future of aviation in western Canada. A transition was beginning that would see the leadership role change from a time when barnstorming and bush pilots showed what was possible to an era when ability in the corporate sphere was often more important than flying skills. A new generation of aviation leaders emerged, quite different from their predecessors, who would take BC aviation into the post-war era of jet travel and the everyday use of aviation by the general population.

This transition period and the leadership that emerged present an interesting challenge for the aviation historian. In their penetrating examination of the reign of France's "Sun King," The Age of Louis XIV, historians Will and Ariel Durant suggest, in an early chapter, that "the historian, like the journalist, tends to lose the normal background of an age in the dramatic foreground of his picture, for he knows that his readers will cherish the exceptional and will wish to personify processes and events." The Durants promptly proceed to demonstrate, with the depth and scope of their research and the intelligence of their interpretations, that they have not fallen into this trap.

Fortunately, whereas journalists are bound by relatively short and immutable deadlines, and so tend particularly to adopt the course of dramatic personification—instant heroes or instant villains—historians are not. They can, unless they have delusions of financial rewards, set their own deadlines and at least attempt to emulate the Durant partnership. In any case, the hope is to make the discoveries in research that allow them to arrive at legitimate overall interpretations (bearing in mind philosopher Friedrich Nietzsche's admonition: "There are no facts, only interpretations"), which are as close as we can hope to get to historical truths.

In this book, by choosing to write about and analyze the province's aviation leaders, the problem of personification comes to the fore because some reputations have been enviably framed by what a fellow aviation historian calls "gee-whiz" journalism. This is particularly true of pilots whose early careers were relatively unremarkable but who later went on to fame as presidents of leading airlines. Aviation, especially bush flying, easily breeds superlatives: flight is exciting and exhilarating; stories of heroism and adventure all naturally encourage exaggeration in their telling. Competence can quickly become dramatic daredevil heroism; routine become high adventure.

As well, there is the problem of defining leadership, because leadership has many manifestations. It may be a powerful politician deciding to found the nation's first airline: a person with enough clout to declare it a monopoly, and command of sufficient public funds to overcome early errors of judgement and ensure eventual success. It may be the first women to fly commercially on a regular basis. It may be a talented person of unusual charm and persuasiveness who enjoys that most precious of attributes: good luck; or it may be another equally competent person who has the great good fortune to team up, more or less simultaneously, with a wealthy mining promoter to provide financial support and a singularly gifted story-teller to promote his image to that of a legend.* Some choices are self-evident; others are bound to be arbitrary.

While it would be difficult to claim that women played a significant leadership role before 1960, female pioneers did emerge. Alys Bryant, for example, flew exhibition flights in BC as early as 1913; and the "Flying Seven," led by Margaret Fane, were flying over Vancouver in the mid-1930s. Fane later also flew, to a limited degree, as the first woman commercial pilot in BC. However, the inclusion of the early stewardesses as leaders seemed to me to be self-evident. They brought a whole new dimension to air travel. They provided moral support to nervous, mostly male passengers at a time when airline flying was not without danger. At a time when the role of most women was seen clearly as homemakers, they logged many hours with their crew colleagues in fog, rain, ice and snow over the dangerous mountains of British Columbia. While at first the workload was relatively light, later their task became more and more onerous: serving meals to larger numbers of passengers in less and less time and dealing with disorderly and often drunken ones. I felt their story

*My dictionary defines "Legend" as "an unverified story handed down from earlier times, especially one popularly believed to be historical"—and goes on to provide a usage note: "The words legend and legendary have come to be used in recent years to refer to any person or achievement whose fame promises to be particularly enduring, even if its renown is created more by the media than oral tradition."
—THE AMERICAN HERITAGE DICTIONARY OF THE ENGLISH LANGUAGE

ought to be included because they were leaders: the first women in Canada to fly commercially on a regular basis.

However, in the arena of bush flying shortly after the Second World War, the successful introduction of a brand new aviation innovation—the helicopter—took place and proved to be an almost instant success. This development produced three outstanding BC leaders: Carl Agar and Alf Stringer, who almost literally staked out the path of commercial helicopter development in BC and elsewhere; and Lynn Henson, who was the first Canadian woman to become president of an aviation company, Vancouver Island Helicopters Limited, after her husband Ted Henson was killed in an accident in 1957. None of the above have been included in this book because, in partnership with David N. Parker, we have written about them extensively elsewhere.

Our final candidate, Herman Peterson, belongs to a very different category. At no time did Peterson aspire to become the president of a large corporation; he was happy throughout his flying career with what he did so admirably: providing, for 25 years, a safe and reliable bush-flying service in the very remote northwest corner of British Columbia. His reputation among the aviation community was known from coast to coast; but more important to Peterson was the unmistakable respect and affection he enjoyed in the community he served for so long.

This is the third book in a series—the first was *Barnstorming to Bush Flying*, in which I narrated the province's aviation history from its beginning to 1930; and the second, *Bush Flying to Blind Flying*, which took the history to 1940. In both, the emphasis was on the overall record of aviation activities in the province, with the role of many early leaders highlighted. In this one, the emphasis is very much on examining and analyzing leadership roles, and it carries the story up to 1960. By this time, the pioneering era was at an end, aviation was well-established as an essential industry and the frontiers of flying had been pushed back beyond the mountains of British Columbia.

As with my previous books, this one deals solely with commercial fixed-wing operations and does not attempt to squeeze in aircraft construction or military aviation—both of which would require more than one book each for adequate coverage.

Unfortunately, only two of the five leaders involved were still alive and available for interviews when I researched this book—Jim Spilsbury and Herman Peterson. There were others, fortunately, who, if not actual leaders, were very influential. For example, Maurice McGregor, one of the first pilots to fly the scheduled service from Vancouver to Victoria for Canadian Airways, and later, the one from Vancouver to Seattle for TCA; Canada's Hall of Fame inductee Sheldon Luck; and Gordon Ballentine, who began his flying career with Don MacLaren's Pacific Airways in 1925—and a number of other experienced aviators too numerous to list here.

This history is not meant to debunk reputations but to provide a realistic assessment of those reputations and the unmistakable importance of all aviation pioneers' contributions to the development of aviation in British Columbia and Canada as a whole.

CONQUERING THE NORTH

Flying well over a million miles the Western Canada Airways has conquered the distances of the North and made possible its early development.

WESTERN CANADA AIRWAYS
LIMITED
HEAD OFFICE   **WINNIPEG**

Development Timeline of Principal Airlines

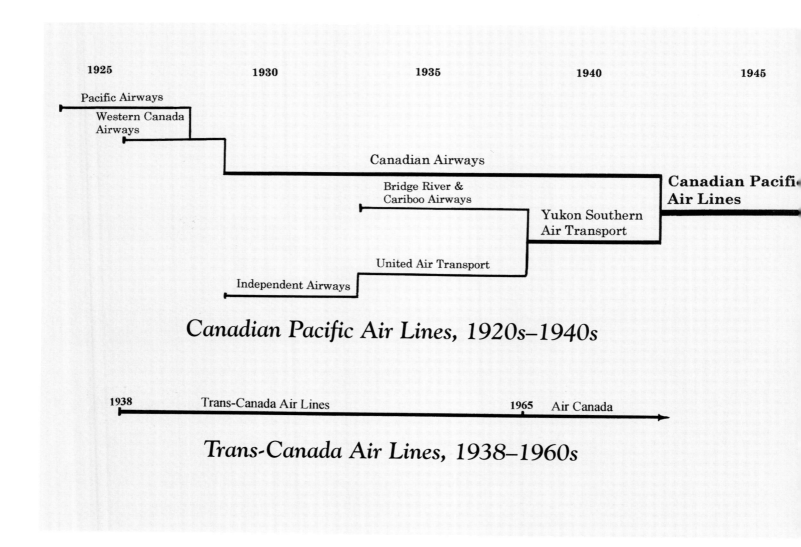

Canadian Pacific Air Lines, 1920s–1940s

Trans-Canada Air Lines, 1938–1960s

1945   1950   1955   1960

Central British Columbia Airways

Pacific Western Airlines

Queen Charlotte Airlines

Pacific Western Airlines, 1940s–1960s

Part One

COAST TO COAST—AT LONG LAST

Chapter One

C. D. Howe and the Creation of Trans-Canada Air Lines

"Unless Canada watches her step . . .
our American friends will control the routes to
Europe and Asia via Canada to the detriment
of Canadian and British interests."

COLONEL R. H. MULOCK

INEVITABLY, no sooner had the young Charles Lindbergh touched down in Paris in 1927 to complete his dramatic conquest of the Atlantic, than people began to dream of trans-Atlantic passenger flights. Some did more than dream about them. Knowing that sooner rather than later aircraft would be developed with both the capacity and range to accomplish this, they began to plan potential routes. Among the earliest was the redoubtable Juan Trippe of Pan American Airways, who quickly visualized the first stage as travelling from the United States, up through the Maritimes to Newfoundland: the obvious jumping-off point for trans-Atlantic service at the time.

Then, as now, Canadians were alarmed at the prospect of an American incursion and eventual appropriation of our airspace. Historian Shirley Render, in her meticulously researched study of Canadian aviation in the 1930s, *Double Cross*, records that, as early as 1931, Colonel R. H. Mulock, "one of the most decorated fliers of World War One," and "considered by many to be one of the top aviation authorities in Canada," was warning the Dominion government of this threat. "You will have noticed in the Press that Pan Am is starting an international air line between Boston and

Halifax. . . . Pan Am is really the effective tool of the United States Department of Commerce for the furtherance of American foreign trade . . . Unless Canada watches her step we might discover that our American friends are gradually in a position that they will control the routes to Europe and Asia via Canada to the detriment of Canadian and British interests."[1]

This threat persisted until Trans-Canada Air Lines was created in 1937; and, although the federal government and, in particular, its transport minister, C. D. Howe, are still frequently lauded as visionaries who gave Canada its first intercity, transcontinental airline, in reality, there was little that was visionary about it. During the last decades of the nineteenth and the first of the twentieth century, Canada only just fended off American railway intrusion. By 1936, the Americans, mainly Juan Trippe of Pan American Airways, were continuing sustained and vigorous attempts to at least gain a foothold in Canadian air space. Once again the existing government only just woke up in time to do the same with air transport, and there was little that was commendable about the way this was accomplished. On the contrary, it chose the wrong aircraft, apparently for the wrong reasons, and its later order to chop up the Avro Jetliner can only be described as bizarre.

In hindsight, Canadian aviation in the 1930s can be compared to a long, high, turbulent mountain pass with several sharp ridges to be overcome. As well, the climb up to this pass during the 1920s and 30s was an arduous one because, as historian R. E. G. Davies put it, "Of the world's leading nations, Canada was about the last to create a nationwide air transport system."[2] Historian Kenneth Molson was even more outspoken: "The action of the Conservative Government during the early 1930s had resulted, by 1936, in a lack of airline connections between major Canadian population centres. Coupled with the lack of an air policy, this situation was rapidly becoming a national disgrace."[3]

There is nothing mysterious about this: it was unfortunate but understandable. The vested interests in transportation at the time were the railway and steamship companies. In the 1880s, the government had sunk millions into the completion of the Canadian Pacific Railway (CPR), and in subsequent decades the company had provided millions more to improve the line and enhance its operational efficiency. In the 1920s, as J. R. K. Main, who later became Director of Civil Aviation, points out:

THE CANADA GREY GOOSE

The bird with the strongest, swiftest and most enduring flight. Chosen by the W.C.A. to be incorporated in their trade mark, a guarantee of delivery completed and the symbol of safe flying.

WRITE FOR FREE BOOKLET "THE BUSINESS OF FLYING"

WESTERN CANADA AIRWAYS
LIMITED
HEAD OFFICE   WINNIPEG

It is not altogether surprising that officialdom showed little interest in establishing intercity air service after World War I. Two transcontinental railway systems and several shorter ones had been pulled back from the brink of bankruptcy and consolidated into the Canadian National Railways System (CNR) in 1918. Intercity airline systems have almost inevitably looked to profitable mail contracts as the first reliable means of sustenance; so have railways. The lack of enthusiasm for supporting a competitive system [i.e. transcontinental airlines], to share the already inadequate source of income, can thus be understood.[4]

A first slight but encouraging updraft helped the climb towards the metaphorical mountain pass. It came as an almost grudging subsidy. Provided by the Dominion government in 1927, no doubt prompted by the knowledge that the Canadian government was the only one in the western world offering no assistance whatsoever to aviation; it was an early form of matching grants. The government would supply two aircraft to an established flying club with an approved airfield from which to operate, if the club provided one or more aircraft from its own resources for flying training. As well, the club had to have a licensed instructor and air engineer. The stinger was that the club also had to cough up a $4,000 guarantee bond for the surplus DH-60X Moths the government would provide.

In British Columbia, the result of this meagre government offering was a surge of optimism that led to the creation of a number of small companies to provide flying and maintenance training in Vancouver. Meanwhile, with this somewhat encouraging omen and a strong economy at the end of the 1920s, existing companies operating in western Canada began to expand. The most stable of these, Western Canada Airways, had been founded in December 1926 by wealthy Winnipeg businessman James A. Richardson—who had made his money in grain—and bush pilot/mining engineer H. A. (Doc) Oaks, to take advantage of the boom in mining exploration and development at the time. Oaks had the flying skills and mining exploration knowledge to run the operational side, while Richardson was well qualified to run the company: he had the financial resources, the enthusiasm for aviation and the business competence.

Two years earlier, Don MacLaren, a First World War fighter ace, in partnership with Ernest Rogers, vice-president of the BC Sugar refinery, had incorporated Pacific Airways in Vancouver with one war-surplus Curtiss HS-2L flying boat and had won a contract to fly fisheries patrols along the west coast. MacLaren, who couldn't afford them, yearned for bigger and more modern aircraft and, in 1928, he sold his company to

Richardson's Western Canada Airways, joining that company as superintendent of its Pacific Division.

Western Canada Airways had not exactly prospered but, by 1930, it had certainly improved its position. Richardson decided to launch an expansion, renaming the company Canadian Airways and merging a number of small, struggling operators from across the country. It became, and remained, the pre-eminent aviation company in Canada for many years.

These developments did not go unnoticed by the two major railways; they were run by canny businessmen and politicians and, as a sort of insurance policy just in case aviation did begin to challenge them, the CPR had, as early as 1919, secured a licence to own and operate aircraft commercially, but done nothing with it until 1930. Then the Canadian Pacific and the Canadian National each invested $250,000 in Canadian Airways, which by then was operating regional services in several provinces, and looked as though it would become a nationwide system in which the two railways would have a growing equity.[5]

By 1928, though, only ten small Post Office Department airmail contracts to various companies were in operation in Canada—all but one of them summer contracts into isolated communities. Nevertheless, the economy appeared to be booming and it was in a mood of growing optimism in 1930—the ultimate effects of the stock market crash at the end of the previous year were yet to become apparent—that the Post Office Department finally awarded its first major airmail contract to Canadian Airways. For the company, the Prairie Airmail was an ambitious proposition. It assigned ten senior pilots and ordered several Boeing and Fokker mailplanes. Together with the training required—particularly for night flying—they added up to a very substantial financial investment. At the same time, the government undertook to provide a series of beacons, as well as emergency landing fields, so that night flying would be possible.[6]

This contract represented the first major ridge surmounted in our mountain pass. Unfortunately, the terrain beyond proved inhospitable. The government's emergency airfields turned out to be, as historian Ken Molson noted, "in poor condition or inadequately lighted. . . . The revolving acetylene beacons between the airports gave a great deal of trouble . . . and when the lights were serviced, they frequently went out again almost immediately."[7]

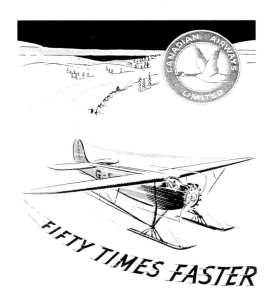

FIFTY TIMES FASTER

Mail by dog team meant months of isolation. Mail by plane provides close contact with civilization and close contact is essential to progress.

The air mail is but one phase of the "speeding-up" which today is characteristic of the Northland.

Domestic, mining and medical supplies are delivered by air fifty times faster than when ground transport only was available.

CANADIAN AIRWAYS
LIMITED
MONTREAL   WINNIPEG   VANCOUVER

Toronto Office—1430 Canadian Bank of Commerce Building.
Edmonton Office— - - Richardson Bldg.

In February 1931 Canadian Airways began to fly the two new routes: Winnipeg, Regina, Moose Jaw, Medicine Hat and Calgary; and Edmonton, North Battleford, Saskatoon, and Regina. From then on, now that the Great Depression had really started to take hold, there were constantly recurring rumours that all airmail contracts were to be terminated. Finally, in March 1932, the Prairie Airmail service was terminated only a little over a year into what was supposed to be a four-year contract. Despite this crushing setback, the air crews of Canadian Airways and other companies across the country managed to survive because, in a generally ravaged economy, the mining industry remained relatively strong and active. Thus, while the next four or five years were far from prosperous, in an arena of fierce competition, bush-flying operators usually managed to keep food on the table. The crews persevered with courage, intelligence and stamina and Canadian bush flying became universally admired and respected—but, for scheduled airline services, the pace of development was slow.

By 1935, Canadian Airways had inaugurated its first regular scheduled passenger service between Vancouver and Seattle. Because a small airmail contract was involved, and at the insistence of the Post Office Department, the aircraft had to be a de Havilland Rapide to meet the government's Empire Preference policy. Unfortunately for Canadian Airways, it was competing with United Air Lines, a US airline equipped with Boeing 247s, the first of the fast new breed of airliners, and returns were dismal. In the first half of June, 1936, Canadian Airways carried 30 passengers over the route compared with United's 256.[8] Most people still travelled on the parallel railway and steamship services that could cover the distance in four to six hours (as opposed to approximately one hour by air), or travelled in private automobiles or buses on the improving highway system.

Nonetheless, 1936 proved to be a year of much promise for Canadian aviation. The government had finally realized that if it did not move to help create a national airline, other countries would. Britain's Imperial Airways was expressing interest, and companies in the United States, who were by now developing airlines rapidly, were looking hungrily to the north. Thus, by the end of the year, control of civil aviation was removed from the Department of National Defence and set up under a new department. At the same time the government clearly indicated that a trans-Canada airway was to be established and it was understood that Canadian Airways would be involved.

This was the last ridge in our pass and, once surmounted, the aviation industry looked forward eagerly to dropping down into a metaphorical era of friendly skies and gentle breezes. Instead they would encounter a good deal more turbulence before these expectations materialized.

James Richardson decided to start preparing for the new airline in 1936 by acquiring a Lockheed 10A—closely comparable to the Boeing 247—to replace the Rapide, and to train crews for airline flying. G. A. (Tommy) Thompson the company's general manager, who appears to have been very cautious about developments, worried about the cost; but Richardson went ahead and pilot Z. Lewis Leigh went down to the Boeing School of Aeronautics in Oakland, California—operated by United Air Lines—to take their course in the then most advanced techniques in airline flying. He came back highly impressed by the course and began to train other company pilots, particularly in blind-flying techniques.

At last, in 1936, there was a promise of real progress, and this is where we encounter C. D. Howe—at a meeting with the two most influential and powerful people in the aviation arena; and the lead up to this event offers an intriguing paradox. The three initial participants in the drawn-out negotiations to set up Trans-Canada Air Lines were the Canadian Pacific Railway's president, Edward W. Beatty (later Sir Edward); Canadian Airways' president, James A. Richardson; and Transport Minister C. D. Howe—who was blessed with the resonant given names of Clarence Decatur, transformed by his enemies, of whom he had many, into Clarence Dictator.

Beatty and Richardson were unequivocal free enterprisers. In a way Howe, born and raised in the United States, was too; but he had followed a more circuitous career. After graduating from the Massachusetts Institute of Technology as a civil engineer, he had been appointed to a full professorship at Dalhousie University in Nova Scotia, when he was 23. There, in addition to teaching, "he performed," according to biographer Leslie Roberts, "a number of consulting assignments for various Maritime Corporations."[9] His next move, after taking out Canadian citizenship papers (at that time becoming a British subject) in 1913, was to become chief engineer for the Board of Grain Commissioners; and his task was to supervise the construction of grain elevators along the Canadian shore of the Great Lakes, as well as along the St. Lawrence.[10]

Richardson made a huge mistake, first in not stating that Canadian Airways' financial stability rested on air mail contracts, and second, in not pointing out that the air mail would generate needed revenues for government coffers. Bennett saw the air mail only as an expenditure, a luxury the country could ill afford. . . .

Double Cross
Shirley Render

Howe soon came to appreciate that there was far more money to be made on the other side of the fence and, in 1916, he resigned from the government to set up his own engineering and construction firm in Port Arthur (now Thunder Bay), Ontario. He suffered an initial setback—his first contract to build a grain elevator in Saskatchewan ended in a shambles when a windstorm destroyed it before completion. Recovering, he went on, before he joined the Mackenzie King government in 1935, to build, as Roberts records, "grain elevators, docks, bridges and factories in Canada to a contract value of more than one hundred million dollars."[11]

The paradox or, if you will, the irony, was that Howe, after becoming a millionaire as an entrepreneur, ran for Parliament as a Liberal candidate and joined the Dominion government; and he did so at a remarkably providential time. By 1935 the Great Depression was at last beginning to show signs of dissipating; and Howe, because of his record of competence as an engineer and businessman, was immediately appointed Minister of Railways and Canals by Prime Minister Mackenzie King. Then, less than a year later his ministry was reorganized, and he became minister of the much more powerful Department of Transport (DoT). He remained with Transport until 1940, but at the outbreak of the Second World War, he was also appointed Minister of Munitions and Supply. This not only moved him up to the rank of senior cabinet ministers, but, under emergency war measures, gave him more or less a free hand in spending.

In politics, the ability to allocate money is power, and Howe's special powers remained with him for 15 years. They enabled him to bypass the traditional tendering for contracts and to award them to the companies he favoured—which in turn enabled him to "get things done" with gratifying expedition; and, when the war ended, he became Minister of Reconstruction and Commerce with renewed emergency powers. By 1950 it was becoming obvious that the country was entering a period of prosperity; but then, just as the reasons for Howe to retain special powers were fading, the Korean War started. Howe became Minister of Trade and Commerce and his powers were renewed once more to be retained until the Trans-Canada Pipelines debates in 1956 when, after his special powers had been rescinded, he not only tripped but fell heavily.

However, it was as Minister of Transport that Howe was able to prevent James Richardson's Canadian Airways, undoubtedly the largest, most competent and experienced aviation company in Canada, from becoming the country's first transcontinental airline in 1937. Instead, the newly created Trans-Canada Air Lines* became a crown corporation with no participation by private enterprise.

Beatty and Richardson had, in fact, been invited to participate. However, after long and involved negotiations, Howe insisted that the Trans-Canada Air Lines Bill should specify "nine directors, of which three were to be appointed by the Canadian National Railways, three by the Canadian Pacific Railway and three by the Minister of Transport."[12] In effect, the Canadian National members of the board would be government, as, of course, would the three appointed by the minister—meaning that, while the CPR and Canadian Airways were to put up the funds to create the airline, the government would have complete control. This, put simply, was anathema to Beatty and, on March 16, 1937, he gave his final answer to Howe.

> I have your letter of the 15th instant and am indebted to you for your further elaboration of the views of yourself and your colleagues respecting the Trans-Canada Air Lines Bill.
> I am sorry, however, that your contentions have not changed the opinion, in regard to the proposed set-up of the Air Lines Company, which is held by our directors.
> It is not, in the circumstances, necessary to continue our correspondence, and I should appreciate it if, in the Bill as introduced, you would omit any reference to this company.[13]

Beatty's determination not to accept subordinate responsibility—or at least have an equal share—with the government in the operation of such an airline may have been a simple doctrinaire free-enterprise response; but it may also have been a reaction to the frustration of his original desire to make sure that the proposed airline did not, or at least did not too rapidly, start to siphon business away from his railway.

During the debate in Parliament to establish TCA (Bill 74), which began in March 1937, Howe practised what can only be described as a barrage of obfuscation. At no time did he mention the names of either Canadian Airways or James Richardson—although both possessed the obvious expertise, experience and structure to establish the airline; and despite Richardson having been assured by Howe in April 1936 that "Canadian Airways from every point of view are in a position to be a very important instrument in advancing the country's interest and that it was his desire that they should become the Imperial Airways of Canada,"[14] Canadian Airways was totally excluded. As well, Howe claimed there was very little time for debate because, without even a plan in place, other

CANADIAN AIRWAYS REPORT FOR A TRANS-CANADA AIRWAY

The proposal gave a complete suggested schedule of operation, equipment required at the various bases for servicing aircraft and where the maintenance personnel should be stationed. In short, it presented the government with a complete blueprint for setting up and operating a trans-Canada airway system based on almost ten years' experience of operating Canadian Airways and its predecessor companies, together with the best advice from several American airline companies.

K. M. Molson
Pioneering in Canadian air Transport

"Howe's trouble seems to be that the sudden acquisition of Cabinet rank and of power has gone to his head and he is not able to deal with ordinary individuals except on the basis of a superior being dealing with inferiors. However, he has undoubtedly been getting the 'breaks' in many ways, and as long as his luck holds out, we need not look for much change in him.

E. W. Beatty *Letterbook* 165, CPR Archives

* The name was changed to Air Canada in 1964.

One of the Boeing 40B-4 mailplanes purchased by Canadian Airways for the Prairie Airmail contract in 1929.—AUTHOR'S COLLECTION

F. M. (Maurice) McGregor who, flying a Sikorsky S-38 amphibian, pioneered the regular scheduled Vancouver-Victoria route for Canadian Airways in 1932. He and E. P. H. (Billy) Wells went on to inaugurate the Vancouver-Seattle route, first with the DH Rapide and later with the first Lockheed 10A Electra to be operated by TCA.
—MAURICE McGREGOR COLLECTION

A de Havilland Rapide, the type of aircraft first used by Canadian Airways, and then by Trans-Canada Air Lines, on the Vancouver-Seattle route. Unfortunately, it was competing against the much faster and more modern Boeing 247s of United Air Lines.—PETERS COLLECTION, ROYAL BC MUSEUM

Competition: a United Air Lines', for those days, high speed Boeing 247A arriving at Vancouver Airport, c. 1936.
—JOE BERTALINO, BC PROVINCIAL ARCHIVES, F-4789

Canadian Airways' first Lockheed 10A, CF-AZY, at Vancouver Airport, 1936. Its predecessor, the DH Rapide is in the background, framed by the 10A's undercarriage.
—MAURICE McGREGOR COLLECTION

CF-TCC, TCA's third Lockheed 10A Electra, on the apron at Vancouver, October 1937, after inaugurating TCA's first commercial airmail service between Vancouver and Seattle. —PETERS COLLECTION, ROYAL BC MUSEUM

countries would pre-empt the vitally important trans-Atlantic route if Parliament spent too much time debating the issue. This crossed the boundary from obfuscation to mendacity, because, in response to a request from Howe, Richardson and his staff had submitted a very comprehensive plan to Howe in September 1936.[15]

And when Howe did obliquely refer to Canadian Airways without actually naming it, he maintained that it would not be capable of running an airline because, in his words, "that company is engaged in extensive services [bush flying] quite foreign to the services we are going to develop here." The truth was that the Canadian Airways plan, ten copies of which were submitted by Richardson, clearly stated that it would set up a separate company called Canadian Airways Limited if it were to run the airline. The existing bush-flying operation would be renamed Airways Limited.[16] As a conclusion to this sordid affair, historian Ken Molson records that Don MacLaren, the first to jump ship, was released (with some resentment) from Canadian Airways to join TCA at the end of April 1937:

Even more disturbing was another event that occurred shortly afterwards. Canadian Airways Limited requested the return of the ten copies of the plan covering the proposed development of the trans-Canada airway system which they had presented during a visit in the latter part of September 1936. Nine copies were received immediately but, in spite of a number of telephone calls to Ottawa, the tenth [the copy given to Don MacLaren] was not forthcoming for several days. When it was received it gave the impression of having been copied prior to its return.[17]

This obviously gave rise to the suspicion that MacLaren and TCA used it to set up their operation—at least initially.

It is interesting to hear MacLaren's recollections of these events recorded in an interview many years later. To begin with he suggested that Howe, the Liberal, did not favour Richardson because Richardson was very much a Conservative in his politics. Secondly he suggested that only Beatty was against the government having majority control on the TCA Board. "I went to see him, but he was adamant. Mr. Richardson tried to talk to him and he was adamant, so Howe wouldn't wait any longer. . . . He said, 'I'm going to form my own company.'" MacLaren went on to say that Howe phoned him and asked him to join the new company, which he did. "So then I moved to Montreal and opened the office there in April 1937. I was the first employee of the company."[18]

Canadian Airways . . . agreed to release the men that Trans Canada Air Lines required but requested reasonable notice so that they could be replaced without disrupting operations. The first pilot to go was Lewis Leigh in the middle of August. By the end of the year the Company had released twenty-two men to Trans Canada Airlines, including D. R. MacLaren and thirteen pilots. Many of these pilots had just recently received extensive instrument flying training at considerable expense to Canadian Airways.

K. M. Molson
Pioneering in Canadian Air Transport

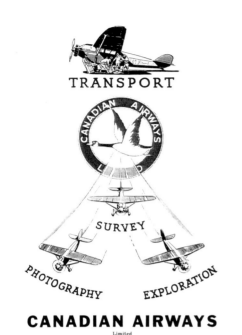

TRANSPORT

CANADIAN AIRWAYS LTD

SURVEY

PHOTOGRAPHY **EXPLORATION**

CANADIAN AIRWAYS
Limited
MONTREAL   WINNIPEG   VANCOUVER

Toronto Office   ·   1430 Canadian Bank of Commerce Building
Edmonton Office   · · ·   Richardson Building

MacLaren also claimed that "I drew up the list of pilots. They were all bush pilots and none of them had ever had any training on instruments, except Lee [Lewis Leigh] who had gone to the Boeing school." In fact, Canadian Airways had fully trained 22 pilots, all with instrument-flight capability up to the prevailing American airline standards. This claim might have been a simple memory lapse, but it sounds very much like a retroactive attempt to elevate the importance of the part MacLaren played in the early development of TCA; because, even though at Howe's request he was the first employee, in the years to come he made little progress in the new corporation's hierarchy.

In any case, it must have been a bitter experience for James Richardson who, despite MacLaren's claim, clearly and no doubt resentfully, refused to participate: first because, as a director of the CPR, he was so closely associated with Beatty; and second, as a businessman he shared Beatty's reasons for withdrawing. He had spent large amounts of his own capital to found and operate Canadian Airways. He bought new aircraft and spent a great deal of money training crews and setting up facilities to operate the Prairie Airmail contract in 1930—only to have the whole operation cancelled by the Bennett government after little more than one year of a four-year contract. The same thing happened again in 1936 and 1937, when he bought new aircraft—a de Havilland Rapide and two Lockheed 10As— one to compete with United Air Lines' Boeing 247s on the Vancouver-Seattle route; the other at Howes's request for use by the DoT to test radio stations on the proposed trans-Canada route; and finally, he bore the expense of instrument training for 22 pilots in anticipation of airline flying.

Instead, Richardson, the man so often called the "Father of Canadian Aviation," was left now to compete with a state-owned airline that was thoughtfully protecting itself against competition on the only potentially profitable routes at the time.

Howe's motives for shutting out free enterprise make for interesting speculation; the most likely seems to be that he cherished power and relished exercising it. As well, there is little doubt that he wanted to go down in history as the creator of what he called "my airline"—Canada's first transcontinental line. In any case, Howe's conduct throughout the debate for the establishment of TCA amounted to a display of egregious duplicity—or, as Shirley Render has so aptly termed it, a Double Cross.

Chapter Two

C. D. Howe and the
Formative Years of TCA

"Who [with a chain saw] chops up
a prototype aircraft that has rocked the world
with its mind-bending performance? Well,
the answer is Canadian politicians, that's who!"

JACK SCHOFIELD

THE RESULT OF Howe's manipulation of the debate on Bill 74 was that the new Trans-Canada Air Lines Corporation began operations with what appeared to be tremendous advantages: a monopoly on potentially profitable routes, secure and generous funding and, for the first time in Canadian aviation history, secure and profitable airmail contracts. In the past, as historian Ken Molson has pointed out:

the Post Office Department kept cutting these contracts down so that almost all routes were being operated at a loss by the airline companies but the Post Office openly stated that they [the Post Office] were making a profit. . . . This is in marked contrast to the policy followed in other countries which were using the mail payments to the aviation companies as a means of building up and supporting a system of national air services.[1]

In fact, the Post Office seemed determined to exploit operators rather than assist them. In a guest editorial for the journal *Canadian Aviation*, James Richardson, using *Hansard* as his authority, pointed out "that the cost of northern airmail services to the Post Office Department for 1936 was $173,512 while the revenue received from those services was $505,592 giving the Post Office a profit of $332,080, a profit percentage of 192%."[2] Yet now that the government itself was involved, this profit taking ceased and the airmail contract granted to TCA was on a straight, guaranteed mileage basis. As C. A. Ashley recorded, "The rate for mail was fixed at 60 cents per mile. . . . The rate of 60 cents was per plane-mile flown with mail, and did not depend on the weight carried. . . ."[3]

Some indication of the importance of mail to a new airline is illustrated by figures revealed in annual reports. In 1937, TCA's passenger revenue was $3,610 (all on the Vancouver-Seattle route), the mail revenue $12,637. In 1938, it had risen to $15,270 and $556,193, respectively; and in 1939 to $643,915 and $1,632,873.[4] In short, the Post Office Department's free lunch was over; and the railways, whose powerful vested interests had done so much to retard the development of aviation in Canada, would now have to compete with aviation for mail revenue.

This did not, of course, apply to private-sector aviation. Many years were to pass before the monopoly was compromised with a breakthrough by Canadian Pacific Air Lines (CPA). When CPA came into being in 1942,* the *Whitehorse Star* reported how quickly Howe responded to any suggestions of competition:

> Private airlines will not be allowed to operate in competition with the projected new Trans-Canada Air Lines service to the Yukon and Alaska, Munitions Minister Howe told the House of Commons last week.
>
> Replying to questions by George Black (Con., Yukon), Mr. Howe said airfields at present under construction would be used for the new route and there would be no duplication.
>
> Only government recompense to an airline using the route was through carrying mail, Mr. Howe said. Mail contracts were on a monthly basis and warning had been given to the company now operating that Trans-Canada Air Lines would eventually operate in that territory.
>
> The minister added: "There will be no question of competing lines; if Trans-Canada goes in the other line must go out."[5]

The following year, in April, came an even stronger assertion of monopoly. Canadian Pacific Air Lines revealed plans for overseas services after the war. In response, Prime Minister Mackenzie King announced that Trans-Canada Air Lines was to be "the sole agency which may operate Canadian international services." In the words of historian W. Kaye Lamb:

> [L. B.] Unwin and [Punch] Dickins [president and general manager, respectively, of CPA] protested vigorously. . . . They had a strong case; the Canadian Pacific had been providing international services by sea for half a century—surely it was logical to allow it to employ aircraft as well as ships. But the wording of their protest was provocative: "If equity and justice have any place in the Canadian Government plan," they wrote, "Canadian Pacific should be allowed to carry traffic in the air to supplement its long-established sea routes."
>
> The key minister concerned, C. D. Howe, was not pleased; he responded in March 1944 with a government order announcing that transport by air was to be rigorously separated

* In 1942, Beatty's Canadian Pacific Railway assumed full control of Canadian Airways and amalgamated a number of other aviation companies into Canadian Pacific Air Lines, later to become a strong competitor to TCA.

from surface transportation, and that railways would be required to divest themselves of all air activities within a year of the end of the war.[6]

In Canada, such a draconian order, directed at a company as powerful and influential as the Canadian Pacific Railway, could only have been issued during wartime, when political power becomes concentrated in the federal government. In any case, neither measure was effected. TCA did not take over CPA's northern route into the Yukon, and the "sole agent" policy of the government was set aside after the war. They did, however, lend some validity to the claim that Howe's middle name was Dictator rather than Decatur, and perhaps foreshadowed the arrogance that led to his eventual downfall.

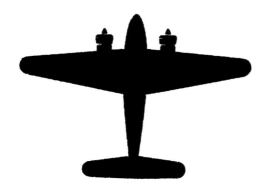

Meanwhile, in spite of all the advantages with which Trans-Canada Air Lines started, it did not fly off into the bright, blue yonder of instant success. As with most such ventures, there were a number of teething troubles—many of them apparently caused by Howe's autocratic style of superintendence. Predictably, having sidelined the best available Canadian experience, training and expertise—Canadian Airways—he decided that Americans should be hired to manage the new corporation; and the experts he had been talking to in the United States had firmly recommended the use of the Douglas DC-3, as Beatty, after he had met with Howe at the end of 1936, revealed in a letter to James Richardson:

In the Minister's view a service at least West of Winnipeg should be commenced by the first of next July and that it should be a passenger and mail service. He considered the Douglas plane best for our purposes, and this, he said, was the recommendation of American experts.[7]

The experts hired from the States were: Philip G. Johnson, as first vice-president, with D. D. Colyer and H. T. Lewis as his technical advisors. H. Oliver West was hired for maintenance and engineering, and O. T. Larson for dispatch and meteorology—all were from United Air Lines. In addition, S. S. Stevens, of Eastern Air Lines, became the radio and communications man; and finally, a Canadian, W. A. (Bill) Straith, then working with Northwest Airlines, also an American carrier, was hired as chief flying instructor.[8]

However, when it came to choice of aircraft, Howe did not follow the experts' advice, opting for the Lockheed 10A instead of the DC-3. His decision may have been influenced by the final appointment of directors. In place of the nine originally proposed, there were seven: C. P. Edwards

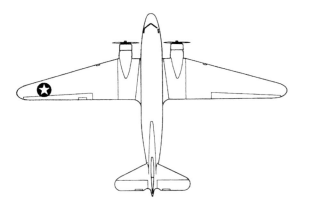

and J. A. Wilson, Department of Transport (who would be unlikely to challenge their minister's decisions) and George Herring, Post Office Department; all the rest, Samuel J. Hungerford (president of TCA and also president of Canadian National Railways), Wilfred Gagnon, J. Y. Murdoch and H. J. Symington were also directors of Canadian National Railways.[9] None had any experience in aviation transportation and they were not capable of making enlightened recommendations about suitability of aircraft. All of them reported directly to C. D. Howe and no doubt deferred to him because he claimed extensive consultation with American airline experts. It soon becomes apparent that Howe seems to have made all the early decisions about aircraft acquisitions unilaterally.

Some support for this speculation is suggested by a letter from Beatty to Howe in November 1936, before Beatty had declined to be involved in the new airline and when he was still confident that Canadian Airways and the CPR would operate it. Beatty had asked Tommy Thompson, then general manager of Canadian Airways, for an aircraft evaluation. In his report, Thompson emphasized that his data were incomplete, but was evidently pessimistic about operating costs of the DC-3, and he recommended the Lockheed 10. As we shall see, Thompson's data certainly were incomplete. First, the 10A could not maintain altitude with a full load over the Rocky Mountains, whereas the DC-3 could; second, even with a half load of passengers, the DC-3 could compete with the 10A in seat-mile costs.

With the wisdom of hindsight, there is a temptation to suggest that this was the second time Tommy Thompson appeared to be unduly cautious. The first, when he was against buying the 10A for the Vancouver-Seattle run; and now this recommendation to pass up the most successful airliner of its time: the DC-3. However one has to remember that Thompson had been general manager of Canadian Airways in 1933 when, after the cancellation of the Prairie Airmail contract, the company very nearly went under. In this context, when he and almost everyone else thought that Canadian Airways would be operating the new trans-Canada airline, his cautious approach is easily understandable.

In his letter to Howe, Beatty reported that

I discussed the matter very fully with Mr. Hungerford [president of CNR] this afternoon and we both feel that it would be wiser to start the service from Winnipeg west with [Lockheed] Electra machines, because it is to be expected that some time will elapse before we will be able to fully use a plane of the capacity of the Douglas type.[10]

No mention here about the safety factor of single-engine performance if the other engine failed. It sounds more like two reluctant railwaymen prepared to step very gingerly into the aviation field; and, for all his self-assurance, Howe, too, may have been influenced by this cautious approach. If not, it is difficult to understand the rationale for the decision. Howe himself had said that the DC-3 was "the recommendation of American experts." This certainly made sense because nearly all substantive American airlines at the time were either operating or waiting impatiently for delivery of their first DC-3s. One notable exception was United Air Lines, which was operating Boeing 247s on the Seattle-Vancouver route; and it was from this company that Howe hired his consultants to set up TCA.

In fact, the "Douglas plane" was produced to challenge Boeing's 247, the first of the fast, twin-engined monoplane airliners with a retractable undercarriage. The DC-1 and its successor, the DC-2, had been operating very successfully since 1934. The DC-1, with its twin 700-hp Pratt & Whitney Hornet engines, carried 12 passengers, compared to 10 for the 247, its cruise speed was 35 mph (55 km/h) faster and it had a superior range. With it, Transcontinental & Western Air (which in 1950 became Trans World Airlines) operating between Los Angeles, California, and Newark, New Jersey, set, according to Kenneth Munson, "the first of 11 US and eight world speed and distance records" early in 1934.[11] Presumably, these were proving flights because the DC-1 was a single prototype, almost immediately superseded by the stretched DC-2, with its modified rudder, more powerful 720-hp Wright Cyclone engines and capacity of 14 passengers.

Moreover, when the DC-3, a stretched DC-2 with an enlarged cabin, came into service in 1935 it was unmistakably superior to the Boeing 247 or the Lockheed 10A. As Munson observed,

the larger DC-3 fuselage would accommodate a third row of seats, so giving an increase of 50 per cent in seating capacity [24] over the DC-2. Airline customers were already impressed with the DC-2's operating costs; when offered a larger aircraft with costs only two thirds those of the DC-2, even with the more powerful (1,200 hp) Cyclone or Twin Wasp engines, they soon produced a flood of orders. Such was the impact of the DC-3 that by 1938 it was carrying 95 per cent of all US airline traffic and was in service with 30 foreign airlines; a year later, 90 per cent of the world's airline trade was being flown by DC-3s.[12]

On the other hand, James Richardson's decision to purchase the first Lockheed 10A Electra[13] was perfectly rational because he had entirely

No mention here about the safety factor of single-engine performance. . . .

Vancouver Airport, February, 1939.

TCA's CF-TCK, a Lockheed 14-H2 Super Electra, over the Prairies in the fall, 1938.

The all-powerful cabinet minister, dubbed by the media, "Minister of Everything," Clarence Decatur Howe.—VANCOUVER PUBLIC LIBRARY 61248

The troublesome Pratt & Whitney Hornet engines that kept the air engineers busy during TCA's early years.—BRITISH COLUMBIA ARCHIVES Z-26679

The ill-fated prototype Avro
Jetliner, CF-EJD-X (X for Experimental).
—ROYAL BC MUSEUM

A TCA Douglas DC-3 on the tarmac at
Victoria, 1948. —BRITISH COLUMBIA ARCHIVES Z-26682

different criteria in mind when he made the purchase. First, he needed to replace the slow and cumbersome de Havilland Rapide[14] to satisfy the Post Office Department, which had initially insisted on the Rapide and was now complaining about its performance; second, to compete with United's Boeing 247Ds on the Vancouver–Seattle run; third, there were no high mountains to be crossed on that route; and fourth, he needed a fast, modern machine to initiate training for the proposed transcontinental airline flying that, not unnaturally, he anticipated for Canadian Airways. Moreover, the 10A was, as pilot and historian Z. Lewis Leigh pointed out later, "good, smooth aeroplane to fly, and considered to be fairly fast for its time. . . . The only problem was that it could not maintain the necessary single-engine altitude required for full-load flight over the Rocky Mountains."[15]

This "only problem" was, of course, a deadly serious one for a scheduled passenger service that would be crossing the Rockies on a regular and frequent basis. This and the knowledge that Howe never had a reputation for economizing on his projects makes it a curious decision. In retrospect, we know that the experts were more than justified in recommending the Douglas DC-3, which had come into service in 1935.

What makes Howe's decision the more puzzling is that the people he appointed as management to run his new airline were nearly all from United Air Lines. Unlike the other major US airlines, UAL had been operating the Boeing 247, an aircraft almost identical in performance, capacity and operating costs to the Lockheed 10A. By 1937, though, Kenneth Munson recorded that United "had to admit the eclipse of its Boeing 247 fleet, now losing money to its Douglas-equipped rivals [and] began its DC-3 service in June 1937." Before long United had a fleet of 45 DC-3s.[16]

Some have suggested that Howe was more impressed with the management style of Lockheed than of Douglas, and based his choice on that. It may well have been that the Douglas people were more concerned with production to meet their flood of orders than salesmanship; whereas the Lockheed brass treated Howe with the utmost consideration and respect because they were very concerned with sales in the light of the DC-3's success. Shirley Render records that "Howe had earned a reputation for making rash promises and allowing flattery to cloud his judgement."[17] And biographers Bothwell and Kilbourn record that "indeed, he was always a relatively easy mark for much less important and charming flatterers than

Murchison."[18] In any case, he would have been wiser to look to the designers and engineers rather than management, as apparently all other airlines had at the time; because, on top of its other superiorities, the DC-3 could comfortably maintain single-engined, full-load altitude over the Rocky Mountains.

Yet another factor may have been that Lockheed was promising a new and more advanced airliner in the near future. H. W. Seagrim, who retired from Air Canada as executive vice-president, provides the background to these early developments. Only a week after the Trans-Canada Air Lines Bill was passed in April, 1937,

C. D. Howe announced that . . . he had had his department place tentative orders for three additional Lockheed 10As and four Lockheed Super Electras [14-H2s]. . . . Howe wanted this order placed as soon as possible to ensure that what he considered to be "his" airline got the earliest possible start.[19]

In this case there appears to have been no debate; according to Seagrim, Howe made an apparently unilateral decision: "As far as can be determined, the orders in question were placed without anything in the way of a formal aircraft evaluation."[20] Although the prototype 14-H2, or Super Electra, first flew in July of 1937, development was slow and the first machine wasn't delivered to TCA until May 1938. Unfortunately, it soon became apparent that still more development was needed. To quote Seagrim again: "From the outset it was apparent that the 14 could not match the seat-mile economics of the DC-3 which preceded it into airline service by more than a year."[21] In fact, the DC-3 had been in service in the United States for nearly three years before delivery of the first 14-H2 to TCA.

Nor was this to be the only seemingly illogical decision about aviation made by C. D. Howe. Twelve years later, in 1949, when the United States was straining to catch up to Britain and Canada in the construction of the first jet airliner, Canada's Avro Jetliner took off from Toronto's Malton airport for its first test flight on August 10. All indications were that the Avro plane exceeded its proposed performance specifications, even though TCA kept upping those specifications; and, after Britain's de Havilland Comet—which had undergone its first successful test flight only two weeks earlier—had suffered its tragic setbacks, the Avro Jetliner could well have led the world in this new technology.

. . . the 14 could not match the seat-mile economics of the DC-3

Inexplicably, the leading aviation journal of that day, *Canadian Aviation*, afforded only one photograph and three columns to the Avro Jetliner in a 69-page issue.

As historian Jack Schofield records:

In typical reticence to laud Canadian achievements . . . this sad, oft told story goes on to relate how Eastern Airlines, United Airlines, TWA and even Howard Hughes himself...were about to place advance orders for the Jetliner when C. D. Howe, the then Canadian minister of everything, blew them away by ordering the Jetliner scrapped—cut into pieces with chain saws! This was a precedent in aviation history—who chops up a prototype aircraft that has rocked the world with its mind-bending performance? Well, the answer is Canadian politicians, and they had even a bigger surprise for the industry and taxpayers a little way down the road.[22]

However, the demise of the Jetliner was a good deal less abrupt and brutal than that of the Arrow. Whereas the Arrow was a summary execution, the Jetliner lingered for several years before suffering a form of euthanasia. After the Second World War, Sir Roy Dobson, managing director of Avro in England, made several trips across the Atlantic to negotiate with C. D. Howe to take over the plant of a Crown Corporation called Victory Aircraft, which had been assembling Lancasters at Malton. Negotiations were successful and Avro Canada took over the plant.

Consequently, after further negotiations with TCA, the decision was made to build the Jetliner as a medium-range, intercity airliner with two Rolls-Royce Avon jet engines. When the design was almost completed, they encountered the first setback: Rolls-Royce advised that the Avon engine was unlikely to be available for civil certification when the aircraft was ready to fly. This necessitated redesign to accommodate four of the older Rolls-Royce Derwent engines to match the power of two Avons and was successfully accomplished. In 1950, however, only a year after the Jetliner had made its successful test flights, further development was halted by the Korean War; and the government decision to concentrate on producing military CF-100 interceptors left the prototype Jetliner languishing in hangars for the next six years before it was destroyed.

Don Rogers, Avro's chief test pilot for the Jetliner, points out that the jetliner flew from Toronto to Winnipeg—with the required reserve of fuel for a diversion—in two hours and forty minutes. That time doesn't raise any eyebrows now, but in 1950 it was spectacular for an airliner to achieve airspeeds of more than 400 mph (640 km/h). Furthermore, "Some unkind remarks were made to explain its cancellation. I really don't understand the press report of C. D. Howe saying that it didn't fly properly and that it had to have sand ballast in the rear of the fuselage. This, of course, was not correct. We did use sand ballast for certification work, to position the centre of gravity we wanted for a particular test, but this certainly was not a requirement for normal operations."

Rogers provides a sad eulogy to this venture:

Unfortunately, the story had a sad ending; I can't imagine anything more unpleasant than seeing an airplane that you have lived with for seven years and enjoyed flying—a really beautiful machine—being cut up with saws, axes and hammers, with pieces falling on the hangar floor. I couldn't go in the hangar for a couple of days while they were doing this job because it was a heart-rending experience.[23]

Mike Cooper-Slipper, an ex-Battle of Britain fighter pilot who was also one of the test pilots on the Avro Jetliner project, echoed much of what Don Rogers had to say. He commented that it was a dream to fly and "could not explain the rationale for the attitude by the politicians of that day." As well he indicated that, "in later years, C. D. Howe took to slandering A. V. Roe as a means of defending what was then being recognized as his own irrational actions."[24]

Once more there were shades of suspicion that, as with the management of Douglas 12 years earlier, Avro's executives failed to demonstrate the respect Howe felt was his due: "There was what government officials would describe as 'arrogance' at A. V. Roe, whose spokesmen seemed to view the project as vital and important for Canada."[25] As well, perhaps almost inevitably, people hinted that being American-born and, as with the later Trans-Canada Pipeline fray, Howe was favouring the country of his birth: in this case running interference to allow the United States to catch up with Britain and Canada in the jet airliner technology.

In 1956, a BC newspaper reported comments by TCA vice-president William F. English while on a tour of western operations. He was commenting specifically on the new "$2,250,000 'jet age' runway just completed at the Vancouver Airport," but "Mr. English declined comment on jet airliners, other than 'I'm not saying jet airliners are not good, we just feel there are still some problems to be dealt with.' Some time ago TCA considered jets but finally placed an order with the American Lockheed Corporation for eight Super-Constellation airliners."[26] At least this time they chose what have generally been acknowledged as the best of the piston-engined airliners before the advent of American jets.

T.C.A. Plans New Fleet of Aircraft

Raised in eight years to the stature of a major airline, Trans-Canada Air Lines is enlarging its fleet and strengthening its organization with many talented ex-service personnel, according to the 1945 review made by H. J. Symington, C.M.G., K.C., president.

Plans call for a new fleet of greater seating capacity than the 10 and 14-seat types currently being flown, with entry into service of three twin-engined 21-passenger DC-3's marking the opening phase of this program which is aimed at having 21 additional DC-3's in service by the summer of next year.

The year 1945 saw the allocation to Canada of six more trans-border air routes into the United States, Halifax-Boston; Toronto-Cleveland; Toronto-Chicago; Port Arthur-Duluth; Whitehorse-Fairbanks, and Victoria-Seattle.

The company hopes to take autumn delivery of the first Canadian-built DC-6's.

Returning to TCA and its earlier Lockheeds, the corporation did eventually purchase DC-3s—three in 1945 and, by the end of 1946, the fleet included 27—but for the moment, TCA was stuck with its Lockheeds. Lockheed, meanwhile, was trying to meet the competition by attempting to boost the 14-H's speed and altitude capability;[27] and this, in turn, led to further problems. The list was extensive: to begin with, a high wing loading was necessary to provide the additional speed in the air which, in turn, resulted in unacceptably high take-off and landing speeds for the airfields then available. The solution attempted was to provide Fowler flaps, a flap system that went beyond the normal function of a flap by providing increased wing area. Unfortunately, the speeds were still excessive; in addition, the machine had disturbing characteristics when it did stall. Consequently, Lockheed produced another modification in the form of a fixed wing-slot. The end result made for considerably improved stall characteristics but the aircraft was still by no means docile, and the wing-slots led to a new hazard in winter flying: an ice build-up in the inlet of the slot—a problem compounded by the fact that the early Lockheeds had no de-icing equipment.

Yet another problem with the early Lockheed 14s (though no fault of the maker's) lay with the new Pratt & Whitney Hornet engines that, while providing considerably more power than the Wasp Juniors on the 10A (875 hp compared to 450), were far from reliable. Jack Dyment, TCA's former director of engineering concedes that "We had trouble with them because of cylinder failures. Not really true was the contention of some rude people who said you could trace Trans-Canada by following the trail of Hornet cylinders on the ground."[28] This deficiency was exacerbated by the icing problem because it called for long spells at full throttle to maintain height and airspeed over the mountains when the aircraft was carrying a load of ice.[29] All of which meant that TCA pilots had their nerves tested with some frequency for the first three or four years of operation, and the engineers had their hands full trying to keep the aircraft serviceable for regular scheduled runs. There was no airline honeymoon for the operating crews: the bride turned out to be both fractious and very demanding.

Meanwhile, it was comforting to learn that pilots evidently had not lost their rather exalted image by the conversion from bush flying to airline flying—at least not with the media. For example, Ken Grant provided this

"... The Hornet suffered cylinder problems and on a cruddy night when the weather was blowing and the mountains were challenging, the crews would taxi out for take-off, lock the brakes and run the shit out of the engines until a cylinder head would pop, and then taxi back in and cancel the flight. I'm not sure that I would have done anything different."

Herb Noble
ex-TCA flight engineer

Howe asked the House to consider a resolution to clarify and extend his powers of which he had given notice several days earlier. On June 18th, the day following the meeting of Hitler with France's leaders in a railway car in the forest of Compiègne to accept their surrender, Howe's Bill was read for the third time and passed. The Minister of Munitions and Supply was now the accredited dictator of Canadian industry.

C.D.
Leslie Roberts

rather breathless newspaper description in the *Vancouver Sun*, under the heading "Heroic Young T.C.A. Pilots and Their Work":

The glistening monster rises imperceptibly from the runway, then vanishes suddenly into the curtain of darkness beyond the last row of colored boundary lights. Slowly the drumming motors fade. The plane's running lights become a dim star travelling steadily down the far skyline.

As simply as that, two young men have hopped off on a midnight jaunt across the Rockies and a thousand miles of prairie. . . .By the time the 9 o'clock gun booms the hour, the silver plane is emerging from the shadowy ramparts of the eastern Rockies. Midnight finds them 11,000 feet [3 350 m] above the Saskatchewan plains. Crews change at Winnipeg at 3 o'clock, and dawn meets the big airliner above the shadowy shores of Lake Superior, a few hours from its journey's end at Montreal.

Who are these unsung supermen who take continents in their stride between dusk and daylight? What are their thoughts as they bore through the night two miles above a sleeping world?[30]

No doubt their thoughts were often in the form of prayers—prayers that there would be no ice in the clouds that night, and that they wouldn't blow a cylinder halfway across the Rockies.

As for Howe, by now repeatedly referred to in the media as the "Minister of Everything," his tenure as the most powerful cabinet minister in Canadian history came to its end with another example of his penchant for making unilateral decisions. This occurred in the Trans-Canada Pipeline debates of the 1950s. Then, in his determination to force through Parliament his bill for the proposed construction of the line by the Trans-Canada Pipeline Corporation, he stumbled seriously. This corporation, 83 per cent of which was owned by United States interests, and which had undertaken to provide all the funding for the project, now required upwards of an $80-million loan of taxpayers' money to start construction. The bill under debate would provide this. In the end, Howe invoked closure to block debate and force the bill through.

There are many similarities between the Trans-Canada Air Lines and the Trans-Canada Pipeline Bill debate, which took place nearly two decades later. When the Pipeline—a line to carry natural gas from the Alberta fields through Winnipeg and on to Ontario and Quebec—was first discussed in Parliament in the early 1950s, one member wanted assurance that, if gas were to be sold to the United States, this would only happen after all Canadian sources had been satisfied. As he phrased it, "Canada first." Howe went one further, offering the guarantee that the policy would be "Canada always." By 1956, without apology, he abruptly reversed himself and, in glowing language, was extolling the virtues of selling natural gas to America, which would not only pay all the construction costs of the line but provide handsome profits for years to come.

Meanwhile, though, in 1955 the Prime Minister, Louis St. Laurent, introduced a bill to once again extend Howe's "temporary" emergency powers. The bill was defeated and Howe complained "that he was now part of 'a government which has fallen into the hands of children.'"[31] Nevertheless, he continued to urge the importance of a Canadian pipeline to the industrial centres of Ontario and Quebec before Texas gas took its place.

So here, once again, as in the TCA bill, urgency came to the fore—because in this case the government loan of $80 million to begin construction had to be passed over to the American contractors before the end of June so that they could place orders with a steel mill for the pipes if construction was to commence in 1957. To make matters worse, while the opposition and the media by this time had reliable evidence of it, Howe refused to concede that in the interim he had received proposals for construction of the pipeline without any public funding from two Canadian entrepreneurs, notably one with impressive credentials: "Frank McMahon of Calgary, the financier and president of Westcoast Transmission, a company that had piped Peace River gas through British Columbia to the Pacific coast, arriving at Port Moody, BC, the previous year."[32]

This led to passionate and persistent accusations in the Commons that Howe was subsidizing big business in the country of his birth at the expense of his adopted country. Eventually, Howe "was forced to admit that he had had it [the McMahon letter] in his hands for five weeks. . . ." Howe's concealment of it was denounced as flagrant contempt of Parliament. "The letter was marked private, 'he told his tormentors.' "I get letters from my sister. I suppose I should announce in Parliament when I receive a letter from my sister."[33]

"About the pipeline?" asked the Conservative Opposition member John Diefenbaker ingenuously.

Once more, in the heat of this prolonged debate, Howe skirted the truth to the point of downright mendacity. His enthusiastic biographer, Leslie Roberts (who repeatedly describes Howe as a man of high integrity), nearly ties himself in a knot trying to rationalize this unsavoury conclusion: "In the pipeline transaction, it is conceivable that he [Howe] nego-

. . . flagrant contempt of Parliament . . .

tiated himself into a situation in which he was confronted by what he could regard as public humiliation unless he asserted his will, and accomplished what he had set out to do."[34]

Whatever history's final assessment of C. D. Howe, the consequence of the notorious pipeline debate—which finally ended with closure in June 1956—was that in the 1957 general election not only did the Conservatives form a minority government but, in the words of historian W. L. Morton, "the Liberal ministers had been decimated . . . [and] Howe, perhaps more than anyone responsible for this debacle, had been defeated in his own seat."[35] Then in another election less than a year later, the Conservatives gained what Morton described as the "greatest electoral victory of Canadian history."[36]

One thing seems fairly certain: it must have been a shrewd awakening for Howe. After two full decades of glorious power as the "Minister of Everything," of getting things done while frequently demonstrating his impatience with, and not infrequently his contempt for, parliamentary procedures—and by extension democratic principles—he finally overreached himself and lost it all. Lord Acton's contention that "power tends to corrupt and absolute power corrupts absolutely" seems to have been validated.

As for Trans-Canada Air Lines, even with the built-in advantages it enjoyed, after a shaky start for the first few years it went on to become an extremely successful airline, able to bear comparison in an international arena. Whether or not this would have been the case if Howe, with relatively limitless access to the national treasury, had not intervened so assertively, is in the realm of pure speculation.

In any case, the advent of TCA was a momentous event in BC. It established major routes to and from the province and overcame the hitherto formidable challenge of crossing the Rocky Mountains on a regular basis. More importantly, it could be compared to the national significance of the CPR's triumph more than 50 years before, as well as signalling the eventual demise of dominance by the railways for passenger and mail transport.

Part Two
GRANT McCONACHIE AND CANADIAN PACIFIC AIR LINES

Chapter Three

The Early Years

*"He sometimes flew on argent wings,
but more often on credit and a prayer."*

ANON

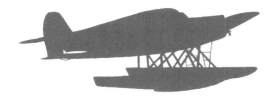

WHILE TRANS-CANADA moved tentatively towards airline proficiency in the late 1930s, the competition was experiencing different problems. The long dreary burden of the Great Depression was at last beginning to ease, but the threatened approach of another world war brought with it many obstacles for commercial aviation. With an increasing emphasis on military production, spare parts became exceedingly scarce; and so, by 1939 was the supply of aviation fuel. The principal competitor, Canadian Airways, also suffered from lack of leadership. The company was now as much controlled by Beatty as Richardson (who died in June, 1939), and Beatty continued to vacillate between his railway interests and the inevitable shift to air transport—at least for passengers and mail.

This ambivalence seems to be grudgingly confirmed by Norris Crump, who worked for the CPR for 52 years, retiring as chairman of the board in 1972:

Donald Bain also requested that I write something on the differences in thinking in the 1940s and 50s between railwaymen and airline personnel. Succinctly stated, we expected to keep the railway operating profitably and were skeptical of the airline ever contributing much to the parent company's profits. Time has proven this assumption to be correct. With the benefit of hindsight, if had we to do it all over again, many of our decisions would have been different.[1]

The ultimate benefactor in the eventual creation of Canadian Pacific Air Lines began his aviation career more than a decade earlier—a young man out in the West who eventually made CPA into a very strong competitor to the national airline; a man who became almost legendary for his charm and persuasiveness, but not always for his veracity.

G. W. G. (Grant) McConachie was born in Hamilton, Ontario, in 1909, and was brought by his family to the whistle-stop, embryonic town of Calder, Alberta (now merged as a suburb of Edmonton), when he was a year old. Grant's father, William, was district chief master mechanic for the Canadian Northern Railway.* Grant grew up with the town but, as his biographer Ronald Keith observed, "It would be difficult to suggest that he had a normal childhood. He worked like a galley slave, although his family did not need the money he earned. The Protestant ethic was deeply ingrained in him, and he worked harder than most full-grown men."[2] In short, we have all the makings of a Horatio Alger story.

McConachie's aviation career began in Edmonton when he was an 18-year-old engineering student at the University of Alberta. Edmonton was then the jumping-off base for aviation in the northwest and McConachie had caught the romantic bush-flying bug. He dropped out of university before the first-year finals. According to Keith, he found a job as a spare-board fireman with Canadian National Railways, and began taking flying lessons at the Edmonton Aero Club with instructor Maurice Burbidge.

The early years of his flying career are difficult to describe with any confidence because, as with nearly all bush pilots at the time, he kept virtually no records; consequently, all accounts have relied almost exclusively on interviews—and anecdotal material, subject as it is to the distortions of time and memory, needs to be viewed with a reasonable measure of scepticism.

In any event, what we know is that by 1931, he had acquired his commercial licence but, since he was broke and, because flying jobs for minimum-time pilots were virtually non-existent as the Great Depression worsened, his prospects seemed bleak. Then, with true storybook fortuitousness, Uncle Harry came to the rescue. Harry McConachie made his living at the time as a salesman: in company with a travelling midway, he sold "Sur-Gro—the miracle hair tonic." He was, in fact, a snake-oil salesman, and evidently a very good one because McConachie was able to persuade Uncle Harry to put up $2,500 for a used Fokker Universal, G-CAGD, conveniently located at Edmonton and registered to H. R. McConachie of Vancouver, who was not related to Grant. Grant

The early years of his flying career are difficult to describe with any confidence because, as with nearly all bush pilots at the time, he kept virtually no records. . . .

* One of the nearly bankrupt lines that was amalgamated into the Canadian National Railways system in 1918.

Fog Banks Delay "Flying Prince"

Titled Russian Held Up at Regina; On Way to Edmonton

WINNIPEG, Jan. 9.—With the avowed purpose of taking pictures in the Great Bear Lake district, scene of recent discoveries of radium and silver ores, a former Russian nobleman, Prince Leo Galitzine, flew into Winnipeg Thursday on a mail plane, bought himself an aeroplane and flew out again Friday.

The prince, who now lives at Edson, Alta., admitted he planned a flight to the Arctic mineral area but insisted he did not contemplate staking claims there. He was accompanied by a commercial pilot, Grant MacConachie of Edmonton, who took the controls of the new machine as the pair hopped off for Edmonton.

Word received Saturday indicated that Prince Galitzine and Pilot MacConachie had been forced to land at Regina, because of fog, and at press time were still waiting for a break in the rolling fog banks.

McConachie's first company, with Uncle Harry as president, was called Independent Airways and began its brief existence in August 1932.

After a spell of not very successful barnstorming, McConachie landed a contract to haul whitefish during the winter months from Peter Pond Lake in northern Saskatchewan to the nearest railhead, which was just over the Saskatchewan border at Bonnyville, Alberta. Whitefish were very much in demand by the Jewish community in Chicago. In his eagerness to win the contract, McConachie had accepted a rate of 1½ cents a pound. This was enough to pay for fuel and operating expenses but not nearly enough to provide for maintenance and overhaul and pay back his uncle as well.

At this juncture, just as his credit was running out, McConachie experienced another of the fortuitous encounters that occurred throughout his career—he met aristocracy: the wealthy Maltese wife of White Russian refugee Prince Leo Galitzine.[3] The Princess owned two aircraft: a de Havilland Puss Moth, CF-APE, and another Fokker Universal. The Moth was registered to Independent Airways on September 22, 1932, but there is no mention of the Princess. The previous owner is listed as W. J. Holland of Edmonton (Bill Holland, the well-known Canadian Airways pilot). This was a registration of convenience because, at the time, only a Canadian citizen—in those days a British subject—could be registered as the owner of an aircraft, and the Princess did not qualify.

The Fokker Universal, G-CASE, was also registered to Independent Airways on September 22, 1932, and was later written off by another pilot, L. A. Vines, while barnstorming at Gull Lake, Alberta, on June 10, 1933.[4] However, this aircraft had an interesting history before then. In January 1932, newspapers announced that Prince Leo Galitzine, a Russian immigrant who had established a fur ranch in Edson, Alberta, had purchased an aircraft from Canadian Airways and intended to fly up to Great Bear Lake. Asked by a journalist if he intended to stake claims, the Prince replied coyly, "I just want to take some pictures up there." The journalist was sceptical.[5] In any event, Grant McConachie was hired by Galitzine to fly the aircraft back from Winnipeg to Edmonton.

The next news, in February, was that the Prince had incorporated a company:

Great Bear Lake Airways is the most ambitious of the undertakings represented on the list of new [Alberta] companies thus far. It has 15,000 shares of $1 and 1,000 shares without nominal value. . . . Commercial aviation, northern mineral development, land and general industrial business are its purposes.[6]

So much for the "few pictures."

Shortly after this sortie, Great Bear Lake Airways was dissolved and Independent Airways now had a fleet of three aircraft. McConachie is listed as president and Prince Leo as vice-president, although it was almost certainly the Princess's money that was involved. With these three aircraft the company won a contract to haul more than one million pounds (454 000 kg) of whitefish, this time from Peter Pond Lake to the railhead at Cheecham, Alberta, and at a rate of 10¢ a pound. Then, as McConachie was getting ready to fly out to start the contract on November 30, 1932, in his Fokker Universal G-CAGD, he left the engine idling while he went into a shack to discuss details with Uncle Harry. When he returned, the take-off was barely successful; he tried to turn to avoid an obstacle and crashed. Ice build-up on the propeller was given as the cause of the accident.

In an interview taped by CBC radio 30 years later, McConachie describes the accident at length: excerpts list the extent of his injuries.

I had to make a turn too low, a wingtip caught on the ground and the airplane started rolling from wingtip to nose to wingtip to tail to other wingtip to nose to wingtip to tail and ended up in a ball and I was in the middle of the ball. . . .

I tried to move my left arm—I couldn't—and my right arm wouldn't move very well. My wrist was broken; I didn't know it then, but I got my arm up and lifted the goggles together with the face mask, and I could see. This was the first good report that I'd had that day. . . . Well, the engine was back in my lap. I'd broken my legs in 17 different places, both wrists, ribs and fingers—I should have been killed; but, I didn't feel too much pain, except in my left knee—the left kneecap was broken in many, many pieces; and the kneecap had slid up my leg, and it was way up above my knee, way up on the thigh. . . . I had one rod right through my left arm, pinning me back, so I couldn't move. . . .

So, they took me into hospital, I was in there for about two months, with a cast on both hips. . . . I came out with nothing but a stiff leg.

There follows, on the tape, a brief interview with journalist Gordon McCallum:

I was among the reporters who dashed out to the scene, and saw them pulling Grant from the wreckage. He looked to be pretty badly hurt. He was rushed to the Royal Alexandra Hospital and to the operating room. No one told him how he was. Then a nurse with a mask over the lower part of her face leaned over him and whispered, "Don't worry, Mr. McConachie, you're going to be all right." Only her eyes showed above the mask. Grant relaxed and submitted to the anaesthetic. Two days later, they couldn't keep the energetic Grant in his room at the hospital. He insisted on a wheelchair and soon he was flying about the corridors. . . .[7]

At the risk of undue scepticism, it requires a considerable suspension of disbelief to credit that, two days after coming off the operating table with

Prince Will Leave For North Shortly

Announcing his intention of starting northward at the end of the month if possible, Prince Leo Galitzine, Edmonton's air-minded royal visitor, reached the city Sunday afternoon after a trip from Winnipeg in his newly purchased monoplane.

Pilot W. G. MacConachie was at the controls.

"I hope to gather an outfit and leave for the north as near the end of the month as possible," said the prince.

He still maintains that he is making the northern flight solely for recreation and "to take some pictures," although possibility of his staking mining claims was rumored.

Fish Fly South To Feed Chicago

Chicago may be full of gang wars and echoing to the stutter of machine guns, but Chicagoans like to eat fish just the same—and fresh Alberta whitefish and trout have a strong appeal to the Chicago palate.

To keep the Illinois residents supplied, Grant MacConachie, Edmonton-trained commercial pilot, does his stuff, "ferryin" the piscatorial harvest of Cold lake, Alberta, to Bonnyville in his universal Fokker cabin aeroplane.

"I've carried about 65,000 pounds of fish so far," he told the Journal when in Edmonton Thursday, "and I'm going back tomorrow for more."

the severe, indeed gruesome, injuries McConachie described, nurses "couldn't keep the energetic Grant in his room. . . . He insisted on a wheelchair and soon he was flying about the corridors. . . ." Those broken fingers and two broken wrists must have healed remarkably quickly. Moreover, ten years before this broadcast was taped, the same journalist, Gordon McCallum who, incidentally, attended the same school in Edmonton as McConachie, gave a far more restrained account of the injuries in an article on McConachie's career up to that time: "When Grant crashed one time near the Edmonton airport, I watched them pull him out with broken ankles and ribs." Next, McCallum records that, "four days later, in a hospital wheelchair," McConachie recognized the nurse, Margaret Maclean, who had whispered encouragement, and "romance blossomed."[8]

McConachie resumes the CBC interview with a description of events when he came out of hospital. He went up to the fish camp where his two remaining aircraft were carrying on with the hauling operation, taking with him some ardent spirits to cheer his crews.

So I went up by train, on crutches. My left leg was completely stiff, there was no doubt about it, and the doctor told me that there were adhesive lesions in the knee—that he had bound the kneecap together with kangaroo tendon and that I couldn't break the kneecap, not to worry about breaking it, and I would never fly again.

That night, the crew celebrated his return and, after several gins, McConachie said to Chris Green, the engineer who had been with him in the crash: "You know, Chris, I think that, if I lie on the table, and put the leg from the knee to the foot out over the end of the table, and somebody jumped on it, that'd break these adhesions down." Chris Green refused to be the jumper. By now, though, they had consumed more than half a case of gin between six or seven of them, and McConachie persuaded Lewt Veweger, "a great, big husky fellow," to jump on his leg.

The result, when Veweger ran across the room and jumped, was that McConachie was flipped into the air and onto the floor, where he lay writhing in agony. His leg swelled up so quickly, he couldn't get his pants off—he had to cut them off. Two days later the swelling subsided and, within another day or two, he regained enough flexibility to climb back into the cockpit and start flying again.

Wherever the truth lies, McConachie recovered; but this accident had brought the company close to bankruptcy (the wrecked Fokker had

Grant McConachie posing in the open cockpit of his first Independent Airways' aircraft, the Fokker Universal G-CAGD, c. 1932.
—NATIONAL ARCHIVES OF CANADA C-61893

TUESDAY, FEBRUARY 16, 1932

Prince at Head Great Bear Lake Flying Concern

Leo Galitzine Is One of Incorporators of New Airways Firm

McConachie two years later at Charlie Lake, BC. This was the floatplane base for Fort St. John.
—FORT ST. JOHN—NORTH PEACE ARCHIVES

More financial support came from a wealthy Princess. With Puss Moth, CF-APE, in the background, *left to right:* Unidentified, Harry McKeown, Bill Holland (pilot), Princess Galitzine, Grant McConachie and "Uncle Harry." Uncle Harry was the president and the Princess vice-president of Independent Airways.

—HARRY McKEOWN COLLECTION

Sluicing on McLaren Creek.

Planes Transporting Equipment and Supplies to Two Brothers Valley.

Two Brothers Valley.

Ginger Coote had landed on a lake to sit out weather. He was able to fly out before searchers spotted him.
—BRITISH COLUMBIA ARCHIVES H-5903

TWO BROTHERS VALLEY
GOLD MINES LIMITED

200 LANCASTER BUILDING
CALGARY
ALBERTA

May 3rd, 1935

Mr. Louis Lebourdais,
Government Telegraph Operator,
QUESNEL, B. C.

Dear Mr. Lebourdais:

You will recall me speaking to you on the telephone regarding the parties who authorized us to take our plane on the search for Ginger Coote. You advised me at that time that the trip was authorized by D. R. McLaren of Canadian Airways and also Mr. Carter Guest. I would very much appreciate you writing me a letter confirming this.

Thanking you,

I am,

Yours sincerely,

TWO BROTHERS VALLEY GOLD MINES LIMITED

Per: _____

JHB/AB

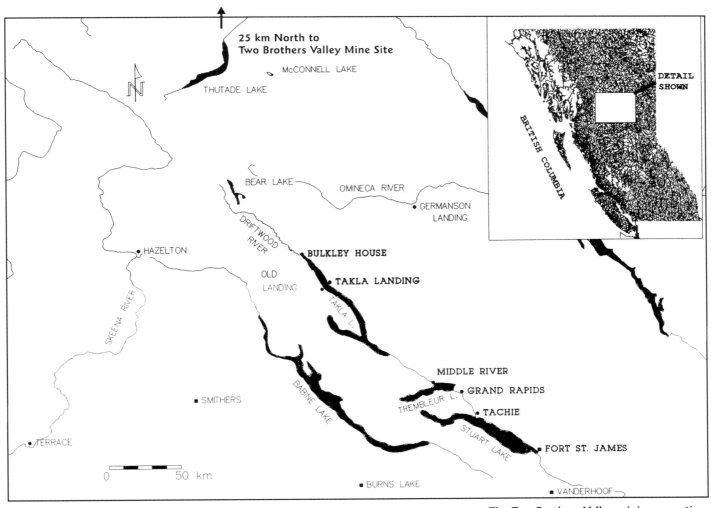

**25 km North to
Two Brothers Valley Mine Site**

McCONNELL LAKE

THUTADE LAKE

N

DETAIL
SHOWN

BRITISH COLUMBIA

BEAR LAKE

OMINECA RIVER

GERMANSON
LANDING

DRIFTWOOD
RIVER

HAZELTON

BULKLEY HOUSE

OLD
LANDING

TAKLA LANDING

TAKLA L.

SKEENA RIVER

MIDDLE RIVER

GRAND RAPIDS

SMITHERS

BABINE LAKE

TREMBLEUR L.

TACHIE

STUART LAKE

TERRACE

FORT ST. JAMES

0   50 km

BURNS LAKE

VANDERHOOF

**The Two Brothers Valley mining operation,
beginning in 1934, was the first in Canada to be
installed and supplied entirely by air.**

not been insured). Then, once again, McConachie made another most fortuitous contact. He was approached by Barney Phillips, an Edmonton mining promoter.

Biographer Keith tells a story that is familiar to most bush pilots—one that was sometimes music to their ears because it meant revenue flying time*—the story of a lost gold mine. In this case, the original prospector to make the strike in 1925, "Black Mike McLaren," had "come back to Seattle [from northwestern BC] with $17,000 in his poke." Returning the following year, he enjoyed the same sort of success but lost everything when a raft overturned. Third time turned out to be unlucky: he went in with a partner and both disappeared. Another prospector had then gone into the area and lived with the Indians for two years before finally persuading one of them to show him where the gold was. The prospector only just made it back to civilization to present his grubstakers with a map before dying. Barney Phillips had bought the map from them.

A report by P. M. Monck, a BC land surveyor who surveyed the area in 1935, lends some credibility to this story. He reported that McClair Creek, at the outlet of which the mine was sited, was a "local name, honoring Chas. McClair,† first discoverer of gold in the creek in 1912. He disappeared later at Thutade Lake, and his disappearance has never been solved."[9]

Phillips, a canny operator, knew that McConachie was in serious financial trouble, and he had chosen McConachie to take him in to the site for the first time because McConachie would then be obliged to maintain the strictest secrecy about where they were going or lose the chance of a lifetime to revitalize his failing company. The only aircraft available was his Puss Moth, CF-APE, and with it, early in the spring of 1933, McConachie moved Barney Phillips and three miners into the lake—a remote one, not far from the headwaters of the Stikine River—with enough supplies to last them for a couple of months.

However, when he returned to Edmonton, he found that the Independent Airways' Fokker Universal had been seized by a sheriff on behalf of creditors. The sheriff promptly repossessed the Puss Moth as well. There is a sad postscript to this part of the story:

Princess Margaret Galitzine of Edson died Friday [May 18, 1934] in Port Said, Egypt, according to a cablegram received here today. No details as to the cause of her death were given. . . .

* Revenue flying time is time paid for by the customer; non-revenue flights occur when the operator has to ferry an aircraft from one area to another at his own expense

† Possibly the "Black" McLaren in Ronald Keith's description.

Princess Galitzine was born in Egypt [presumably of Maltese parents] 27 years ago, the daughter of a wealthy merchant. Later she moved to Alexandria and thence to London, where she was educated. She was married to Prince Leo Galitzine in 1928. In 1929, the Princess came to Canada with her husband, intending to settle in British Columbia. During a visit to this district, they became so impressed with its climate and natural advantages that they decided to locate at Edson, where the Prince established a fur ranch.[10]

Meanwhile, because of the secrecy Barney Phillips had insisted upon, McConachie was the only person who knew where the prospecting crew was—and he now had no means of getting back to resupply them. After weeks of anxiety, he managed to persuade pilot Charlie Elliott, who had recently become the owner of his own company, Pacific Airways, to meet him at Burns Lake and fly a load of supplies into Two Brothers Lake in the Junkers F-13, CF-AMX. Just after take-off, after refuelling at Takla Landing, the engine failed and they were forced down on the lake. They made temporary repairs, but Elliott, after dropping McConachie and the supplies back at Burns Lake, returned to Vancouver to have the engine overhauled.

After more weeks of harrowing anxiety, at the end of July, when "the supply mission was more than six weeks overdue," McConachie finally managed to persuade Ken Dewar, a Consolidated Mining & Smelting pilot, to fly in supplies. Since the original intention had been to preserve total secrecy, this was something of an irony, but Barney Phillips and his three-man crew were rescued in the last stages of starvation.[11] The failure of McConachie, in the interests of secrecy, to approach the authorities—either the Department of National Defence, which was responsible for civil aviation at the time, or the Provincial Police—when he knew that four people were in imminent danger of starving to death seems curious, but that's how the story goes.

Despite this discouraging start, Phillips, who had proved enough gold at the site to warrant a mine, decided to stick with McConachie. He purchased two Fokker Universals, to be operated by McConachie, thus enabling McConachie to set up a new company, United Air Transport, in 1934. The mine to be served by the two Fokkers was the Two Brothers Valley Mine, situated close to the lake of that name (now Toodoggone Lake). It was a placer gold operation running some distance to the west of the lake and north up McClair Creek. It became the first mine in Canada to be installed and supported solely by aircraft.

The help given to McConachie by Barney Phillips was obviously substantial. The two Universals were registered to Phillips in November 1933, and were not transferred to United Air Transport until December 1934. Then, in January 1935, McConachie was able to acquire a Ford 4-AT-A Trimotor G-CARC[12] and based it in Burns Lake. This aircraft could not be equipped with floats, thus it could not be used for summer hauling into the mine; instead, it made some winter trips on skis with heavy and bulky loads into Two Brothers Lake, and it served very well in McConachie's winter fish-hauling operation out of Peter Pond Lake. United Air Transport also took over another Universal, G-CAFU, in November that year, so its fleet was beginning to expand.

In 1936, another pilot who was scraping a living, and who was destined to enjoy a long and distinguished aviation career, Sheldon Luck, managed to find a job with Columbia Aviation.* He joined Grant McConachie to haul fish in northern Alberta, using an aircraft that had been designed as a mailplane, the Boeing 40B-4 (redesignated in Canada as the 40H-4), powered by the same Pratt & Whitney Hornet engine that was to give TCA so much trouble a year or two later.

Luck went down to Vancouver to pick up another Boeing, CF-AMQ. While he didn't know it at the time, McConachie had apparently bought out Columbia Aviation early in 1936. By August 1936, Luck was working for United Air Transport and stayed with it and its successors, Yukon Southern Air Transport and Canadian Pacific Air Lines, until he joined the Trans-Atlantic Ferry Command in 1942. From 1936 to 1942 he worked out of Prince George and Fort St. James, flying a variety of aircraft, but for the last two years almost exclusively Lockheeds on the Whitehorse scheduled runs.

By the beginning of 1938, therefore, McConachie was emerging from the "gyppo" operation phase of his aviation career into something more substantial. His company now had the impressive name of United Air Transport Company Limited, and he owned what could reasonably be called a fleet of five aircraft.

One of the people who went to work for McConachie during this period offers an interesting illustration of McConachie's persuasiveness as well as the unfailing optimism and good luck that led to his eventual success. What follows is based on an interview by Karen Woodward in 1975.[13]

By the beginning of 1938, therefore, McConachie was emerging from the "gyppo" operation phase of his aviation career into something more substantial.

* Columbia was one of the small companies that had started up during the surge of optimism early in 1930.

Jack Baker . . . had suddenly decided he didn't want to become a bean counter; instead he decided to travel to the north country.

The man McConachie persuaded to work for him was as adventurous and optimistic as McConachie himself. Jack Baker had started to study accounting at a Winnipeg college, but then suddenly decided he didn't want to become a bean counter; instead, he decided to travel to the north country. He travelled all the way to the Arctic Ocean. He caught the train to Edmonton; then another to Waterways (Fort McMurray), where he transferred to one of the Hudson's Bay sternwheelers. Travelling down the Athabasca River, through Lake Athabasca, down the Slave River to Great Slave Lake, he eventually reached Fort Simpson.

At Fort Simpson he joined up with an old trapper, and together they built a 40-foot (12-m) river boat and travelled down the Mackenzie River with supplies and eight dogs. Arriving at the delta, they took the east branch of the river and set up camp close to the site of what would later become the settlement of Inuvik. The old man left after a year, but Baker moved to the west side of the delta (to Aklavik) and, for the next seven years, made a good living as a trapper on his own.

His next move was to join the Hudson's Bay Company's main competition in the north, the Northern Trading Company. He became its manager at Fort Liard, in the Northwest Territories, still very isolated but far less so than Aklavik. Two years later, in the winter of 1938, he met McConachie for the first time. The arrival of an aircraft at Fort Liard was still an important event, and Baker recalls it very clearly:

An aeroplane landed nearby in what we called the Black River, a tributary of the Liard. I went down to meet the pilot and he said, "My name is Grant McConachie. Would you mind if I stayed overnight with you?—it's getting late and I'm on my way to Fort Simpson." I said sure, because I was glad of the company. So, he bedded down his aeroplane and stayed. At about eight o'clock I told him I had to keep a radio sked with the Hudson's Bay man at Fort Nelson, and I dragged out the most awful looking contraption of a radio you ever saw.

Baker explained that he had built it himself from parts of an old, broken-down receiver in the store, with the aid of a book called *The Radio Amateur's Handbook*. He had made a little key; then he learned the Morse code and was able to set up a schedule with the Hudson's Bay man in Fort Nelson, which was only about 130 miles (210 km) away. Baker takes up the story again:

McConachie was watching and he said, "Where did you get that thing?" and I told him that I built it. He found this hard to believe—but he said "Well, I think it's wonderful." Then he said to me "Would you be interested in going to work for me?" I said what doing? "Well," he said, "It's like this, my company, United Air Transport, can get a mail contract from the Dominion government from Edmonton to Whitehorse; but we lack one stopping place. They won't give the contract unless I can get a place in between Fort Nelson and Whitehorse. There is a place there, we call it Watson Lake because of an old trapper who lived there—his name is Frank Watson. If you would go in there and establish a radio station and a weather-reporting station, I think we can get this mail contract."

I told him I couldn't just walk away from the trading company. "Oh," he said, "I wouldn't expect you to do that, but keep it in mind."

Shortly after this encounter, the Northern Trading Company sold out to the Hudson's Bay Company, so Baker contacted McConachie and agreed to go into Watson Lake for him. He was dropped there by Ralph Oakes, on the ice, in February 1939, "with a broad axe, a whipsaw and some grub." He was met by "Frank Watson* and a 'big fellow' named Vic Johnson [who] had already got out a set of building logs" and completed part of a building.[14]

With engaging understatement, Baker describes his experiences:

That was quite a little struggle at Watson. You had to haul in logs out of the bush with a hand-made sleigh, and hew them with the broad axe and whipsaw lumber by hand. Fortunately, I was pretty adept at those things in those days. So we built up four good buildings: a radio shack, a bunkhouse, a main station and the cache. It was sledding right along. We were going to put in our own little runway; then war broke out in the fall of '39, and the government decided to start moving into that country. They sent in some surveyors who stayed with me. That was in 1940. They surveyed what is now the present airport at Watson Lake. Shortly thereafter, Vancouver General Construction sent in a number of men and equipment and began punching out the airport.

The arrival of the construction crews in 1940 marked the beginning of what came to be known as the Northwest Staging Route. The United States had become increasingly concerned about the growing military strength and aggressiveness of Japan; and both the US and Canada realized that they had no air bases along the northwest coast from which to mount any defence, either along its coast or inland into Alaska and the Yukon. The first step was to set up the Canada-United States Permanent Joint Board on Defence—and the Board's first decision was to set up a string of air bases stretching from Edmonton, Alberta, to Fairbanks, Alaska—Grand Prairie, Fort St. John, Fort Nelson, Watson Lake and Whitehorse. The next stage, of course, after the jolt of the Japanese attack on Pearl Harbor in December 1941, was to use these bases to facilitate the construction of the Alaska Highway, which began in 1942. "Just how important the road might become was made even clearer in early June

CAPT. DON PATRY
CHIEF PILOT YUKON DIVISION C.P.A.
TRANSFERRED TO COAST

Capt. Don V. Patry, chief pilot for the Yukon Division, Canadian Pacific Air Lines since last May has been transferred to Vancouver where he will be in charge of the Vancouver–Fort St. John run.

For several years past Don has made his home in Edmonton and is one of the most popular pilots to fly the air lanes of the north. He became chief pilot of the Yukon Division, C.P.A. when another pilot, Capt. Sheldon Luck, was "loaned" to the R.A.F. Atlantic Ferry Command last spring. Up until recently Don was flying one of the company's large Lodestar airliners between Edmonton and Whitehorse.

His many friends here hope to see him again in Whitehorse when time and circumstances permit. In the meantime "Happy Landings" to you Don always.

Whitehorse Star
February 5, 1943

* After whom the lake was named.

[1942] after the Japanese attacked Dutch Harbor and occupied Kiska and Attu in the Aleutians."[15]

The initial problem was how to reach these remote places with the heavy equipment required to construct an airfield which, in turn, would provide support from the air before the highway went in. Whitehorse was easy: it was served by the White Pass & Yukon Railway from Skagway. Fort St. John and Fort Nelson could be supplied overland provided the ground was frozen. Watson Lake was by far the most difficult, with no access except by floatplane in the summer or skis in the winter—and by the old fur traders' river road. This was a long and very arduous route from Wrangell, Alaska, up the Stikine River to Telegraph Creek, overland by what was then a rudimentary trail-cum-road to Dease Lake; and from there by some form of boat down the often narrow, winding and treacherous Dease River to its junction with the Liard River at Lower Post— 26 miles [42 km] southeast of Watson Lake on the BC-Yukon border.

The solution was somewhat inept. Boats were provided, with scows that were 45-feet (14-m) long, strained solid with cables and ratchets to the forward end of the boat, making the units over 70 feet (21 m). Consequently, the whole unit had to take the extreme outside of every bend all the way down the river. This was accomplished more or less successfully but, inevitably, there was a good deal of spillage.

Returning now to Jack Baker's account, he describes what it was like to work during McConachie's earlier ventures.

In the days when I was first in there, it was landing on the lake in the summer on floats, and on skis in the winter. So I got then a grounding in weather observing, with the old Dominion weather bureau out of Toronto. I used to have to send three weather reports daily on the radio— by this time, of course, I had learnt to become a reasonably good operator. This was a very onerous job because it had to be seven days a week and there was no let-up—even on Christmas Day, I still had to get up at four o'clock in the morning, take my morning observation, code it and send it out to Fort Simpson, where it would go on down through to Edmonton and Toronto, as well as the noon one, and a four o'clock one in the afternoon again. I did that for three years at Watson.

By this time, the company had changed its name to Yukon Southern and then that was amalgamated with smaller companies into Canadian Pacific. There was a man, Grant McConachie, who had more personality than I could ever imagine in any man before. He was full of BS but he had great organizing power. For instance, take a man like myself, who would work for him, and I worked for McConachie—I'll bet you I worked many times 15-16 hours a day—and in the wintertime do all sorts of things for McConachie. Often, I didn't get a pay cheque—not that it really mattered, because I still had money left over from the trapping days, but you still expect to get paid for doing the work. There were many other fellows. I can remember young mechanics, young fellows coming up in the world, just boys, who would go way up into the far north

The line [north to Whitehorse] progressively grew in size and equipment until, at the outbreak of war, it was the most important factor in the northern air transport picture. Pioneer work done by this company in laying down landing strips and airfields assisted materially in locating the joint defence airfields and the Alaska Highway.

Canada's Northern Air Routes
[CPA Booklet]

country and live a desolate existence—all for McConachie. They wouldn't have done it for anyone else.

He welded it; he made that airline out of three or four smaller companies who had been at one time tremendous rivals. And you can imagine taking pilots and personnel—pilots are sort of prima donnas. Everyone looked up to the old bush pilots. Each bush pilot felt that he was just about as good as anyone else. So when you got a bunch of them together and you tried to weld them all into one company—well, of course, it took a long time to do that; but he did it.

Ironically, when this success was achieved, Jack Baker became dissatisfied. CPA trained him and sent him up to Whitehorse as chief dispatcher. He stayed for four years and then left because CPA had become too bureaucratic. "You had to adhere to regulations—you had to make report, report, report. I had to sit down and make reports to someone down there who I'd never seen—and we didn't get paid very much in those days. Nothing like the American airlines used to pay their fellows— Northwest, United—so I thought to hell with it and went back trapping."

Another observer, Jack Petley, a Canadian Pacific Railway employee, had considerable contact with McConachie and displays a similar mingling of admiration tinged with a faint hint of deprecation:

McConachie was just like a big kid: about six foot tall [183 cm], good looking and he was a pilot. He was a great guy. He could convince anybody of anything—a bit of a womanizer, too, you know—but a great guy.[16]

It would be a mistake, though, to attribute too much of McConachie's success to charm and good luck. Clearly, he possessed more substantive abilities to complement those enviable assets.

Chapter Four

Faltering Steps

*"As you know, we have been operating
for seven years without the loss of a passenger,
and they are killing them off regularly
in the States."*

GRANT McCONACHIE

REALIZING THE FUTILITY of attempting to compete with TCA along the profitable east-west corridor, McConachie was now concentrating on a north-south route in the late 1930s, starting from Edmonton in Alberta and, to begin with, leading up to Whitehorse, Yukon. It is difficult nowadays to appreciate why this route, leading as it did into very sparsely inhabited territory, was worth pursuing. This is because we are so accustomed to flying non-stop across oceans, but before the Second World War things were very different. A number of far-sighted people like McConachie saw a future in the huge Asian population and, to reach that potential market at that time, one had to fly up through the Yukon and Alaska, cross Bering Strait and then fly south again to reach Asia. From very early on, McConachie's objective seems to have been to develop this route.

However, the problem, as with all operations during the interwar period, was to secure a substantial airmail contract to provide funds while developing what we now call an infrastructure. That was the first priority, but McConachie had also realized that the future lay not on floats and skis but on wheels which, in turn, meant airfields—or at least airstrips along the route.

In fact, McConachie had been operating a small, eight-times-a-year mail contract in north-central BC since 1937. Working out of Prince George, UAT's first mail service ran from Fort St. John to Fort Nelson, back to Fort St. John and then to cover much of the area that is now under Williston Lake: Gold Bar, Finlay Forks and Fort Grahame. There was also an additional service from Prince George to Fort St. James, Manson Creek and Takla Landing.[1] This was one of the contracts from which the Post Office Department was making a profit and the operator losing money.

However, progress had been made in his efforts to initiate a north-south airmail service. United Air Transport had, from early 1938, a contract to fly mail out of Edmonton, through Prince George and Fort St. John to Whitehorse. Like so many of the Post Office Department's actions during the 1930s, this contract seems to have been covert and arbitrary. G. A. Thompson, at that time Canadian Airways' general manager but writing in 1944, comments that Canadian Airways was planning to bid on this postal contract, but

These plans unfortunately were brought to naught through the Post Office awarding the United Air Transport, as it was then called, the mail contract from Edmonton to Whitehorse without calling for tenders and so quietly that the first public knowledge of this was an announcement in the papers. . . .[2]

McConachie's ambition was to link up with a service from Vancouver, but he had failed to get Vancouver as a starting point. Instead, in January 1938 he initiated an experimental run from the small town of Ashcroft, about 200 miles (320 km) northeast of Vancouver, to link up with the Edmonton flight. Sheldon Luck, who was working for UAT at the time, describes this development: "The Post Office approved [the Ashcroft venture]. I think it was on a trip basis just to help pay expenses, and we ran weekly Ashcroft, Fort St. John, Whitehorse. The Edmonton mail trip had come up, and we joined it at Fort St. John and carried on to Whitehorse."[3]

However, this did not solve the problem of Vancouver passengers having to make the train journey to or from Ashcroft, and the airmail situation continues to be confusing. As Sheldon Luck describes it:

It was probably about May [1938] when they decided we'd start operating right out of Vancouver, but still without a formal, official mail contract. What was happening, although I didn't find this out until later, was that McConachie was being bumped on a mail contract from Vancouver to Whitehorse because of a political thing. Colonel Coote, Ginger Coote's father, had a lot of political clout.

The Post Office approved . . . I think it was on a trip basis just to help pay expenses, and we ran weekly Ashcroft, Fort St. John, Whitehorse.

GINGER COOTE

Ginger always came to know all the miners and camps in B.C. and the Yukon, accounting for thousands of miles through all kinds of weather, over some of the roughest terrain imaginable, as well as flying patrols for the provincial police. Yet he never lost his nerve or faith in aviation, maintaining flying to be the safest method of travel, even after a crash and several precarious forced landings. His most serious injury was a sprained leg—sustained when stepping out of his plane

"Mercy Pilot"
T. W. Paterson, *Victoria Daily Colonist*, June 28, 1979

Ginger Coote had been running his own company, Bridge River & Cariboo Airways, for several years. As Luck points out,

> He [Colonel Coote] was pulling for Ginger to get it out of Vancouver and he had the Board of Trade or Chamber of Commerce, backing it.[4] At the same time, Aubrey Simmons, who had a number of government appointments in the Yukon—and who, of course, had a lot of political clout—was pulling to have his brother George with Northern Airways at Carcross get it. . . . But McConachie found out that the easiest way to get that mail run was to amalgamate with Ginger Coote Airways. I can't tell you to this day whether they bought Ginger Coote Airways.[5]

As an obvious beginning, McConachie opened a company base in Vancouver early in 1938. In a letter dated April 25, addressed to George Herring, superintendent of Air Mail Services in Ottawa, he offers his own explanation of what had occurred:

> I have been in Vancouver for the past four or five days and find a great deal of interest being shown in our run to Prince George. . . .
> The United Air Lines Corporation had registered the name, United Air lines, before we registered United Air Transport in British Columbia, and as soon as we opened our office in Vancouver, they immediately forced us to stop using our name in this district. We, therefore, revived the company of Ginger Coote Airways, Limited, and are operating in British Columbia under this name. This company is a wholly owned subsidiary of United Air Transport Limited.[6]

McConachie goes on to complain that United Air Lines' reason for objecting was that, in the event of an accident to a United Air Transport aircraft, it would reflect on UAL's record. "As you know, we have been operating for seven years without the loss of a passenger, and they are killing them off regularly in the States. . . ."[7]

The phrase, "revived . . . Ginger Coote Airways," is interesting because that title was not mentioned in the Companies Register until 1939.[8] However, McConachie had exchanged the name United Air Transport for Yukon Southern Air Transport (YSAT) in January 1938. So, while the financial details of this transaction remain obscure, McConachie got his airmail contract to fly out of Vancouver, and Ginger Coote continued for a while to fly it with him in the North. YSAT struggled on from one financial crisis to another, always saved at the last minute, according to biographer Ronald Keith, by McConachie's silvery tongue.

Then, in 1938, McConachie agreed to lease three of the newly designed Fleet 50 Freighters. They were produced, according to Fleet president W. J. (Jack) Sanderson, after extensive inquiries among bush flying crews for their suggestions.

These interesting if not very elegant aircraft were twin-engine biplanes with fixed undercarriages. In fact, despite some excellent design features, they were very much a compromise machine. They fell between the de Havilland Rapide and the new breed of fast, twin-engined monoplanes with retractable undercarriages. The fixed undercarriage obviously reduced speed, but their biggest problem lay with the engines: two Jacobs engines of 300 hp left them almost cripplingly underpowered.[9]

Less than a month after YSAT began to operate the first one, CF-BDX, on August 14, 1938, Sheldon Luck took off from the Liard River at Lower Post and ended up in the trees. The aircraft was damaged beyond repair. Sheldon Luck explains what happened:

When I took off, there was some fog but it was patchy. As I flew into a patch two things happened. The airspeed indicator went out[10] and the starboard engine lost power. I was using full left rudder. I opened the starboard engine to full power but it began to vibrate fiercely; so I cut back on it just as we came out of the fog. Unfortunately, we had swung so far right that I was flying right up the side of a mountain. I had to pick an old burn and put her down—I stalled to drop into the second-growth trees.[11]

Luck made a fine job of this forced landing. Neither he nor his two passengers were injured. The company's second Fleet Freighter, CF-BJT, was picked up by McConachie at Fleet's factory in Fort Erie, Ontario, early in February 1939 and he flew it west, landing at Chicago where he arranged for insurance for the three new Freighters he had leased with a firm of underwriters. Then, after what Ronald Keith calls a "convivial luncheon in the executive dining room," he invited the three insurance executives, one of whom was the president of the firm, to inspect his new acquisition.

He started the starboard engine but, when he tried to start the port one, it backfired and caught fire, setting fire to the wing as well. McConachie's story, as told to the CBC some years later, was that the fire spread so quickly he had no time to shut off the engine before running back through the cabin, where the seats were already burning, and jumping out of the aircraft. It continued to burn until the fuselage broke in half. This "put the engine into wide open, and twisted the undercarriage askew so that the plane jumped the chocks, and away it took off across the field. . . ." There were numerous commercial aircraft on the tarmac and "here was this flaming thing going round and round on one wheel, spraying gasoline all over the Chicago airport."[12]

"... here was this flaming thing going round and round on one wheel, spraying gasoline all over the Chicago airport."

As biographer Keith describes it: "A wide gyration headed the projectile directly toward the row of airliners. Then, suddenly, the engine spluttered and quit. The remains of the Fleet Freighter subsided in a heap of smouldering rubble."[13]

This is a dramatic story but, once again, there are hints of exaggeration. A photograph exists showing not a heap of smouldering rubble but the skeleton of BJT with most of the fabric burned off, its back unbroken and standing squarely on its undercarriage with the chocks still in place in front of the wheels. Several people are standing within a few feet of it, dousing the last smouldering remains of the fire.[14] It must, nevertheless, have been one of the speediest insurance claims after a policy had been issued in aviation history, and affords another example of McConachie's extraordinarily good luck.

So this aircraft, too, became a write-off and McConachie gave up on the Fleet, cancelling the third one he was to lease and turned to another compromise aircraft, but this time closer to the Boeings, Lockheeds and Douglases: the Barkley-Grow.

In January 1940, McConachie pulled off another deal that almost strains credibility. He contacted Canadian Car and Foundry Co. Ltd., Canadian distributors for the Barkley-Grow T8P-1 twin-engine transport, much like the Lockheed 10 (except that it had a fixed undercarriage): a sturdy, all-metal plane with good performance on wheels, skis or floats.[15] Powered by Pratt & Whitney Wasp Junior engines of 400 hp, it had a very respectable performance, with a claimed cruising speed of 216 mph [350 km/h] at 9,600 feet [2 900 m]—although pilots who later flew the Barkley-Grow said the actual cruising speed was more like 160 mph [260 km/h].[16] The only drawback, apparently, was that it could not maintain altitude with a full load on a single engine without serious overheating of the remaining engine.

Grant Moore, who was "business manager and pilot with Grant McConachie in the very early days," offers the following account of the deal:

Grant went in to see Canada Car who, as it happened, had just taken over five aircraft from an ailing Barkley-Grow company. Can-Car knew that Grant had this contract for the airmail to Whitehorse and they had hoped they could make a sale because this would be a good demonstration for these aircraft.[17]

According to Moore, McConachie praised the aircraft and was asked if he could use them. McConachie said yes, "but I want to make one thing

United Air Transport's Waco Custom, CF-BDM, about to take off on the
first mail run from Whitehorse to Prince George, 1938. Left to right: Jack Wilson;
J.B. Williams; Louis Labourdais, MLA; J.G. Turgeon, MP; Ginger Coote; and
Sheldon Luck.—NATIONAL ARCHIVES OF CANADA, PA-124219

McConachie had two stiff competitors in the Yukon. One was George Simmons' Northern Airways, operating out of Carcross. This Ford Trimotor was operated by the other, the British-Yukon Navigation/White Pass Route, operating out of Whitehorse.
—HAROLD DAVENPORT COLLECTION, BRITISH COLUMBIA ARCHIVES F-4771

What appears to be the end of McConachie's first Ford Trimotor, CF-BEP, after an RCAF Hawker Hurricane swung on take-off and collided with it at Vancouver airport in March, 1939. However, after McConachie had won a handsome award from the government for its loss, it was sold to Northern Airways, repaired and operated for another two years.—PETERS COLLECTION, ROYAL BC MUSEUM

The first of McConachie's ill-fated Fleet Freighters. CF-BDX made a forced landing on an old burn when one engine failed just after take-off out of Lower Post. Although the engines were salvaged, the rest of the aircraft was not.

—PETERS COLLECTION, ROYAL BC MUSEUM

McConachie and Sheldon Luck in front of the Lockheed 18 Lodestar, "Yukon Emperor", after the first scheduled flight from Whitehorse to Vancouver.

—NATIONAL ARCHIVES OF CANADA, PA-124226

From Edmonton comes the report that the Yukon Southern Air Transport through its president, Mr. Grant McConachie intends making application to both the Canadian and United States government to extend its airlines from Whitehorse, Y.T., to Fairbanks, Alaska.

Mr. McConachie is also reported to have made the statement that the first survey flight on a proposed air route from Edmonton to Vladivostok will probably be made this summer. If this proposed route becomes established it is understood that the local airport will be included therein.

It will be remembered that when Mr. Le Bourdais and Capt. Bell, manager of the Edmonton airport were here some time ago it was stated that Whitehorse would be the most southern airport to be used in the Trans-Pacific air service to the Orient when it is eventually inaugurated as Imperial Airways and the Trans-Canada hook up.

Whitehorse Star,
May 17, 1940

clear: I don't have any money." The Can-Car representatives responded with what they called a nominal price, $20,000 apiece. McConachie repeated that he had no money and eventually persuaded them to let him have the aircraft for a dollar down and a $500-a-month lease.[18]

It seems, to put it mildly, curious that Can-Car would in effect give away three brand-new and perfectly serviceable aircraft, and one can only speculate. One possibility is that Can-Car had its attention focussed on potentially large and lucrative military contracts and, since the Barkley-Grows were its only venture in civil aviation, they got lost in the shuffle.

In any event, the first of these aircraft, CF-BMG, was in service with several different companies until 1947; the second, BLV, until 1960; and the third, BMW, until 1965.[19] By any yardstick, then, this must rank as the most profitable deal ever afforded an aviation operator and the worst ever suffered by a vendor.

Yet another instance of McConachie's apparently endless good fortune occurred at this time. The proposed purchase of the much faster Barkley-Grows would have rendered the lumbering Ford Trimotor virtually obsolete. However, on March 3, 1939, BEP was parked on the tarmac at Vancouver Airport. By this time, the training of military pilots was gathering pace and a young RCAF Sergeant-Pilot, who had just graduated from Camp Borden, Ontario, with his wings, was practising what were known as circuits and bumps—take-offs and landings. During one take-off, he failed to correct for torque; the Hawker Hurricane fighter he was flying swerved off the runway and, just below flying speed, collided with the parked Trimotor.

The result was what looked like an unmistakable write-off. McConachie's response was to sue the government and he won. Yukon Southern was awarded $53,000 for loss of air-freight contracts and collected $5,200 for the loss of the aircraft.[20] In fact, BEP was sold to the White Pass's British-Yukon Navigation Company who, presumably, restored and flew it until 1941, when it was scrapped.[21]

Nevertheless, McConachie was, in spite of his good luck, constantly on the verge of a financial collapse. He describes his fiscal woes and what he did about them and, in doing so, his visions of a route to the Orient:

Barney Phillips Jr.,[22] who was handling the financing and traffic end of the airline, was continually in trouble with all our creditors, particularly the credit manager of Imperial Oil. So I decided to try to consolidate our debts into one—and only one company.[23]

McConachie goes on to describe his meeting with the board members of Imperial Oil in Toronto. He had plans to fly north through Whitehorse and Alaska, cross to Siberia and then down to China. He had the aircraft to do that. He claimed he had an agreement with the Russian Amtorg trading company in New York to have airports installed in Siberia and that the Chinese would be delighted to have a reliable mail service in the remoter areas to the north. As McConachie portrayed it:

[The Board members] were pleased with the idea: how fast the mail service would be through to Vladivostok and North America, and we'd take passengers and their mail for a dollar a mile to the Bering Sea. They [Amtorg] agreed to all this, and to putting in any airports we needed, over and above the ones they had. All we had to do was use Russian crews, Siberia to Shanghai. We didn't mind who the crews were. We'd check them out.

The outcome was that, "after some hesitation," the Imperial executives agreed to extend to McConachie a $100,000 credit without interest. As usual, McConachie was taking a good deal for granted. Some might doubt that the Russians would, when it came to it, build airfields to accommodate him, and the Chinese had not been consulted; but he brushed that aside with the suggestion that they were bound to be delighted to get modern transport in such remote areas. It was a remarkable piece of salesmanship on McConachie's part. But, despite the Great Depression, Imperial Oil was still a very prosperous corporation and the loss of $100,000 could be weighed against the possibility of handsome revenue in gasoline and oil sales if McConachie succeeded with his vision.

This [McConachie concludes] put all our debts into one account—because we hadn't paid any debts for about a year or a year and a half—and we were able to pay off all our outstanding bills. Imperial Oil were a tremendous help in getting us out of our financial difficulties. So it was the route to the Orient that put the Imperial Oil deal over and eventually put us on a sound financial basis in northwestern Canada.
    We never did fly the route, of course, as Yukon Southern Air Transport—but only because the war intervened and we were instructed by Ottawa to wait until after the war.[24]

While McConachie doesn't mention it in his CBC interview, Keith claims that this was the first time McConachie demonstrated the great circle route concept.* "Using a schoolroom globe and a piece of string, he spread the string from Edmonton up to Whitehorse and then swinging down over the Aleutians, across the ocean and down to Shanghai. Then he marked the string with a pen. Next he moved the string from Edmonton to Shanghai via Honolulu around the bulge of the Pacific, and marked the string again. This illustrated that the route over the Pacific was

* The arc of a circle on a globe is the shortest route between two points, not a straight line on a map.

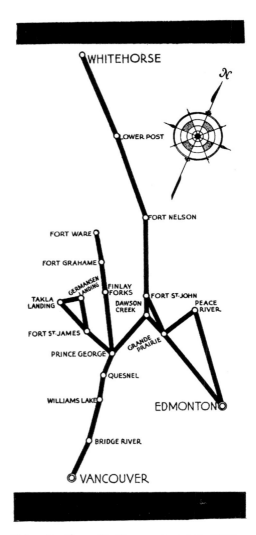

Yukon Southern Air Transport routes, 1938.

2,000 miles (3 300 km) longer than the great circle route via the Yukon."[25] Keith's Bush Pilot with a Briefcase leaves a strong impression that McConachie was the first to appreciate this approximate great circle route; whereas, of course, many people—most notably James Richardson and Juan Trippe—were aware of its possibilities as early as 1931.[26]

McConachie's claim that Imperial Oil's line of credit solved all Yukon Southern's debt problems is, of course, an exaggeration; but his exaggerations all seem to have been remarkably effective. He certainly did not experience aviation's version of rags to riches, but he did gradually expand his services, both to the north and further south.

While McConachie favoured—and in a sense pioneered—the concept of great circle routes to the Orient and to Europe, his second important realization was that the use of floats in the summer and skis in the winter was becoming obsolescent except in very remote areas. Wheels, particularly now that the concept of retractable undercarriages had been adopted, were the wave of the future. They would, for the most part, do away with the downtime forced on bush operators by the freeze-up and break-up periods; and, where lighted runways were available, they would make night flying feasible—particularly important during the short daylight hours in the north in winter. In this case, too, McConachie pioneered the development of wheels in the north, as witness Jack Baker's work to construct an airstrip at Watson Lake.

Meanwhile, though, his company was still far from profitable. Apart from the airline route to the north, it was still involved in bush flying, competing with the experienced and well-organized Canadian Airways—particularly for the mail runs in the Omineca district, and the general bush flying in that area, where Sheldon Luck, among other pilots, was competing with Russ Baker of Canadian Airways from the base at Fort St. James. As well, McConachie's fleet was made up of Fokkers, Norsemen, Wacos, Fairchilds, Barkley-Grows and a lone Boeing 40-H4, originally used for fish hauling. Such a diversity inevitably complicates maintenance as well as the necessary inventory of spare parts. All this was compounded by the early wartime restrictions on commercial flying, which brought reductions in the supply of aviation fuel and the growing difficulty of finding the spare parts required to keep aircraft flying.

If, however, you read the newspapers, you would never have guessed McConachie was in trouble; on the contrary, they suggested rather persuasively the appearance of affluence and success. For the next 18 months there was a stream of announcements and advertisements in the Whitehorse Star and the Prince George Citizen—all, naturally enough, couched in the most positive terms.

On June 9, 1939, the Star reported that "Mr. Grant McConachie . . . has completed arrangements for operating a regular tri-weekly service between Vancouver, Oliver, Vernon and Kamloops. Thus will the fertile Okanagan Valley be served with a transportation service which is bound to prove valuable to its residents and shippers in the future."

In May 1940 the same paper, under the heading "YUKON SOUTHERN AIR TRANSPORT OUT TO EXTEND ITS OPERATIONS," reported that McConachie intended to apply to both the Canadian and the United States governments to extend his route from Whitehorse to Fairbanks, Alaska. Furthermore, he would probably make a "survey flight on the proposed air route from Edmonton to Vladivostok later that summer."

The next one, in August, is worth quoting at some length:

The sleepy traveller, unshaved, hurriedly dressed with his coat and tie clutched in his hand, who just makes the airport as the pilot is gunning his ship, need no longer worry about an overlooked breakfast according to an announcement made by officials of the Yukon Southern Air Transport Ltd.

A new service is being inaugurated on the Yukon Southern's twin-motored Barkley-Grow airliners operating on a thrice-weekly schedule to the Yukon, the Peace River area and the British Columbia Interior from Edmonton and Vancouver to Whitehorse. As an added courtesy, beginning July 24th, the company will serve lunches to their passengers in flight. This service will be offered not alone for the benefit of our late arrival but more to alleviate the common pangs of hunger which assail many air travellers when flying at high altitudes.

This latest effort on behalf of the company to provide further passenger comfort will be the pleasant duty of the co-pilot. The smartly uniformed hardy assistants of northern flyers whose job it is to warm motors in sub-blizzardy weather, help load furs and other northern express now take on, along with their other duties, the more glamorous role of male hostess. This lighter work of theirs will be carried out with the same efficiency that has marked other services of Yukon Southern's personnel and in the future many a fair lady's heart will skip a beat when she is offered a second cup of coffee by the gallant riders of the airways.[27]

The reporter obviously had fun with this; and one suspects that, when the co-pilots read it, the atmosphere crackled with virile profanities. As well, it sounds like a delightful twist on the "witticism" that stewardesses found so objectionable: "Coffee, tea or me?"

By this time the $100,000 credit by Imperial Oil was diminishing rapidly and there were, as pessimists had forecast, not enough passengers to sup-

CIVILIAN AIRCRAFT GROUNDED IN B.C. BY ORDER IN COUNCIL

An order–in–council gazetted Saturday in Ottawa bans all flights over British Columbia and its waters by civilians aircraft not engaged in training pilots or operating on regularly scheduled passenger flights, except with the express permission of the civilian inspector of aviation

Previously a 200-mile [320-km] zone inland from the coastline had been declared a prohibited area, and the ban on civil flying applied to this region. The whole province and the contiguous waters now are regarded as prohibited areas.

Charter aircraft come under the ban. Few others are affected because there are practically no civilian aircraft being flown for private transport apart from charter planes.

Whitehorse Star,
January 30, 1942

port the service to the Orient, or even to Whitehorse. By the middle of 1940, McConachie was looking around for another of his "incredible deals." The deal, when it developed, must have convinced McConachie that the angels really were on his side. It was the offer of a merger.

One of the first indications that a substantial merger was in the making appears in a letter from Walter Gilbert, superintendent of the Pacific Division of Canadian Airways, to F. B. (Russ) Baker and C. G. (Gordon) Ballentine, dated February 25, 1941. Baker was based in Fort St. James at the time, and Gilbert advises that "As you are aware it has been necessary for reasons of Company policy, for operational control of our Fort St. James district to be placed under Yukon Southern, under a 'pooling' agreement recently arranged."[28]

Stepping back a moment to 1939, a host of small bush companies were competing for business that inevitably shrank with the outbreak of war. In the same year, on June 26, the man who had done more than any other in Canada to promote aviation, James Richardson, died of a heart attack. Then, in 1940, Canadian Pacific Railway's Sir Edward Beatty, apparently at last realizing that air transport had come of age, took over Richardson's place as president of Canadian Airways.

In the words of historian Ken Molson: "It had long been an understanding between Sir Edward Beatty and James A. Richardson that if the CPR ever wished to enter the air transport field they would always be able to do so through Canadian Airways Limited."[29] Beatty set his people to work organizing a merger of as many smaller companies as possible and, with the enviable resources of the CPR, he was able to accomplish this within two years. For people who worried about too much concentration—in other words, monopoly, an accusation to which the CPR had long become accustomed—Beatty advised the government that his motive was to rationalize northern air transport in time of war. Optimists greeted this move with approval; sceptics spoke snidely about enlightened self-interest.

Altogether the CPR took over ten smaller aviation companies, including Yukon Southern, eventually merged in May 1942 into Canadian Pacific Air Lines Limited. The potential for friction between the former owners of them under the merger was, of course, manifest.

Change is never easy to encompass and the change from bush flying to the inevitably more structured and bureaucratized world of airline flying

First airmail covers flown by United Air Transport in 1937 and 1938.—SHELDON LUCK COLLECTION

was often difficult to assimilate. The cultural shock was the more severe because bush flying crews were, almost by definition, individualists. It was very hard, even for a well-organized company like Canadian Airways, to keep a close check on bush operations with their multitude of unforeseeable contingencies.

In short, it was very difficult to maintain anything approaching close control over bush flying crews; thus the jolt of abruptly becoming involved with a highly structured and very controlled airline schedule was severe; and, perhaps inevitably, air crews felt, if not exactly disfranchised, at least diminished. On top of all this was the obvious difficulty in any merger of who was to be the controller and who the controlled; and this aspect appeared almost immediately with Canadian Pacific Air Lines, even before it had formally adopted that name.

In his February 1941 letter to Russ Baker and Gordon Ballentine, Walter Gilbert, after advising them of the "pooling" agreement that put the Fort St. James base under the control of Yukon Southern, went on to say that Baker will have to be moved out of Fort St. James because he could not work under McConachie.[30] There were, of course, many other similar difficulties to come—but Grant McConachie had the personality and ability to come out on top in the end.

Chapter Five

Room at the Top

"The government said, 'If you can find a way, any way, privately, go ahead; do what you like.'"

MAURICE McGREGOR

INTERESTINGLY, in his interview with the CBC, McConachie jumps from a description of his coup—the $100,000 credit from Imperial Oil in 1938—all the way to 1947, when he became president of CPA. This is hardly surprising because these were not really his glory days. The Imperial Oil credit was soon expended and Yukon Southern did not prosper in the early 1940s.

Evidently, though, the "pooling agreement" mentioned in Gilbert's letter of February 1941 was well advanced. In April, a Vancouver newspaper announced, under the headline, "World's Fastest Commercial Planes for Yukon Run," that McConachie had taken delivery in Vancouver of the first of two Lockheed 1808 Lodestars. To do so, he must obviously have had access to CPR's financial resources; and, as always, he elicited maximum press coverage from the new acquisitions. The event earned two large photographs on the front page of the newspaper, with the caption, "Grant McConachie, president of Yukon Southern, who rode up from the south in the plane; standing beside him is L. D. Parker, Lockheed test pilot, who delivered the ship."

The caption goes on to record that

The big 14-passenger ship, which will shortly be placed on the run from Vancouver to Whitehorse, cruised at an average speed of 228 miles an hour [370 km/h] on the trip to Vancouver with less than 60 per cent of power and a 30-mile-an-hour [50 km/h] headwind, and will prove a great asset when the company increases its services between here and the Yukon to three trips weekly on June 1.[1]

That Yukon Southern could acquire these two aircraft at a time when the United States and Britain were rapidly developing their air forces is intriguing, because the Lockheed 14 (Super Electra) and the 1808 (Lodestar) were also produced as the Hudson and the Ventura, respectively—both as bomber and reconnaissance aircraft.[2] The Lodestars were a big improvement over the 10As and the passenger capacity was adequate for the traffic on that route. In any case, it is very unlikely that Yukon Southern could have acquired the superior DC-3s even if they'd wanted them because the military were purchasing as many as they could get their hands on as war with Japan became more and more of a threat; and the Allies in Europe were doing the same.

As it turned out, the utilization of the Lodestars was brief: although both were registered to Yukon Southern in April 1941, they were returned to the United States in September.[3] They did however start the tri-weekly service on June 1. As well, Barney Phillips Jr., now assistant general manager of the company, "informs us that commencing on June 14 there will be a stewardess service inaugurated."[4]

Once again, McConachie made the best of press coverage when the Lodestars went back to the United States to be refitted as military aircraft before being ferried across the Atlantic:

Two of the newest and largest commercial transports in Canada flying between Vancouver, Edmonton and the Yukon are to be stripped of their comfortable trappings and fitted out as troop transports for use by the British Government in Egypt.

At the request of the British government, and in accordance with their own policy of all-out aid in the war effort, Yukon Southern Air Transport Ltd. are sacrificing their recently purchased Lockheed Lodestars for service in Egypt.[5]

Nevertheless, while these changes were taking place, McConachie was being assimilated into the austere atmosphere of the CPR's western headquarters in Winnipeg in 1942. The contenders for the job of running CPR's Air Services, Western Air Line (in other words, the western division of CPA), had to be chosen from ten companies, each, as McConachie recorded, "with its own president, most of them senior to me in age, if not experience. . . ."[6] The main contenders seemed to be Wop May and Punch Dickins, of Canadian Airways, and Leigh Brintnell of Mackenzie Air Service. These two companies had been fierce competitors on the route from Fort McMurray to Aklavik. There were, of course, several other hopefuls among the other companies involved in the merger, so the CPR had a difficult task on its hands sorting out these conflicts before things settled down to the smooth, hierarchical administration they were accustomed to.

Railwayman Jack Petley describes his experience at that time:

I was working as secretary to the general manager, Western Lines, Winnipeg (CPR), Mr. [W. A.] Mather. In 1942, Mr. Mather became vice-president [of Canadian Pacific Air Lines], and Mr. [W. M.] Neal went to Montreal as vice-president of the CPR and I became secretary to the vice-president, Mr. Mather. Somehow, they had picked up Grant McConachie of Yukon Southern out of Edmonton and made him the western manager and got rid of Wop May. Punch Dickins was in Montreal, CPA's head office. After the merger, we set McConachie up in the boardroom right next to where I worked, and I bought his furniture for him. He wanted a liquor cabinet. We didn't buy one for him so he said, "I'll buy one myself."

He wanted me to be his secretary but he didn't offer me as much money as I had been getting on the railway, and I'd been on the railway since 1929. So I said I didn't want to move; so he got Hugh Main from Moose Jaw. Hugh had been working in the claims department in Moose Jaw. He wasn't a secretary—he never had been. Then Grant took Harry Porteous, the assistant chief clerk in the vice-president's office, and made him office manager. Hughie had such a time with Grant, because Grant had always worked on his own. And about three o'clock one afternoon Grant came into the office and shouted across the desks, "Hey, Hugh, let's to go down to the Y for a swim." This shook everyone up because it wasn't the sort of thing that happened in the CPR.

Then, in 1942, came the construction of the Alaska Highway. McConachie had pioneered the Northwest Staging Route to Whitehorse, and the construction of the highway would obviously necessitate a dramatic increase in air support. Yukon Southern—by then taken over by Canadian Pacific Air Lines—was just as obviously in the best position to provide this support. Unfortunately, though, construction of the highway was being paid for by the United States. Consequently, the United States insisted that the majority of the flying should be contracted to an American airline: in this case, Northwest Air Lines.

The end result was that Canadian Pacific was barely breaking even during the war years, even though the volume of business was further increased by the construction of the Canol Pipeline from Norman Wells, on the Mackenzie River, to Whitehorse. However, as Kaye Lamb points out, another factor intervened: "Unfortunately the outlook was anything but promising. About 90 percent of the existing traffic was related to the war effort; how much traffic there would be to take its place when the war ended remained to be seen. Price controls were holding rates at uneco-

PILOT SHELDON LUCK LEAVES YUKON SOUTHERN FOR FERRY SERVICE

Captain Sheldon Luck, one of the most popular pilots to traverse the air lanes of the north and who, after three years service with the Y.S.A.T. was raised to the rank of chief pilot of the Y.S.A.T., division of the Canadian Pacific Airlines, has resigned this post in order to join the Ferry Command with headquarters in Montreal.

Sheldon has more than six thousand flying hours to his credit and hitherto has been a familiar figure in Whitehorse and throughout the Yukon Territory. His many friends here wish him every success and happy landings at all times. He is being succeeded in the Canadian Pacific Airlines service by another popular pilot, Capt. Don Patry who has also been in the service of the Y.S.A.T. for the past three years. Congratulations are extended to Don who will merit his promotion.

Whitehorse Star
June 5, 1942

nomic levels, and to Montreal's annoyance the airlines, though working to capacity, were operating at a loss."[7]

Meanwhile, friction had developed between east and west. In Montreal, L. B. Unwin had been appointed president of CPA with the celebrated Punch Dickins as general manager. To quote Lamb again, "Financial control lay in Montreal, with Unwin and Dickins, both of whom were inclined to pinch pennies, but so far as the west was concerned, policy matters were dealt with by W. M. Neal, the railway's vice-president in Winnipeg. Neal had been much attracted by Grant McConachie's enthusiasm and ambition and he appointed him general manager of western airlines. Since, in the words of close associates, McConachie 'defined success as expanding the airline rather than making money,' some friction with Montreal was inevitable."[8]

In fact, Punch Dickins was comfortably ahead in seniority. In 1940, Sir Edward Beatty, in co-operation with G. E. Woods-Humphrey, previously the managing director of Imperial Airways, had set up Canadian Pacific Air Services to provide a trans-Atlantic air service. This was one part of the CPR's contribution to the war effort, and was designed primarily to ferry military aircraft to Britain. The first flight of seven Lockheed Hudsons took off from Gander on November 10, 1940, and landed in Britain 10½ hours later. On February 1, 1941, C. H. (Punch) Dickins of Canadian Airways was appointed vice-chairman of Canadian Pacific Air Services and became general manager of ferry operations a month later.[9]

Dickins' tenure in this capacity lasted only a few months because the responsibility for trans-Atlantic ferry services was taken over by the Royal Air Force Ferry Command in August 1941. Because the Canadian Pacific Air Services operation had been successful—in its short career it had ferried more than 300 aircraft to Britain—one can speculate that Dickins must have felt secure in his prospects of becoming the top man in Canadian Pacific Air Lines when it was formed early in 1942. As we know, in the end McConachie came out on top, and Dickins left early in 1947 to join de Havilland as a sales representative.

In any event, CPA continued to be fully occupied if not profitable during the war years. It had started in 1942 as a merger of ten different operators and a fleet of 77 aircraft of almost every conceivable size and shape.[10] Consequently, the administrative difficulties reached well beyond the problems of crew seniorities. Considerable credit is due to the people who managed to sort all this out and produce, eventually, a viable airline.

CANADIAN PACIFIC AIR LINES LIMITED

Additional modern aircraft were added to your Air Lines. To provide for the traffic, extensive new radio communication installations were also required, as well as additions to ground equipment, shops and airport facilities. To finance these capital expenditures your Company advanced an amount of $4,027,000 during the year.

Canadian Pacific Railway Annual Report for the Year 1943.

As for McConachie, even though Northwest Air Lines had won out on most of the early contracts for the Alaska Highway flying, he received tangible recognition from the Canadian government for his management of the Alaska Highway and Canol Pipeline air support operations. In 1946, newspapers reported that

Air Minister [Colin] Gibson announced last Wednesday that Mr. Grant McConachie, manager of Western Lines of the Canadian Pacific Air Lines Ltd. . . . had been awarded the McKee Trans-Canada trophy. This much-coveted trophy is awarded annually for the greatest contribution to Canadian civil aviation. In making the award, Mr. Gibson stated that: "Through his exploration and pioneering, both the Alaska Highway and the Canol project were brought to an earlier successful conclusion than otherwise would have been possible.

Through his pioneering on the Whitehorse run the delivery of much needed aircraft and supplies to Russia was greatly speeded up. His companies were the first to use radio facilities, both in the air and on the ground, and in that part of the country to operate multi-engined aircraft, both of which were major factors in promoting safe aerial transportation."[11]

Nevertheless, and despite this distinction, the CPR brass remained dissatisfied: the airline was failing to make a profit. One obvious difficulty it faced during the war was the acquisition of new aircraft to meet the growing passenger and freight traffic on the northern route. Fortunately, the route had such strategic importance that CPA managed to purchase a number of Lockheed Lodestars. Apart from the two it had almost immediately returned to the military in 1941, it acquired ten more from 1943 to 1945, as well as six Boeing 247Ds. During this period, the schedule on the Whitehorse run increased from three a week to daily except Sunday. However, there was still the problem that CPA was confined by C. D. Howe's ruling: it could not compete on any of TCA's routes—indeed, it would have to relinquish all air services after the war.

During wartime businessmen-politicians like Beaverbrook in Britain and Howe in Canada enjoyed what amounted to a moratorium of democracy. As long as they produced results they were given virtually dictatorial powers. When the war ended, however, so did the moratorium and Howe was obliged to quietly rescind this draconian edict. For CPA, though, there was still the problem that, when the military necessity of most of its routes ended, these routes became in effect feeder routes to TCA's main tracontinental ones. Whether or not these feeder routes were economically viable remained to be seen. The railwaymen in the CPR were clearly pessimistic.

In 1946, CPA began to re-equip, replacing the Lodestars with the more efficient DC-3s; and, in 1947, CPA was granted licences to operate, in

C.P.A.L. PLANES FLYING THROUGH TO WHITEHORSE

Important northward extension from Vancouver of the Canadian Pacific Air Lines air route has been made.

The company is now operating planes directly from Vancouver to White Horse in the Yukon, a 1196-mile [1 925-km] air trip occupying seven and a half hour's flying time. Previously, Canadian Pacific planes northbound from Vancouver went only as far as Fort St. John, where passengers transferred to the Edmonton–White Horse planes.

The new service means that better equipment and more of it will be operated out of Vancouver. Instead of 10 passenger Boeings 14 passenger Lockheed Lodestars are to be used.

Planes for White Horse leave Sea Island Airport, outside Vancouver daily except Sunday at 9 a.m. and arrive at their destination at 4:45 p.m.

Prince George Citizen
June 3, 1943

CF-BMW, one of Yukon Southern's bargain-basement Barkley-Grows in Vancouver, 1942, shown here in CPA livery.—CANADIAN AIRLINES ARCHIVES

Sister ship, CF-BQM, taking off from the Fraser River at Quesnel.
—GEORGE YOUNG, PETERS COLLECTION, RBCM

Ginger Coote, the quintessential image of the dashing bush pilot in the 1930s. He joined forces with McConachie briefly before operating on his own during the latter part of the Zeballos gold rush.—MARGARET RUTLEDGE COLLECTION

◄ Sheldon Lake, BC, 1942. The advantages of the Barkley-Grows were that they were fairly fast but still available for bush flying as well as airline service.—A. FINNIE, BRITISH COLUMBIA ARCHIVES, F-4402

Sheldon Luck, the grand old man of Canadian aviation. He began his flying career in 1930. He left CPA in 1942 to join the Trans-Atlantic Ferry Command and was still flying commercially into the 1970s. In 1980, he was inducted into Canada's Aviation Hall of Fame.—ROYAL BC MUSEUM

British Columbia, routes between Vancouver and Prince Rupert, and between Vancouver, Penticton and Calgary. The service from Vancouver to Penticton began with a DC-3 on September 8, 1947; it was followed by the first Vancouver-Calgary flight on September 22, 1947.[12]

Air engineer Mansell Barron joined CPA in 1946, working on maintenance in the hangar at Edmonton Municipal Airport. His comments are revealing. Among other things, they demonstrate the CPR's ambivalence about getting into the airline business in the first place:

CPA wasn't an airline at that time [1946]; it was a conglomerate of companies. The idea was to fly people to the railway centres where passenger trains would take them across Canada. They couldn't see—McConachie could, but the railway people couldn't—any sense in flying all the way across Canada when they had a good railroad system. Marvellous passenger service and food and silverware and God knows what. I'm telling you, you couldn't travel under nicer circumstances than on the CPR. The food was better than anything you can get today, because it was all fresh—there was no refrigeration, just ice boxes, and they bought it as they went along.

So they [the CPR] were satisfied with the north-south feeder lines. When I started they had Cansos, Barkley-Grows, Norsemen. . . . Then they bought the DC-3s.[13]

In 1946, then, even with the DC-3s, CPA was still some way from becoming a substantial airline. We have already seen evidence that the CPR brass were disturbed by the lack of profits, but the break evidently came in the spring of 1948, when the Fraser Valley communities suffered the worst flooding of the century. It was then that the CPR recognized what the first helicopter operators were beginning to exploit. With most disaster situations, aircraft can still operate. When floods or avalanches cut off roads and railway lines, this is particularly so.

McConachie, now president of CPA, was quick to seize this opportunity because, as Mansell Barron describes the situation:

The whole country here was flooded. Both railroads were washed right out. . . . The CPR had to stop at Sicamous because the whole Fraser Valley from shore to shore was a mass of water. It looked like a huge lake with little hummocks covered with cows or chickens; it was an unbelievable sight. So TCA flew their passengers in North Stars—from Penticton to Vancouver. They also flew them from Prince George.

The CPR didn't have any aeroplanes like a North Star; they had a bunch of DC-3s. They gathered all 14 of them and moved them all to Penticton.[14] We moved 2,800 passengers for the railroad to Vancouver. All the baggage, and 290 carloads of express—newspapers and lord knows what else.

It lasted for almost a month. The railroad was so impressed with this use of aircraft; they'd never dreamed that this would help them. They had no real vision of what an aeroplane could do for them. So when McConachie wanted his airline to step in, they said okay, go ahead. and that's when it really started. If it hadn't been for that flood, he'd still be looking for his airline. That flood was the turning point for McConachie.

I didn't go back north again. In those days, the top wage I was getting with CP Air was $280 a month. You never got any overtime—seven days a week.

Mansell Baron, CPA

CANADIAN PACIFIC AIR LINES LIMITED

* The modifications consisted mainly of replacing the American Pratt & Whitney engines with British Rolls-Royce Merlins in accord with the government's policy of Empire Preference, even though the Pratt & Whitney engines had proved far more reliable in airline service.

The newspapers gave extensive reports of the operation. Under such headings as "Aircraft Set Records as Sole Link for City," the comments were invariably, and sometimes fulsomely, positive: "In four days since flood waters severed British Columbia's surface transportation links, Western Canadian aviation has been transformed from lusty adolescence into capable, dependable adulthood."[15]

While Barron's enthusiasm, and the newspaper reports, may suggest exaggeration, the flood of 1948 really did open many people's eyes to the true potential of aviation. There was still no Trans-Canada Highway, but everyone had come to take it for granted that the CPR and the CNR would get people across the country. It was almost a traumatic experience to discover that this comfortable illusion could be shattered for a whole month.

Once again, what had been a disaster to most people turned into shining good fortune for McConachie. Now, with the success of the flood operation behind him, he was able to go ahead with his ambition to expand CPA. Attempts to provide direct transcontinental competition to TCA would not bear fruit for another decade; C. D. Howe was still reluctant to concede; but between them, McConachie and Neal won some concessions a year before the flood. As historian Kaye Lamb points out:

Their first success came in 1947, when the Air Transport Board required the C.P.R. to give up all nonscheduled and charter licenses but gave it permission to operate a network of regional services in the west and one or two in Quebec. In 1948, the network was extended to the Yukon and the Arctic. The same year, the Canadian Pacific finally secured the concession that McConachie coveted—permission to fly across the Pacific. It is said that C. D. Howe, the minister of transport, granted it after consulting the president of the government-owned Trans-Canada Airlines, who took a dim view of the financial prospects of a service to the Orient and was not interested in providing it. Howe for his part attached two conditions to the concession: C.P. Air Lines must fly the route with Canadair Four aircraft, Canadian-built modifications of the Douglas DC-4,* and in addition to service to Japan and China they must provide one to Australia as well.[16]

The Canadair Four was powered by four liquid-cooled Rolls-Royce Merlin engines, which had enjoyed a good reputation in British military aircraft during the Second World War but which had not been designed with much regard for weight and fuel consumption. TCA had experienced a good deal of trouble with them during its early trans-Atlantic venture, operating Avro Lancastrians and, later, the North Star version of the DC-4. In short, its range was barely adequate for transoceanic routes.

As well, the Canadian government's permission to fly these new routes was only a beginning for McConachie. Now he had to get permits from Australia, New Zealand, Japan and China. Among his contemporaries, McConachie had few equals when it came to salesmanship, and part of this talent was to tell a good story—which he could. He used the classical formula: a slow build-up of disappointments and frustrations and then an abrupt reversal of fortunes, usually brought about by himself. So it was with these initiatives. For a permit to fly into Australia, he had to apply to the Labour government of Joseph Chifley, and his Minister of Air for Civil Aviation, A. S. (Frank) Drakeford, both of whom were staunch socialists who opposed private control of public transport. After two weeks of what appeared to be immutable negatives in Canberra, he finally got to meet with both Chifley and Drakeford at a lunch—a farewell lunch for his delegation.

Sitting next to Chifley (he had learned earlier that Chifley and Drakeford were both ex-railway engineers), he rose to make a speech. McConachie recalled, for the CBC, that he began it with a brief resumé of his career:

I started on the railway when I was 17, so the only common field we had was the railways. I started to explain how I'd started in as an ash wheeler—that's wheeling ashes from the pits—and then I became a wiper, then I became a watchman, then I became a hostler, then a fireman and finally an engineer.[17] They were dumbfounded, to hear that a man who started on the ash-pit could become president of Canadian Pacific. . . . This appealed to them and, though I had been assured by Mr. Drakeford before we went in for luncheon that they were not going to issue the permit to us, Mr. Chifley, in thanking me for my talk said, "Mr. McConachie, we are very interested in this and we would like very much for you to go back with a good impression of Australia, and we are not really as bigoted as you may think we are . . . and I think that Mr. Drakeford may have some good news for you after this luncheon."[18]

Biographer Keith adds some embellishment to this story that is not on the CBC tape. He quotes "Lofty" Croft, the senior Canadian trade commissioner for Australia, telling McConachie that Chifley and Drakeford were both ex-railway drivers, or engineers.

"'Railway engineers, you say?' McConachie set his Scotch on the sidetable, fished for his wallet, began to search through the assortment of cards and papers [for his railway union card]. Suddenly he grinned cheerfully. 'All is not lost, fellows,' he said. 'This luncheon tomorrow may not be a total waste of time after all.'"[19]

COMMERCIAL AVIATION ADVANCED AT LEAST TWENTY YEARS BY WAR.

Within the space of three years the war has advanced the development of commercial aviation by at least twenty years. This is the expressed opinion of Mr. L. B. Unwin, president of Canadian Pacific Air Lines Ltd., who was in Whitehorse recently on a tour of inspection of the various air routes under his control. In all parts of the north, Mr. Unwin stated, he saw his company's planes performing herculean tasks of transportation with the stepped-up tempo of war-time production. "It is impossible of course" he said "to discuss details of air transportation in the Canadian North-West since so many defence projects are involved but the general picture is one of intense and increasing activity."

It does seem a little odd that a dedicated free enterpriser had cherished his union card in his wallet for 16 years after he had left the union for good—but that's how the story goes.

Next, McConachie's party travelled across the Tasman Sea to Auckland, New Zealand, for the next permit, which was quickly granted on the precedent of the Australian approval. Then, in 1949, McConachie flew to Tokyo for a permit to fly into Japan. For this he had to go to General Douglas MacArthur, whose title was Supreme Commander for the Allied Powers, a position that made him, if not a dictator in Japan, at least a czar. Here once again McConachie makes a good story of his venture. He endured weeks of frustration while he was passed around from one lesser general to another seeking permits: one for food, another for staff and passengers, another for fuel for the aircraft, another for housing and office space—and so on. Each general had to issue these separately, and each told him nothing could be done until he had acquired overall approval from MacArthur. Finally, he did get a 15-minute appointment to meet the great man. Expecting to find him at the centre of furious activity, with banks of phones ringing off the hook and a desk covered with papers to sign, he carefully prepared a 15-minute presentation.

Instead, when he was shown in, the desk was bare of papers and there was only one phone. Moreover, MacArthur promptly led him to a comfortable chair by the fire. McConachie suffered the frustration of a conversation that went on and on without letting him talk about his request for the permit. MacArthur asked, first of all, for ships from the CPR to help bring supplies. (The CPR had ended its trans-Pacific steamship service in 1940, transferring two freighters from the Atlantic to ply between Vancouver, Victoria and the Orient.)[20] Then MacArthur pulled out his celebrated corncob pipe, began to fill it with Hudson's Bay Mixture, and spent several minutes extolling the virtues of the tobacco and the Hudson's Bay company in general. In McConachie's words, the interview ended as follows:

He went on for another 10 or 15 minutes and he didn't seem to be in any rush, and then, all of a sudden, he looked at his watch. "Well," he said, "I've got to go to an embassy dinner tonight. I'm awfully sorry I can't spend more time with you, Mr. McConachie, but when you get back to Canada say hello to my friends in Canada. It was nice meeting you; and, certainly if you can get those ships for us, we need them. I'm sincere about giving you charters."

I said, "Yes, right, General MacArthur, but I came here on another problem. . . . We are going to fly the Pacific, representing the Canadian government in this area, as the Canadian flag carrier, and we need permits."

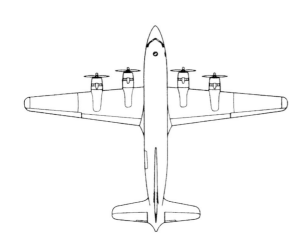

He said, "Oh, you just go down tomorrow morning and see General Wedemeyer and it will be all fixed up. You don't need to worry about any of the permits."[21]

The next stop was Shanghai. Here, in brief, McConachie was working with the Canadian ambassador, Tom Davis, who invited him to a reception where he met Mme. Chiang Kai-shek, wife of the president of Nationalist China. At the end of that evening Davis reported that Chiang had approved the Canadian airline's application to serve Shanghai on a trans-Pacific route.

"It was the easiest permit I ever got, but the least fruitful," McConachie later reflected.[22]

In fact, it was no easier, apparently, than the permit from New Zealand. It was, however, decidedly fruitless. McConachie had been able to lease two North Stars from the Royal Canadian Air Force and, two weeks later, on April 14, 1939, Captain Charles Pentland, with a CPA crew on board, took off in one of them for the first survey flight of the Orient route. By the time they reached Shanghai, the Communist forces were on the outskirts of the city. Pentland fuelled up and departed for Manila that night. He was the last aircraft to leave before the Communists over-ran the city the following day. This was a severe blow because China, with its huge and growing population, had seemed to promise an abundance of passengers for years to come.

As a consequence of the Asia-Pacific initiatives, the CPA's centre of operations was moved to Vancouver International Airport in 1949, where the company acquired, at a bargain price, the very large hangar used by Boeing as an aircraft factory during the war. As Kaye Lamb wrote in 1977: "From it, Canadian Pacific's domestic and international services now radiate on routes that total well over 50,000 miles [80 500 km]."[23] At the time, though, this did not represent an auspicious start, certainly not a surge of prosperity. Instead, these new routes led to more anxiety, if not dismay, among the directors of the CPR. Some time was to pass before the routes even began to break even; and another potential source of revenue McConachie had hoped for was very slow to materialize. He had planned for tourist traffic into Hawaii, and a possible stopover there for passengers on the Asian and Australian runs. To the directors it began to look as though the TCA brass had been more astute in refusing these routes.

Consequently, for Canadian Pacific Airlines, things remained depressingly slow until, as with the Alaska Highway construction in 1942,

FLIGHT FACTS—CPA INFLIGHT BROCHURE

SEAT BELT Please fasten your seat belt when the plane is taking off or landing. Your Stewardess will gladly help you and explain its use.

YOUR EARS Chewing gum will be provided by your stewardess. Its use is suggested while the plane is descending; it makes you swallow. This equalizes pressure in you ear drums. If your throat is congested by the effects of a "cold" be sure to tell the Stewardess. She will provide assistance to ventilate your ears.

SEAT ADJUSTMENT If you wish your seat adjusted, call the Stewardess. She will be pleased to assist you.

MAGAZINES Current issues of a wide variety of magazines are available. Playing cards may be obtained from the Stewardess.

SMOKING Cigarette smoking is permitted after the plane is in the air, but is restricted during take-off and landing. In consideration for other passengers it is requested that you do not smoke a cigar or pipe.

STATIONARY Pencils, post-cards and portfolios of stationary are on board for your use . . . let the Stewardess mail your correspondence . . .

MEAL SERVICE Full course meals are served at usual hours—complimentary, of course

PILLOWS AND ROBE Just ask your Stewardess for these if you feel like napping a little.

GRATUITIES These are not accepted by personnel . . . you are "a guest of the line."

BAGGAGE Will be removed from the plane. Please claim in the station.

RETURN RESERVATIONS Let your Stewardess or passenger agent furnish you with information.

DON'T FORGET Your brief-case, book, top-coat, etc.

another war came to the rescue, at least on the South Pacific run. By the time the Korean War started in June 1950, CPA had begun to operate charter flights to carry military personnel from McChord Field, near Fort Lewis, Washington, to Tokyo.[24] As well, a surprising influx of emigrants from Hong Kong began to fill many seats.

As business began to pick up, McConachie began to press for more expansion—this time to South America. Here, once again, TCA had had first pick and turned the routes down as financially unattractive. So CPA stepped in; but first, the airline's officials had to negotiate reciprocal agreements with the several different countries involved.

In the early 1950s, Maurice McGregor—who had been one of the first pilots to transfer from Canadian Airways to TCA in 1937 and became a senior executive—left TCA to join CPA as director of development. His first task was to survey and assess potential routes to South America—a line down through Mexico, Peru, Chile, Argentina and Brazil. McConachie probably delegated this important task because, at the time, he was engaged in what he considered an even more important one. In 1949, he attended the Farnborough Air Show in England and saw the first de Havilland Comet demonstrated. As we shall see in the next chapter, he tried to make CPA one of the first airlines in the world to operate jetliners. Meanwhile, McGregor had his hands full with the South American venture.

During his initial survey, McGregor managed to do some preliminary negotiating for landing rights: he found and appointed, as his agent, a lawyer in Peru who was a close friend of the president—so Peru was in the bag. Argentina was a washout, but "in Brazil the Director-General assured me, a gentlemen's agreement, that we would obtain bilateral rights in Peru for traffic to Sao Paulo and Rio."[25]

On the strength of this preliminary report submitted by McGregor, the CPA directors approved service to South America but they didn't have the necessary domestic approvals. So McGregor went to the Canadian government and asked them: "'Will you please obtain the necessary approvals, have your government people negotiate bilateral agreements?' The government said, 'Sorry, we have been trying for some time; we can't deal with these people [South American officials]—completely impossible.' So CP said we have to find a way. The government said, If you can find a way, any way, privately, go ahead; do what you like.'"

The first priority was Mexico because KLM was after a route from Montreal to Mexico City with bilateral rights, and to carry the traffic on from there. McGregor started his negotiating trip with a stop at Mexico City, but found things very uncertain and decided to move on down and return later. He went down to Lima and came back to find that the Mexicans were just not interested. He couldn't get anywhere—it was impossible, just as the Canadian government had discovered. However, a friend of his in the Canadian legation, Max Stewart, said he thought he knew a man who could help McGregor—a financier who had left Czechoslovakia ahead of the Nazis in the 1930s and prospered, both in North and South America. This contact in turn introduced McGregor to another lawyer with influence—in short, a fixer. Such people were known in Mexico as "coyotes." This person's advice was brief and to the point:

"Frankly, if you expect to get into this country, you're going to have to pay something."

"This is Canadian Pacific," McGregor responded, "that's unheard of!"

This revelation gave McGregor pause and he wisely decided to involve the company before going forward. He advised McConachie of the situation and insisted that he wasn't going to work alone. He asked for Jack Gilmore, CPA's controller, to join him. An uncharacteristically cautious McConachie responded that the directors would have to know before he could sanction it. The board's decision was to carry on and Gilmore joined McGregor in Mexico City. McGregor resumes his account:

We met with the coyote and he could only speak Spanish. Fortunately, we got Arthur Blanchet, first secretary of the legation, to interpret for us. So we proceeded with these endless negotiations and we didn't get anywhere; they kept raising the ante: starting at $12,000, it went up to $50,000—but, as I said at the time, amortize that over a period of a few operations and it's nothing; but there was no settlement because they were playing us off against the Dutch KLM group.

Then finally we thought we had the deal all settled and agreed when this coyote said, "There's one little thing that's been overlooked before we can conclude this matter: The president's wife wants a large, pink Cadillac—it must be a seven-passenger; it must have whitewall tires, a heater and radio; if you want this agreement, this is another condition." So I replied, "We will deliver the Cadillac to the border of California and Mexico and you can take it across and pay the duty and do what you like with it." He was shocked. He said, "Oh no, that would be very wrong for us to have to pay the duty." In the end, I reluctantly agreed that we would pay the duty; so at last the arrangements were concluded and we signed the agreement. Now we had agreements with Mexico, and thought we had them with Brazil and Peru.

Peru came through, but not Brazil. After considerable negotiation, McGregor learned that Panagra Brazil had kept CPA out. "They were

Daily Province Goes Through Despite Flood

Subscribers in the Okanagan and other Interior points get The Daily Province earlier than usual due to the delivery methods employed to bypass floods.

Papers are flown to Penticton by C.P. Airlines and distributed from this point to central and Eastern B.C. by rail and truck.

Papers for Kootenay subscribers go by way of Spokane by truck. Last Saturday's issue, however, did not reach destination. The truck is still "missing" —behind a slide at Orville, Wash.

Trucks still get through with newspapers in the Fraser Valley. Trucks reached Dewdney on Monday. Loads have reached Hope on the south bank daily.

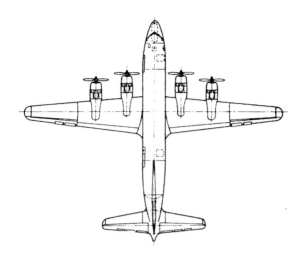

owned 40% by Pan American and they paid the appropriate minister to keep us out."

McGregor's group arrived in Mexico City on a final tour with a host of technical staff to complete arrangements before the service began. "But again—those officials! They wouldn't allow the people aboard our old DC-4 to disembark; they said, 'You can't leave the aircraft because everyone has to be paid,' and I had to come up with a bundle of money; all those people on duty had to be paid: everybody—customs, immigration, security—the lot."

Asked how he handled the money, McGregor replied, "Larger amounts in the bank but the smaller amounts you carried in a briefcase."

By now the Canadairs had been sold and, after a brief spell with DC-4s, they were replaced by the new, genuinely long-range DC-6Bs. The inaugural South American flight took off from Vancouver for Mexico City and Lima, Peru, on October 24, 1953.

While these initiatives were taking place, the company's investment was approaching $400 million, but CPA was still losing money. One fortuitous development in 1955 helped to slow the bleeding somewhat: an offshoot of the Cold War, it was the decision by the Canadian and United States governments to build a string of radar sites along the Arctic coast from Labrador to Alaska. The DEW Line, or Distant Early Warning Line, was a massive construction project that needed substantial air support—though this, of course, would be charter rather than scheduled flying. Consequently, in addition to two DC-4s and five DC-3s, CPA leased eight Curtiss C-46Fs from Flying Tigers airline to use on charter flights, hauling in freight and equipment to the various supply bases and radar sites. The airline operated mainly in the western Arctic—exclusively in the Edmonton, Fort Nelson, Yellowknife, Norman Wells and Cambridge Bay areas. In support of the construction of the DEW Line, Canadian Pacific aircraft carried 36.5 million pounds of freight: after the company completed its contracts on January 31, 1957, six of the C-46s were soon disposed of.[26]

Canadian Pacific Airlines was slowly—too slowly for McConachie's satisfaction—emerging from bush leagues to the big league.

Chapter Six

The CPR:
Deep Pockets and a New Era

*"First indications were
that the Comet was going to
scoop the airline industry."*

E VER SINCE its turbulent creation in the 1870s, a creation preceded and surrounded by corruption and scandals, the Canadian Pacific Railway has been characterized by many as a huge monopoly earning excessive profits. As well, it has been seen as too conservative, if not reactionary, in its outlook. A more objective scrutiny suggests a rather different picture.

During the construction stages of the railway, particularly through British Columbia, many engineering compromises were necessary. For example the choice of route: the most favourable route through the mountains, from an operational standpoint, would have been through Yellowhead Pass and down the North Thompson Valley to the Fraser, and then on down to the coast. Instead construction went through the Rockies and Selkirks via Kicking Horse Pass and Rogers Pass. This latter route presented a daunting 4.5 per cent grade on the western slope of the Rockies and required helper locomotives, based at Field, to move trains over this obstacle. It also made for a dangerous descent when heading the other way. Another obstacle was posed by an ongoing danger of slides and avalanches, which required the building of an extensive network of snowsheds to keep the line open in the winter—most notably through Rogers Pass and in some other hazardous areas: "In the first years of operation

By 1950, close to the end of the steam era, equipment was more powerful, but avalanches and wash-outs still had to be contended with. This photograph was shot just east of Banff, Alberta.
—NICHOLAS MORANT, CPR ARCHIVES

of the line, 54 sheds were built. . . . The cost of the snow sheds was enormous. CPR Annual Reports for the years 1886 and 1887 recorded expenditures of over two million dollars for snow sheds alone for the main line through British Columbia."[1]

These initial compromises had been determined by political and economic considerations. Politically, the compromises were adopted as a barrier to American railroads which seemed poised to build into southern BC and the Prairies, and so funnel traffic to the south to their own railroads in the United States. Economically, the southern Prairies were still relatively sparsely populated and the CPR hoped to attract new settlers to farm the land grants it had received as part of the incentive to build the line—new settlers who would provide both freight and passenger traffic.

Ironically, the person who would eventually become the CPR's most active competitor, James J. Hill, was on the original CPR board of directors. "Hill's overriding interest was, however, still with his American railroad and it had been his hope that the CPR would abandon its all-Canadian route around the northern shore of the Great Lakes in favour of connecting to his lines for a faster, cheaper route to the south. . . . Hill [soon] realized that his logical route from a cost perspective would not outweigh the logic of national interests . . . [and], in mid-1883, Hill resigned from the CPR board. . . ."[2] For the CPR, this patriotic imperative, imposed by the government, turned out to be an expensive one for many years.

While they took some time over their deliberations, once the directors were convinced that long-term operating efficiencies, leading to economic benefits, would ensue, they did not hesitate to spend money on improvements or new technology; and they continued to provide large capital expenditures to improve the line for more than a century. For example, the necessity to provide helper locomotives to surmount the grade of the Field Hill was costing too much and creating a bottleneck for traffic—in addition to the dangers of the downhill run into the Kicking Horse Valley. The solution was a major engineering undertaking: the building of two spiral tunnels, both of which steered the trains through almost three-quarters of a complete circle to reduce the grade to approximately 1.6 percent. The eventual cost for this and other improvements was $1,500,000, a very substantial sum in 1909; and there was yet another improvement when the Connaught Tunnel through Mount Macdonald in the Selkirks was

At the turn of the century operating a railway through the Rockies and the Selkirks was no picnic. Rugged snow ploughs saw plenty of action and had to be manned by rugged personnel. This rotary plough is working in Rogers Pass, *circa* 1910.
—BRITISH COLUMBIA ARCHIVES, 59121

constructed between 1913 and 1916. Double-tracked and five miles (8 km) long, at the time it was the longest railroad tunnel in North America. The cost of this project added $8.5 million when the upgrading was completed—but it undoubtedly provided a safer, more efficient and thus more economical operation.

Later, while some have questioned how slow the company was to adopt dieselization, once it was convinced of the advantages it spent more than $17 millions to convert from steam to diesel power. Meanwhile, all these improvements were from the beginning accompanied (at least until the 1970s when Via Rail took over passenger service), by the highest standards of food, comfort and services for passengers—standards that must have brought frustration to the managers of the government's railway, the Canadian National who, if they tried to match the CPR's luxurious standards, were in constant danger of accusations that they were playing fast and loose with the taxpayers' money.

So it was when the CPR became involved with aviation. The directors took their time before they decided on heavy investment. As historian Kaye Lamb records: "As early as 1919 the C.P.R. had secured authority to own and operate aircraft commercially, but no practical steps were taken until 1930, when the Canadian Pacific and the Canadian National each invested $250,000 in Canadian Airways Limited."[3] Still, while Sir Edward Beatty had kept in close touch with the president of Canadian Airways, James Richardson, the CPR did not become actively involved in aviation until it bought out that company from Richardson's widow in 1942 and merged it with nine other aviation companies.

However, once the directors were committed, although they frequently complained about the lack of profit, McConachie as usual received generous financial support in his efforts to expand CPA. In 1949, after a visit to the Farnborough Air Show in England, he quickly petitioned the directors, urging them to be in the vanguard of the new jet age.

In 1949, Empire Preference was still a strong sentiment with the Canadian government (as witness the insistence on the British Rolls-Royce engines in the Canadair Four and the North Star). At the same time, the aircraft industry in post-war Britain was becoming alarmed by the big lead the Americans were gaining in the design and construction of airliners. Nevertheless, "Britain held the lead in jet-engine development," and felt that if it could produce a practical jet airliner, this was its oppor-

FLY
to
Prince Rupert
in 5½ hours
1½ HOURS TO PORT HARDY,
3¼ HOURS TO SANDSPIT
Leave Vancouver 10:15 a.m. P.S.T. daily except Sun.
NOW! SAVE 10% on round trip
Effective June 5
For information and reservations, phone MA 6161.
USE AIRMAIL REGULARLY
Canadian Pacific
AIR LINES
PHONE PA 4211 — THE BEST MEDIUM FOR CLASSIFIED RESULTS

tunity to jump ahead of the American industry.[4] Hence the de Havilland Comet, the first jet in the world to go into airline service.

At first, as usual, the directors responded to McConachie's request cautiously. At that point, BOAC—British Overseas Airways—had been the only airline to order Comets. The Comet 1's range would not span the Pacific from Vancouver to Honolulu; but McConachie persuaded the directors that, if CPA continued to use the DC-6Bs on the Vancouver–Honolulu leg, the Comet, even with two fuel stops (Fiji and Canton Island) on the Australian leg, would with its superior cruising speed of 490 mph (750 km/h) still put the airline comfortably ahead of its existing schedule.[5] As well, the directors themselves may have been influenced by the Empire Preference sentiment. They agreed, and two Comets were ordered. The order was placed in December 1949, but the first aircraft did not become available until February 1953. By then, nine Comet 1s had been delivered to BOAC, three Comet 1As to Air France, two Comet 1As to UAT [Union Aeromaritime de Transport, another French airline based in Paris] and one to CPA.[6]

Two years after the inauguration of the South American routes, McConachie achieved his long-standing ambition to start a trans-polar route to Europe. No doubt to his chagrin, the Norwegians beat him to it. By 1955, when he started his polar route from Vancouver to Amsterdam, SAS (Scandinavian Airlines System) had already begun its first polar flight in 1954 with a DC-6B, flying from Copenhagen to Los Angeles via Sondrestrom, in western Greenland, and Winnipeg. Canadian Pacific's first survey flight was in a DC-4, from Vancouver to London, via Churchill, Sondrestrom and Keflavik in April 1955. The first passenger flight, in June, with a DC-6B was from Vancouver to Sondrestrom and Amsterdam. Fortunately, as Donald Bain points out, "Although the service barely crossed the Arctic Circle, the term polar route caught the public's imagination."[7] It certainly worked for CPA and McConachie looked forward eagerly to the day when he could put jet airliners on the route.

Unfortunately, though, the CPR's willingness to move with the times and purchase the de Havilland Comets foundered through no fault of the directors. First indications were that the Comet was going to scoop the airline industry. BOAC had found them gratifyingly successful. It was using them on the Johannesburg-Colombo route and, by 1953, Comets were in service on the Singapore–Tokyo route. Unfortunately, CPA's

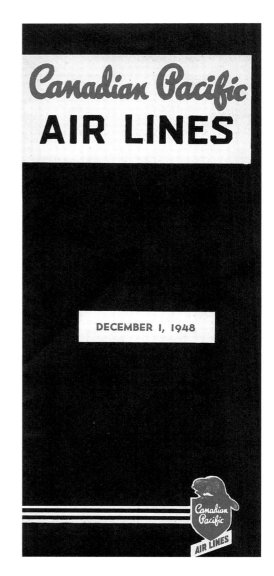

Mailbags waiting to be loaded onto CPA's
Lockheed Lodestar, CF-CPB, at Prince George, 1942.
Mail contracts were vital to sustain BC aviation
just before and during the Second World War.
—FORT ST. JOHN–NORTH PEACE MUSEUM ARCHIVES, I-986.52.06

Lockheed had made considerable strides since
the original 10A Electra. Although still no match for the
incomparable DC-3, the Lockheed 1808, Lodestar, had
become a solid performer for CPA on the
Vancouver–Whitehorse route.—CANADIAN AIRLINES ARCHIVES

While the Lodestar still failed to match the seat/mile economics of the DC-3, it provided the bridge to the most successful of the post-war conventional-engined airliners: The Lockheed 049 Constellation in 1946, and the less successful L-1049 Super Constellation in 1950.
—CANADIAN AIRLINES ARCHIVES

In the search for revenue, Grant McConachie was persuaded by local businessmen men in 1948 to attempt a service to and from Kelowna. Despite the apparently enthusiastic reception on this, it's inaugural flight into Kelowna, the service did not prove profitable.—ROYAL BC MUSEUM

As it developed into a major airline, CPA determined to keep up the standards of luxury travel it had set with its railway and steamship services.
—CANADIAN AIRLINES ARCHIVES

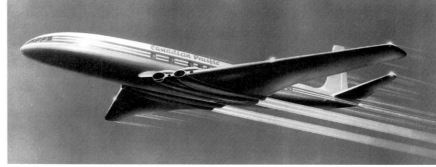

An enhanced PR representation of the de Havilland Comet, an ill-fated but far-sighted attempt by CPA to move into the jet age in the early 1950s.—CANADIAN AIRLINES ARCHIVES

BRITANNIA to be built in CANADA

It has been announced that a license has been signed with the Canadian Government to manufacture the "Bristol" Britannia in Canada.

Canadair Limited in Montreal has been authorized to build a maritime version of the "Bristol" aircraft.

The civil Britannia offers a payload-range performance of entirely new breadth. The full volumetric payload of 30,000 lbs. may be carried over a range of 4,700 miles; maximum range is over 6,000 miles, yet for ranges as short as 500 miles the direct operating costs are low enough to be competitive with the smaller airliners.

The "Bristol"

AEROPLANE COMPANY of CANADA LIMITED

INTERNATIONAL AVIATION BUILDING, MONTREAL

After abandoning the Comet, CPA turned to the turbine-engined Bristol Britannia which, in spite of some frustrating electrical problems, gave excellent service while the company waited for the appearance of the first North-American jets: the Douglas DC8 and the Boeing 707.

—BUSINESS NEWSPAPERS ASSOCIATION

R·112·78

The original design drawings for the CPA's
logo in 1942. Evidently the artist grew frivolous.

—CPR CORPORATE ARCHIVES

VICTORIA
SEATTLE VANCOUVER

Canadian Pacific

B. C. COAST STEAMSHIPS

The Boeing 747, one of the most successful of the jetliners.—CANADIAN AIRLINES ARCHIVES

This publicity photograph, entitled "Strange Cargo," demonstrates that glamour was still an important asset in air travel.—CANADIAN AIRLINES ARCHIVES

initial proving flight to the Orient was less auspicious. Evidently, McConachie was in too much of a hurry this time and too eager for another coup. Knowing that the Comet's range was not up to the trans-Pacific leg from Honolulu to Vancouver, he had decided to base the first one in Australia to operate as far as Honolulu, where it would connect with the slower but longer-range, piston-engined DC-6B for Vancouver.

When the first Comet was ready for delivery, the two senior pilots in the company, captains Charles Pentland (manager of overseas operations) and North Sawle (chief pilot, overseas) flew to London for a short familiarization course—too short as it turned out. When they were ready to depart, McConachie decided to publicize the flight by using it to set a new record for a flight from England to Australia. Pentland and Sawle set off with three additional crew members and six de Havilland technicians aboard.[8] After stopping briefly at Karachi to refuel, they began the take-off run before dawn and at maximum gross weight. The attempted take-off ended when the aircraft ran out of runway and crashed into a drainage ditch, killing all aboard.

After investigation, the verdict was pilot error. Still unaccustomed to jet techniques, Pentland appears to have rotated too soon: "It was found that if the nose were lifted too soon, the engines' effectiveness was reduced and the aircraft could not reach flying speed."[9] A similar accident had occurred to a Comet at Rome four months earlier.

Obviously this was a severe blow for McConachie. CPA lost interest in the Comet and the second one ordered was sold; but in time it became less of a blow because the Comets turned out to be defective. After two Comets had apparently disintegrated in the air with the loss of all on board, lengthy investigation proved that metal fatigue had developed, causing cracks at the corners of windows after repeated pressurization. It was a sad end to a very promising venture. BOAC continued to use later marks of the Comet for some time, but the damage to its reputation had been severe and most airlines waited until manufacturers in the United States produced their first serviceable jetliners: Boeing with its 707 and Douglas with its DC-8.

McConachie now turned to the next best aircraft available: turbine engines mated to propellers. As a short-haul airliner, the Vickers Viscount had been an unmistakable success, but it did not have the range for CPA's major routes; so McConachie decided on Bristol Britannias and the directors agreed. With a cruise speed of 360 mph (590 km/h)—50 mph (80 km/h) faster than the DC-6B—and a capacity of up to 140 passengers,[10] the Britannia had the makings of a fine airliner. Unfortunately, it had two handicaps: it was plagued with minor electrical problems, and it came too late. Only about two years after it went into service, the first of the successful American jetliners, the Boeing's 707 and the Douglas DC-8, began operating.

Captain W. C. Cross, one of the pilots who flew the Britannia liked the aircraft:

> It is 30 years since I was introduced to the Bristol Britannia and 26 since I last flew the type, yet my memories are fresh and very positive. It was a fine aircraft, one that served to bridge the interval between the piston-powered mainline transports of the early '50s and the successful first-generation turbojets of the 60s. . . .[11]

Cross goes on to describe the complexity of the electrical, hydraulic and fuel systems, but points out: "Much has been made of the aeroplane's electrical snags and other problems; but it should also be stressed that Britannias spent very little time on the ground and performed extremely well." He also talks about the frequent flame-outs experienced with the early Proteus engines. "Fortunately the aircraft had ample power, and could operate safely with an engine out. When an engine on the Britannia 'flamed out' it would restart within seconds due to the rapid re-light feature. Except for the annoyance of having the autopilot disengage every time it happened, we became quite used to the occurrence."[12]

It was at this time that CPA executives made another determined effort to divest themselves of most of the feeder lines they had inherited in 1942, and to secure approval to compete with TCA on the main transcontinental routes. In the spring of 1958, the media certainly seemed supportive. After half a page of praise for McConachie, an article in *Saturday Night* leads off with more bullish talk:

> And it is in the controversial question of Canadian cross-country routes that the present interest in the man's meteoric career is found.
>
> The core of the question is: will CPA be allowed to operate cross-country routes in limited competition with Trans-Canada Air Lines? CPA's application, naming specific cities that it is proposed to link, has been filed with the Air Transport Board in Ottawa. The ATB has asked interested parties to be prepared to appear to present arguments. . . .
>
> The outcome, whether a success or failure from CPA's standpoint, will be a milestone in the career of the big smiling man whose driving energy built an airline that carried the name of his country to every continent except Africa. If CPA is successful in gaining trans-Canada routes, it will mark a revolution in Canadian air policy.

The prudent, assertive Scot Gordon McGregor, [was] president of Trans-Canada Air lines, 1948-68. He was appalled and irritated by McConachie's tactics and never failed to wonder why Ottawa allowed CPA to exist.

In 1946, I was in London on an inspection trip regarding our government trans-Atlantic air service operations; the senior boss in the company sent me a cable to get back immediately because they wanted to make a survey flight to South America.

Maurice McGregor

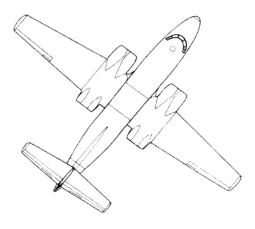

Some people in the industry believe they have a better chance under the Conservative administration than under the Liberals of getting cross-country routes. It was always argued that C. D. Howe, the father of TCA, was the man who torpedoed any such proposals before June 10, 1957.[13]

The article continues in this supportive vein: "Perhaps it is only a happy historical conjunction of events that BC's centenary should be marked by two striking developments for CPA under [McConachie's] guidance: introduction of the turboprop Britannias on overseas routes, and a vigorous and persuasive effort to gain a cross-Canada franchise."[14] The article leaves a clear impression that McConachie had done his homework for the application; yet, according to Ronald Keith, this was his first outright failure because he had failed to prepare.

Full of confidence because the new Diefenbaker Conservative government was in power, with the flashy George Hees as Transport Minister, he prepared his brief to the ATB as a rhetorical tour de force rather than a reasoned marketing study, designed to prove the viability of competition that would produce profits for CPA without deficits for TCA. In Keith's words:

> The written presentation, while skimpy on research and fact, was impressive in the force and eloquence of its assertions. . . . Typical was the president's affirmation, "I am firmly convinced that only under competition does the public secure the best service at the lowest price. . . . Competition will benefit not only the public but TCA as well. . . . TCA's monopoly within Canada is the largest non-competitive pool of aviation business in the free world. . . . If this market cannot support competition there are few in the world that can."
> But when the Air Transport Board hearing began on October 20, 1958, it soon became apparent that the hearing was to be conducted in deadly earnest. The three-man board, flanked by its own economic advisers and legal counsel, betrayed not the slightest disposition in favor of the CPA contention. It was soon also evident that TCA had come to the fray with a thoroughly-researched brief. . . .[15]

The ATB's lawyers evidently made mincemeat of McConachie's rhetorical claims and, "On the fourth day of the hearing the conduct of the CPA case was in the hands of Ian Sinclair, the brilliant, towering black-thatched chief counsel of the CPR."[16] As Keith observes, being pulled off the case so early in the hearing must obviously have represented a public humiliation for McConachie. For the first time his celebrated charm and persuasiveness had let him down. The end result was that the ATB awarded a small consolation prize: one return flight daily serving Vancouver, Winnipeg, Toronto and Montreal.

By 1960, the sometimes quirky Britannias were already being made obsolete by the new jetliners. In October 1959, CPA ordered five DC-8s.

The first four were delivered two years later; and the first one to fly a revenue trip was on the polar route. As Donald Bain records, "DC-8, CF-CPH. Substituting for an unserviceable Britannia, made the first jet flight from Vancouver to Amsterdam via Edmonton on April 30, 1961. Earlier the same day CF-CPH had operated the first Canadian Pacific Air Lines transcontinental flight by a DC-8 between Vancouver and Toronto, also substituting for a failed Britannia."[17] The fifth of these jets ordered in 1959 was delivered in 1963; a sixth had been ordered for delivery in 1965. By 1970, with Boeing 737s operating the shorter routes, CPA was virtually an all-jet operation that was tolerably profitable.

Before then, however, the man who had moved from the cockpit of a beat-up Fokker Universal to the CEO's chair of a jet-age airline suffered a heart attack in Los Angeles and died on June 29, 1965, when he was just 56.

Both the media and the public love to enshrine individual heroes, or villains, for that matter. Because of this, a great deal of purple prose has been written and spoken about McConachie, making it difficult to offer an objective analysis of his career without appearing to be a typical revisionist, bent on demolishing popular icons.

In McConachie's case, his eventual success speaks for itself. Like most other successful businessmen, he used hyperbole and gross exaggerations and, with his boyish charm, could stretch the truth a long way while still maintaining a bland air of innocence and credibility. He could and did exploit people, particularly in the earlier years of Yukon Southern, yet he seldom seemed to evoke any lasting animosity. Even when people were well aware they were being manipulated, they found it hard to dislike him. With all this, there is little doubt that he had more than a fair share of good luck. As Shakespeare put it, "There is a tide in the affairs of men/ Which, taken at the flood, leads on to fortune." During his career, Grant McConachie, who was admirably equipped to do so, captured numerous tides on the flood.

This does not, though, diminish his accomplishments. His place in the history of Canadian aviation is secure.

Part Three

LEGENDS OF THE WEST—BAKER AND SPILSBURY

Chapter Seven

Russ Baker: The Early Years

"About 10 years ago Russell Baker could inspect his one-plane 'airline' in jig time. Now at age 44, he is president of Pacific Western Airlines."

VICTORIA COLONIST

AT THE SAME TIME that Grant McConachie was rising to aviation prominence in the west, another young man was carving a successful flying career there, too. Frank Russell (Russ) Baker was born in St. James, Manitoba, near Winnipeg, in January 1910. Like McConachie, Baker started flying in the bush but made the transition to management in the growing airline industry of the post-Second World War years; and, like McConachie, he was a complex, intriguing, often contradictory personality—one whose story is not easily summarized because it is clouded by expansive publicity and sometimes purple prose. Behind all this, however, lies an important figure: a man who certainly deserves a place among British Columbia's aviation leaders.

With Baker it is sometimes more difficult than with McConachie to separate fact from self-promotion and newspaper hyperbole. He claimed that he had learned to fly when he was 16 but, as his biographer John Condit points out:

"Russ Baker learned to fly at sixteen," says a biography written for him by Vancouver public relations man Al Williamson. Russ boasted of his youthful start in several newspaper interviews as well. Other versions make him as young as fourteen. A photo accompanying one article shows

Russ Baker beside Ginger Coote's Bridge River & Cariboo Airways' DH 83 Fox Moth, CF-API, at Kamloops, 1937.
—NATIONAL ARCHIVES OF CANADA, PA-102378

the allegedly sixteen-year-old Russ standing helmeted in front of his Avion trainer. But the flying school did not acquire that plane until he was eighteen, and for a lad of sixteen, the young aviator had raised a pretty good moustache.[1]

Other records confirm that he enrolled with the Western Canada Airways flying school in August 1928, when he was 18.[2] This penchant for embellishment of his accomplishments stayed with him. He earned his commercial licence on October 29, 1929 but, during the early 1930s, flying jobs were few and far between. According to John Condit: "Russ took up with a bearded mystic, a 'Major Cross,' who planned to have Russ fly him across the Pacific Ocean. . . . The trans-Pacific flight never got off the coast . . . but later at PWA, Russ told executive assistant Duncan D. McLaren of having flown to Manchuria and of having driven a limousine for a man who, when they encountered a flock of sheep, waved his hands and made them disappear."[3] Baker recorded a similar supernatural experience when he was based at Fort St. James in 1938 and found a new, hitherto undiscovered—and still undiscovered—stretch of territory. The Prince George *Citizen* carried Baker's whimsical description:

I was flying above the weather at 9,400 feet [2 850 m], about 35 miles [56 km] east of McDame Creek. From Deadwood Lake, I flew due west down a big river, which seemed to be about twice as large as the Nechako. By its size, and my position, I thought I must have been flying down the Dease River, but I soon realized that I, or my map, was in error.

For suddenly, out of nowhere, great hulks of mountains emerged out of the fog in front of me, like giant icebergs on the sea.

I was surprised—amazed. To be flying at nearly 9,500 feet and suddenly to be confronted with huge mountains towering above gave me a feeling that is difficult to describe. Never in all my years of flying have I had such an experience. . . .[4]

As for the romantic Manchuria experience, in Condit's words, "The unromantic reality was that from 1931 to 1933 Russ, with his brother and Gardiner Niven, laid gypsum over ceilings to insulate homes and churches for his father's Western Gypsum Products. . . . During the 1930s he swung a sledge hammer on the railway and . . . later Russ sketched out the skimpy record of this part of his career by assigning one flying job to each year, claiming jobs with Dominion Skyways, Rouyn, Quebec; General Airways, Toronto; and Mackenzie Air Service, Edmonton. He did work briefly with Dominion and Mackenzie, but the former chief pilot of General was sure he had not worked for them."[5] Earlier, Baker had applied in vain for a job with Canadian Airways; and his brief stint with Mackenzie Air Service terminated abruptly following an encounter "with Boss Leigh Brintnell in

. . . Russ told executive assistant Duncan McLaren of having flown to Manchuria and of having driven a limousine for a man, who, when they encountered a flock of sheep, waved his hand and made them disappear.

1936 after Russ dunked a Mackenzie plane and blamed Brintnell for the faulty maintenance that caused a strut to give way."[6]

During this period, he earned an air engineer's licence and his career as a commercial pilot really began when he moved west to British Columbia and was hired by Ginger Coote's Bridge River & Cariboo Airways late in 1936—though even then he was employed, not as a pilot, but as an engineer to restore Coote's de Havilland Fox Moth, CF-API, which had been damaged in an accident at Gun Lake.

Now another quirk of Baker's showed up. In the first six years of his flying after he had obtained his licence—from 1930 to 1936—he padded his first and only available log book, recording brief stints with various companies. Yet once he had completed the restoration of Coote's Fox Moth and began to fly in 1937, he also began to display an ongoing reluctance to concede that he had worked for anyone but himself—a reluctance that grew stronger later in his career, particularly when he became president of an airline.

When he joined Ginger Coote's company (which, according to the BC Companies Register was still officially Bridge River & Cariboo Airways), log-book entries of Baker's flying CF-API for Ginger Coote Airways, commenced in July 1937. They show him flying to Vancouver once, and then generally in the Quesnel area, with one trip as far north as Fort St. James. As well, in the log-book heading the words "flying for" (Ginger Coote Airways) are crossed out and "rented from" substituted, together with "see attached" written in by hand.

The attachment is an agreement, on Ginger Coote Airways Ltd. letterhead. It stipulated that Baker chartered CF-API for one year "from [this] date for the sum of Ten Dollars per flying hour, and that [Baker] will pay all operating costs of the said aircraft." The agreement is signed by both Ginger Coote and Baker and is "dated this 9th day of our Lord 1937"; the month is missing.[7]

Presumably, therefore, according to the letterhead, the company was operating unofficially as Ginger Coote Airways, because it wasn't incorporated as such in the Companies Register until April 8, 1938.[8] Perhaps in the lean years of the late 1930s Baker and Ginger Coote had reached an agreement for Baker to see what business he could come up with to support Coote's operation at his own risk (which would be similar to the one reached by Okanagan Helicopters' pilots with management in the early 1960s).[9]

. . . he [Baker] also began to display an ongoing reluctance to concede that he had worked for anyone but himself—a reluctance that grew stronger later in his career. . . .

Here, somewhat confusingly, Baker's and McConachie's careers come together. In the summer of 1937, Sheldon Luck was working for Grant McConachie's United Air Transport, based at Fort St. James. He recalls meeting Russ Baker for the first time:

A little Fox Moth came in. We were held up for weather for a couple of days—it wasn't so much weather as wind—this lake [Stuart] was like the ocean. We were sitting at the dock. We all recognized the type, but didn't even know who it belonged to. We were horrified when he decided to land out on the lake. In a wind like that, when it was rough, we always used to land down on the river.

By the time he taxied into the dock you could see the airplane rigging had all just sprung. It had flexible rigging; you could tighten up the wires with turnbuckles. If they were pulled, but not broken, you could re-rig it—and that's what my boys did. I had two engineers anyway because we had two airplanes.

It was Russ Baker. He told me he had been freighting for Ginger Coote Airways. He had been working with Ginger all summer out of Wells—Jack of Clubs Lake—and he said he had just finished a job there and Ginger said to run up and see what was going on here. Now, by this time Ginger and Grant [McConachie] probably had been talking. Ginger probably knew that he was going to become a part of this United Air Transport. That's what I think although I'm only assuming this. But anyway, he took off and left the next day.[10]

The date on which the merger of UAT and Ginger Coote Airways took place is difficult to pin down. In Vancouver, on January 6, 1938, the *Province* reported under the headline, "Two Air lines to the Yukon:"

Vancouver, which has been agitating for direct airmail service to the Yukon, will have two lines to the North this winter.

Mayor G. C. Miller announced on Wednesday that Northern Airways Ltd. of Carcross will start service on Saturday.

Today, R. L. "Ginger" Coote of Bridge River and Cariboo Airways announced that a new company has been formed to operate a service between Vancouver and Fort St. John to connect with the present Edmonton-Yukon airmail. . . .

Mr. Coote is at present in Edmonton completing arrangements for the service. He states that negotiations have not been opened with the post office regarding carriage of mail but that will follow later.

George Simmons of Northern Airways had also begun his run without a mail contract. He had been confident enough to acquire a brand new Waco and undertake several dry runs between Vancouver and Whitehorse—using Prince George, Telegraph Creek and Atlin as stages—in proof of his company's ability to provide the service. He was to receive considerable encouragement. The Vancouver Province published a long description of a meeting of the Vancouver Board of Trade, called by president Murphy, which gave a ringing endorsement to Northern Airways, recommending that "wires be sent from this meeting asking the assistance

"We have shipped the floats for 'ET' to Vancouver along with the floats belonging to another machine, as by doing so we could save considerable money, and you can therefore figure that you will go to Vancouver for changeover to floats. You will have to arrange to get to Vancouver on wheels whenever the time appears to be appropriate. Do not take any chances with bad ice conditions. I hope the weather has improved considerably, as you no doubt have had a poor time of it.

C.H. (Punch) Dickins to F.R. Baker, March 23, 1938

Details Told of Discovery Uncharted Peaks, Rivers

Russ Baker's Story of Amazing "Mystery Mountains" Five Hundred Miles Northwest of Prince George

Details of an unsurveyed range of mountain peaks and uncharted rivers larger than the Nechako in Northern British Columbia, were told here Sunday by Russ Baker, noted pilot and northern representative of Canadian Airways. . . .

Russ Baker is known as a cautious and experienced pilot (he has been flying since he was fourteen years old) and he describes this trip of January 19 as "the most surprising and amazing flight I have ever taken . . . [with] mountain peaks, not seen on any map, towering 10,000 or 11,000 feet [3 050-3 350 m]."

Prince George *Citizen*
February 2, 1939

of Olof Hanson, M.P., and the Hon. W. J. Asseltine, Provincial Minister of Mines, to do all they can to secure the requested subsidy."[11]

Then, on April 8, Ginger Coote Airways was officially incorporated, with Ginger's father, Colonel Coote, as president and McConachie and Ginger as directors.[12] Thus, at this time, Baker was working for both Coote and McConachie. "His log shows that he flew the mail as a UAT pilot in January 1938, from Prince George to Fort McLeod, Fort Grahame and Finlay Forks. This was the eight-times-a-year mail run. . . ."[13] In February, the *Vancouver Province*, reporting on the northern route, quoted Ginger Coote as saying that he was expecting to take delivery of a new Noorduyn Norseman, and that "Sheldon Luck is to be placed on the run from Prince George to Ashcroft, and later on into Vancouver. Pilot Russ Baker will handle the route north of Prince George."[14]

If acknowledging that he was really working for Coote was distasteful, the idea of working for Grant McConachie was evidently anathema. Later in his career, Baker dissembled about the early days. In a newspaper article written in 1955, under the headline, "Baker's Airline Once Lone Moth," the writer records that "About 10 years ago Russell Baker could inspect his one-plane 'airline' in jig time.[15] Now at age 44, he is president of Pacific Western Airlines. . . ."[16] Nowhere in the article is there any hint that he flew for airlines other than his own. While this foible has no great significance, it is interesting because it demonstrates that the old Victorian Horatio Alger ideal (the self-made man) still held powerful sway in Baker's time—even if one had to do a little fudging to qualify.

While the details of the deal between McConachie and Coote remain obscure, as we know, it paid off. The northern airmail contract was quietly awarded to Ginger Coote Airways/UAT.[17] But the merger did not endure for very long. In January the following year, newspapers announced that "An important change in the aviation set-up in Vancouver is announced in the withdrawal [of] R. L. Coote from the U.A.T. at Edmonton. 'Ginger' has formed his own company, British Columbia Air Transportation."[18]

Sheldon Luck remembers that he saw "Coote fairly often in his office in Vancouver; then, abruptly, he disappeared—he just wasn't around any more."[19] Coote had evidently taken the new Norseman, CF-AZE (which was not exactly new—it had been registered to R. Cochrane in Ontario in 1936), with him because AZE was registered as being transferred to the British Columbia Air Transport Company from United Air Transport on

March 8, 1939. Then, less than a year later, it was transferred back to Ginger Coote Airways,[20] and Ginger Coote concentrated for the next two years on the Zeballos gold rush, which was peaking at the time. Similarly, McConachie too changed the name of his company from United Air Transport to Yukon Southern Air Transport.

Getting back to Russ Baker, if he worked for McConachie on the mail run in January, it was probably just for one or two trips because he left UAT to join Canadian Airways, and his seniority with that company is listed as February 15, 1938.[21] As historian Ken Molson records, in 1938 activity in the Omineca area warranted the establishment of a new base at Fort St. James. Russ Baker, who had just joined Canadian Airways and was familiar with the area, was chosen to open the base with a Fairchild 71.[22] During this period Baker wrote frequently and at length to Punch Dickins, the veteran and celebrated bush pilot, then Baker's immediate superior. In these letters, he demonstrates the energy, resourcefulness and knack for portraying things in the best possible light that pointed towards his eventual success. For example, on February 28, 1938, he wrote:

I am tied up here with the weather. Elliott and Bronlund[23] are stewing here with me. We have had the worst storm of the season. . . . I have, however, been using my time to good advantage. Grant McConachie was after Forfar in the hotel here as his agent but you notice by enclosed forms that they are our agent. You can't beat the good old Canadian Airways name. McConachie has also approached Harold Smith here but I beat him to that. Although two agents may seem a lot for here still the hotel will all be passengers and Smith will be mostly freight and I believe in sinking our roots deep. I have forwarded agent's forms to the Prince George Hotel who are to be our agents in Prince and will forward them as soon as they are signed and returned to me.

Sheldon Luck approached Bronlund of C.M. & S., but Bronlund told him not to bother him. He apparently has no use for U.A.T.

Captain Bob Adams is opening up at Manson soon and as Harold Smith looks after all his shipments, we are assured of this business. Adams' account with U.A.T. last summer netted them several thousand dollars.

Today I contacted Chris Beaton, General Superintendent of De Ganahl's outfit at Germanson [sic], made a contract with him to bring out 50 men this fall and contracted to fly 12 of them to Vancouver from Germanson for $100 each. Beaton puts his own men into Germanson on a contract basis. I made two charters from Germanson to Vancouver last summer for them.

Baker ends the letter with some conspicuous stroking: "Thank you very much for the ad in the Prince George paper. It sure makes a fellow feel good to have the co-operation that I have had from the different departments in our office there."[24]

From the beginning, he was competitive to the point of unscrupulousness, but he shared with Grant McConachie a talent for hyperbole—

especially self-promoting hyperbole—as well as invaluable persuasiveness. He did not, evidently, possess the charm that evoked a mixture of respect and affection from the people who worked for McConachie. Nevertheless, the result was that Baker managed—starting with a Fairchild 71, CF-AKT, and later, in 1939 after he had put the Fairchild through the ice at Pinchi Lake, with a Junkers W-34, CF-ABK—to capture a reasonable share of the business available out of Fort St. James.

Baker was particularly successful with two of the major customers in the area: Emil Bronlund, of Consolidated Mining & Smelting, and the American De Ganahl exploration company. Charles De Ganahl was evidently playing the competitive game in reverse: trying to get the competing operators to cut their rates. In a letter to Dickins dated March 23, 1938, Baker complained that "De Ganahl has offered me all their work if I will cut the price to 5¢. I think this is too cheap, but told him I would write you about it."[25] However, Frank De Ganahl, son of the owner, had become very friendly with Russ Baker and then things became rather more than competitive as Sheldon Luck of UAT (who was based in Prince George but frequently worked out of Fort St. James) remembers with some resentment.

Coming up from Prince George, Luck had refuelled at Fort St. James and flown all day for De Ganahl, clearing out a camp. On the last trip, there was only the Chinese cook, a small man, left and Luck decided to take him out rather than do another trip; otherwise the cook would have had to remain on his own with no supplies—and the weather looked chancy. A few days later, Luck had a letter from Carter Guest[26] advising him that there had been a complaint that he had been carrying overloads. The young Frank De Ganahl was a good friend of Baker's, and Luck was convinced that all the information had come from his books. "He had engaged a law firm at Prince Rupert—the name Brown is in the law firm. I never wrote it down so I don't remember it.[27] This law firm had written Carter Guest and reported this overloading. I carried an extra passenger and they worked it out to a 126-pound overload as well as one extra passenger. That wasn't too important because we had the seats out of the Waco and the people were piled up on stuff on the bags anyway. But somebody had to supply the information. Frank De Ganahl was a non-flying man. He wouldn't have known himself."[28]

Guest merely warned Luck to "keep my nose clean. He wasn't going to take any further action; but this law firm then went over Carter's head,

The Junkers W-34, CF-ABK, with which Russ Baker, based in Fort St. James and flying for Canadian Airways, established a considerable reputation.—BC FOREST SERVICE

The Canadian Airways' base at Stuart Lake, Fort St. James, winter 1939-40. *Left to right* the Junkers W-34, CF-ABK; Fairchild 71, CF-AOP; and Bellanca C-300 Pacemaker, CF-BFB.
—ROYAL BC MUSEUM

went right to Ottawa, then Carter got a blast, and I got my 90-day suspension."

While Sheldon Luck doesn't actually name him, there's no doubt that he meant Baker and, as we shall see later with a very similar incident in Kamloops, it would be in character. As it turned out, Luck's suspension never really came into effect because, just after this, Len Waagen, of Ginger Coote Airways, went missing on Vancouver Island in CF-AUX, and the DoT waived the suspension so that Luck could join the search.

During this period a battle for the hearts and minds of the public took place between Baker and McConachie in the columns of the *Prince George Citizen*. McConachie was getting a good deal of space because he was rapidly introducing new aircraft and services to the area; but Baker was adept at turning what were more or less routine flights to bring someone out of the bush into heroic mercy flights. A typical example reports that he was "bucking snow, hail and rain and wind squalls for a total flying time of seven and a half hours. . . ."[29] John Condit records another episode in which Baker demonstrated his talent for "keeping the public posted on his flying. On September 1, 1938, the *Citizen* recorded a flight to Aitken Lake to help eight men who had been foodless for three days after a fire wiped out the CM & S mining camp. The men, said the report, had been reduced to eating porcupine meat." However, when Condit checked with Emil Bronlund, the geologist who had been in charge of the camp at the time, Bronlund denied that there had been any crisis. The camp had been evacuated after the fire without undue hardship to any one.[30]

It seems likely that in the end Baker came to believe his own legend. "Pierre Berton said Russ once told him he had lost count after two thousand [mercy flights]."[31] Judging by Berton's later canonization of Baker, Berton probably believed him, too. A simple calculation demonstrates how improbable this claim was. The only log book available in the two Baker collections—one at the National Archives, the other at Canada's Aviation Hall of Fame—is in the latter. It begins in August 1928 and ends in February 1938, when Baker joined Canadian Airways, and there is no mention of mercy flights in the just over 400 flying hours logged. Realistically, he could expect, at a conservative estimate, to lose an average of three weeks a year for the freeze-up, another three for the break up, or 42 days; and—bearing in mind that, because of weather, it took him nearly two weeks to travel the 400 odd miles [650 km] from Prince George to the Nahanni Valley with Berton—at least another 30 days a year grounded by weather. Allowing another 30 days for other factors such as mechanical problems and other operational contingencies, this leaves about 265 flying days a year, or 2,386 total flying days during the nine-year period, 1938-1947, before he met Berton. As well, Baker claimed he had stopped counting after 2,000; so we have to assume that he accomplished very close to one mercy flight every flying day during those nine years.

At the same time, he told Berton that he had logged 10,000 hours of flying time. This would represent an average of three hours every single day, without any allowance for seasons or weather. However, in spite of his hyperbole, Baker's growing reputation as a bush pilot was deserved. Although cautious with the weather, he was clearly competent, conscientious and he kept his customers happy.

Until January 1939, Baker was operating with the Fairchild 71, CF-AKT. Then, after he put that machine through the ice at Pinchi Lake—a surprising occurrence in the middle of winter—the company provided him with a Junkers W-34, CF-ABK. It was with this machine that he was remembered for his bush flying. On July 12, 1991, the community of Fort St. James celebrated "Junkers Day" to commemorate its bush flying heritage. The ceremony began with a parade through the town—a parade of floats with an aviation motif that was successful despite a heavy downpour. Later, after speeches and reminiscences, a one-third-scale model of ABK, mounted on a pedestal in the town's lakeside Cottonwood Park, was unveiled and a good deal of the talk was about Russ Baker. People praised him as a bush pilot. "Of course, he was absolutely full of bullshit" almost inevitably entered the conversation, but this was evidently such common knowledge that it was shrugged off as simply part of the Baker legend. Perhaps the hard-flying, hard-drinking, story-telling image was so much expected of a macho bush pilot that he couldn't escape it even if he had wanted to.

Gordon Ballentine recorded his impressions of Russ Baker in an article. "In December 1938, Walter Gilbert [Canadian Airways' operations manager in Vancouver] sent me to Fort St. James for the winter, partly because it looked like a slow season at Vancouver, partly because Canadian Airways liked its pilots to have some experience on all its operations, and mine had been almost entirely on salt water: flying boats and seaplanes." Earlier that year, in April, Baker had been down to Vancouver where he was checked out by Ballentine on the Junkers on floats before flying it back up to the Fort for operations. Now it was Baker's turn to check Ballentine out on skis in the winter, and Ballentine gives this appraisal of Baker:

Knowing nothing of ski operations or the territory I spent the first part of January riding with Russ in ABK. Having had a couple of nasty experiences early in my career I was seldom comfortable flying with another pilot, so I hadn't looked forward to this useful familiarization business very eagerly. However, contrary to all my apprehensions I discovered Russ to be just as cautious as I, and a darned good bush pilot.

This is a pretty respectable endorsement from a fellow pilot. Ballentine goes on to describe one of the first trips he made with Baker:

One trip we made together was to Bunshaw Lake to pick up the Stanwell-Fletchers who were coming out after a year in the Driftwood Valley. . . . It was on that trip that I learned about overflow and about sleeping under a tree at 20 or 30 below zero.

Overflow I had heard about, and of course Russ and Paul had experienced it many times, but it wasn't expected at Bunshaw.[32] We landed on smooth, unbroken snow and as Russ slowed to do a 180 and head back to our passengers' camp we sank through the insulating snow into the slush underneath, and bingo, we're locked in concrete. We chopped and jacked the Junkers free, managed to get to the camp and on to poles without getting re-stuck, and then we had to tramp a runway for next morning's take-off.[33]

These were typical of the conditions that Russ Baker encountered and handled very successfully during the several years he was based at Fort St. James. A year later, it became clear that Canadian Airways now regarded him as a valued employee. In a September 23, 1939, memo from Walter Gilbert, marked confidential, Russ was informed that "I might advise you in complete confidence that you have been placed on the 'essential' list of Canadian Airways and that according to this, you will not be permitted to enlist for armed service without the permission of the Minister of National Defence."[34]

Previously, the mining activity in the Omineca and Finlay River area was almost exclusively placer gold mining. Then, in 1937, J. S. Gray, a geologist with the Geological Survey of Canada, discovered an outcrop of cinnabar, the mineral from which mercury derives, near Pinchi Lake. When his report appeared the following year, there was at first little interest. Compared to gold, mercury had no great financial rewards to offer. But when war began to appear more and more imminent, people realized that it had considerable strategic value—it was widely used in, among other things, detonators and precision instruments—and its value soon became apparent.

I might advise you in complete confidence that you have been placed on the "essential" list of Canadian airways

Meanwhile, one prospector, Andy Ostrem, had been to the outcrop and staked a claim. He took samples to Bronlund, of CM & S. When assayed, they proved very high grade.[35] CM & S now realized that it was a valuable property, but Bronlund found that

Eight claims had been filed around Ostrem's original three, including claims for Lawrence Dickinson and Frank Cooke, who later became stand-in president and secretary treasurer, respectively, of Central BC Airways.

Bronlund was obliged to make deals with all the claims' owners, including Ostrem. He persuaded them to form a syndicate, take $45,000 cash each and a 15 per cent interest in the mine output. Each received more than $200,000. . . .[36]

This development meant a gratifying increase in revenue flying for both UAT and Canadian Airways. By February 1941, however, a complication arose for Russ Baker. Unknown to most people, the CPR had begun an initiative to merge many of the existing bush-flying companies, ostensibly to put an end to the cut-throat competition prevalent at the time. A letter Baker received from his superior, Walter Gilbert, addressed to both Baker and Gordon Ballentine and dated February 25, 1941, advised that

Mr. F. R. Baker will be coming to Vancouver on about March 1st, and will be stationed here thereafter, for an indefinite period. As you are aware it has been necessary for reasons of Company policy for operational control of our Fort St. James district to be placed under Yukon Southern, under a "pooling" agreement recently arranged.

For reasons familiar to all of us, it would be difficult for Mr. Baker to work under Mr. McConachie, and for this reason he is moving to Vancouver.

Mr. Ballentine has for some months occupied the position of Chief Pilot at Vancouver and has done very valuable work, in checking out and instructing new personnel and in arranging useful schedules for operating.

Mr. Baker's and Mr. Ballentine's seniority with Canadian Airways are almost identical, with the actual difference in favor of Mr. Baker.[37] On this account it is quite understandable that Mr. Ballentine should feel slightly perturbed at Mr. Baker's coming to Vancouver in an apparently senior position to himself, and regardless of Mr. Ballentine's share in building up the Vancouver establishment. So a few words of explanation, at this juncture, should be in order.

First, it is sincerely hoped that the coming move will be a temporary one. Mr. Baker does not wish to leave Northern B.C. for any longer than is necessary, and any more than we wish to take him away from there.

Secondly, his move from Northern B.C. must be arranged so as to save "face" both for himself and for the Company. For this reason he is being posted to Vancouver as "Assistant Superintendent"

Gilbert ends with a rather winsome appeal: "So, 'for the good of the order', it is up to us to forget any petty differences and settle down to the business of making this Division pay. For if we don't, there won't be any promotions and probably not even any 'jobs'!!"[38]

This development meant a gratifying increase in revenue flying for both UAT and Canadian Airways.

Gordon Ballentine, who was the chief pilot in Vancouver at the time, doesn't recall any specifics of "the reasons familiar to all of us", but does remember that Baker engaged in some dubiously sharp practices and that it was probably "a mixture of 'face' and rivalry."[39] As a speculation, this may well have had something to do with the actions that led to Sheldon Luck having his licence suspended. In any event, the move was successful and, before long, Baker was back in Fort St. James. This incident is probably typical of the administrative manoeuvres necessary to keep the peace before the new hierarchy of CPA settled down.

In 1942, after Baker had returned to Fort St. James, the *Citizen* announced that he had kept his new title: "Russ Baker, popular pilot of central and northern British Columbia, has been made assistant superintendent of the BC division of Canadian Pacific Air Lines with headquarters in Fort St. John."*[40] Just how he would be able to superintend flying in the whole of BC from there is not clear, but obviously the face-saving was still going on. Baker had earned his stripes and, to management in Vancouver, he was worth hanging on to.

For Baker the return from Vancouver to Fort St. James brought him to one of the most interesting, highly publicized and ultimately controversial adventures of his flying career.

* This was almost certainly a slip by the reporter, because Baker was still based at Fort St. James when he returned from Vancouver.

Chapter Eight

The Legend Begins

*"Twenty-four American flyers trapped in
Million Dollar Valley and not a pilot willing to
chance a landing in the wilderness? Baker
would chance it, not once but six times and
get a medal for it."*

PIERRE BERTON

BUSH FLYING has always been romanticized; and, in the 1930s, two bush flying endeavours in particular—mercy flights and successful searches for downed aircraft—received considerable media attention and consequent publicity for the pilots involved. Russ Baker made the most of these two opportunities for distinction.

In January, 1942, Baker was involved in a search-and-rescue operation that, after the war, vaulted him into the headlines. Until then he had a measure of local fame; but, in 1947, an award for that operation brought more beneficial publicity: he was reported in newspapers across the country. The story becomes an intriguing example of differing descriptions of this event, and also illustrates aspects of flying in the north in the 1930s and 1940s. Of the several versions, we begin with Baker's own description, written four years after the event, but which should presumably be the most reliable. Nevertheless, cumulatively, other accounts suggest he exaggerated some aspects and even fabricated others. Baker's veracity aside, these accounts shed more light on one of the most celebrated forced landings and rescues during the 1940s.

Baker's involvement began with a routine flight to Watson Lake from Dease Lake. Some drums of aviation gasoline bound for the new airport at Watson Lake had been stranded in Dease Lake by the freeze-up and he was sent to transport them. While doing so, he was called into the administration office at Watson Lake and advised that three US Army Air Force Martin B-26 (Marauder) bombers had gone down on a flight from Fort Nelson to Watson Lake. He was also told that the Watson radio was in touch with them and had learned that they had "crash landed and that some of the crews were seriously injured."[1] There were eight men in each aircraft, and the navigators had taken an astro fix and reported they were above timberline on a mountain in the Teslin Lake area, approximately 130 miles (210 km) west of Watson.

Baker, who was familiar with that area, doubted this because the mountains around Teslin were heavily timbered. He thought they were more likely to be east of Watson, in the Rockies, where the timber was sparse. Nevertheless, he was told to search west to Teslin Lake, which he did without success. The following day, he was allowed to head east with his engineer, Frank Coulter, after further radio communication with the crews indicated that "their position was serious as some of the men were in very bad condition . . . their food supplies were low . . . and that they were without firewood to keep them warm."[2] During the afternoon, while searching to the east, he received word by radio that another flight of bombers heading from Nelson to Watson had spotted the downed aircraft. Baker checked the new fix "but [was] unable to locate any aircraft. We continued searching and eventually located the missing aircraft approximately fifty miles (80 km) west of the latitude and longitude given."[3]

According to Baker, the B-26s were "lying in a gully, rather high in the mountains," and were spaced about a mile apart. "After surveying the scene, I decided that it was not practical to try and make a landing beside or near the crashed aircraft as the terrain was extremely rough . . . and snow conditions were very deep." Baker then returned to Watson Lake and suggested that he fly two policemen who were in Watson Lake, Keith Alexander and Jack Purdy (both of whom doubled as game wardens), together with a dog team, into the nearest lake—Toobally Lakes, 30 miles (50 km) to the north of the downed aircraft.

However, when they got there, the two policemen estimated that it would take two weeks for a round trip from Toobally to the downed planes

. . . their position was serious as some of the men were in very bad condition.[and].their food supplies were low. . . .

and, because of the heavy snow and rough terrain, only one man could be brought out at a time. They stayed the night in a cabin beside the two lakes on the Smith River and tried again in the morning for a landing at the site before returning to Watson Lake for the second time. "In the meantime a search and rescue flight had been brought in from Fairbanks, Alaska and a twin engine Beechcraft had surveyed the wrecked aircraft but decided against trying to make a landing" [hardly surprising because the Beech was on wheels]. Curiously, the authorities seemed as eager for Baker to land so that he could retrieve the Norden bombsights and secret papers as they were for him to bring out the crews. But perhaps in the context of the times, not so curious because the Americans, just after they came into the war, were almost paranoid about the security of this supposedly uncannily accurate device—they claimed the ability to put a bomb in a pickle barrel from 20,000 feet (6 000 m).

To continue with Baker's account, the following morning he returned to the site with Coulter and the two policemen and, after three attempts to spot at least a tolerably safe landing, Baker finally decided to try one near the middle aircraft. In his own words:

> The landing was made and we walked to the nearest of the crashed aircraft. We gave the crew our emergency rations and other food stuff that we had brought to drop to them if a landing was found impossible. On snowshoes we then proceeded to the second crashed aircraft. . . . As we did not have a toboggan we removed engine cowlings from the crashed aircraft and hauled the injured back to our aircraft. We also secured the secret orders and the Norden Bomb Sights. We then walked to the third crashed aircraft . . . and brought the crew back with us to the centre aircraft beside which we had landed.
>
> I then loaded the injured aboard and took off for Watson Lake, leaving my engineer [Frank Coulter] and the two policemen [Keith Alexander and Jack Purdy] to consolidate the crews . . . and to make a passable runway for further landings.[4]

Because of the limited runway, and the altitude, he could handle only four passengers at a time. The weather was kind, much warmer than usual for the time of year, and the wind strong but not threatening. Baker succeeded in getting everyone back safely after what had evidently been a long search, followed by a difficult and dangerous rescue.

It is interesting to compare Baker's account with two other reports. One, written immediately after the event, comes from Keith Alexander, one of the two members of the British Columbia Provincial Police (BCPP) who accompanied Baker and is dated February 5, 1942, a few days after Alexander had returned to his base at Fort Nelson. It contains some significant differences:[5]

So that he could retrieve the Norden bombsights and secret papers . . .

On Saturday morning, January 17th, 1942, while on business at the Fort Nelson Airport, two American Transport Planes and Seven Pursuit Planes arrived at the airport. Lieut. Smith i/c of the flight informed me that he had just received word that three American Bombers of the 77th Medium Bomber Squadron had been lost from a flight of six, the previous day, somewhere between Fort Nelson, B.C. and Watson Lake, Y.T. Same date at 12:15 p.m. the lost bombers were contacted by the radio station at Fort Nelson Airport. . . . At that time they gave their position south of the Liard River fairly close to Watson Lake. . . . I suggested that . . . [if they needed medical equipment or dogs], the Nelson Detachment was at their service.

Same date at 10:00 p.m. Lieuts. Smith and Krebes . . . stated that they had received the exact location of the three lost bombers. . . . The position now given was forty miles [65 km] north west of Nelson forks in the Beaver River country. Smith asked me if I could accompany them first thing in the morning and bring my medical kit with me. . . .

On Sunday, January 18th, 1942 at 9:30 a.m. I left Fort Nelson Airport with Lieut. Krebes in one of the American Transports. Lieut. Smith left at the same time to convoy the seven Fighters through to Whitehorse, Y.T. At 10:30 a.m. while searching over the Beaver River Country we received a report that Lieut. Smith had spotted the Bombers, we then headed direct to Watson Lake. At 11:30 a.m. we spotted the three Bombers, lying approx. two miles apart at the bottom of a big valley about thirty miles [48 km] south and east of Toobally Lakes, altitude 4000 feet [1 220 m], in a direct line about 90 miles [145 km] east of Watson Lake in British Columbia. We flew low over the Bombers and then in to Watson Lake, arriving there at 12:30 p.m.

Upon arrival at Watson Lake I was met by Major Cork. . . . Pilot Russ Baker and Game Warden Jack Purdy[6] were also there, having arrived in a Canadian Airways plane, Junkers on skis. At the request of Major Cork and Pilot Russ Baker, Purdy and I agreed to accompany Russ Baker in the Junkers to the location of the Bombers to see what could be done. Same date at 3:00 p.m. we left Watson. . . . Upon arrival at the Valley, we flew in circles over a spot near the middle bomber. . . . Baker stated that he did not feel like landing because daylight was fading. We then flew to Toobally Lakes to spend the night in a trapper's cabin.

The rest of Alexander's report differs only in detail from Purdy's recollections recorded many years later. When they had settled in for the night at Toobally Lakes, both Alexander and Purdy advised Baker that, if he couldn't land by the bombers, it would take at least a week just to get to the site with a dog team, and then only "if the fine weather that had never been known in that season," didn't change; and, in any case, they would only be able to bring one man out at a time. When they circled the site again and landed the next morning, Alexander describes the landing as "none too smooth." Next he gives the names of the injured in the southernmost bomber—which landed wheels down—and the extent of their injuries: "We found Lieut. Dancer i/c of that plane with a broken nose and slight internal injuries, Lieut. Smiley with a cut on his head and weak from loss of blood. I pulled the bombsight on one engine cowling, while Purdy pulled Dancer on another. . . ."

While this was being done, Baker put the crew of the nearest bomber to work stamping out a runway for take-off—a standard practice on deep snow—then took off and flew the injured men to Watson Lake.

The same B-26, serial 40-1464, was eventually salvaged in 1972, fully restored to flying condition and now resides in the "Fantasy of Flight" Aviation Museum, Polk City, Florida. Taken in 1999, this photo shows Howard Smiley, the original co-pilot, beside pilot/Museum owner Kermit Weeks.
—HOWARD SMILEY COLLECTION

B-26, Serial 40-1464. Fortunately, there were no serious injuries and the crew quickly assembled an adequate shelter, using a wing cover as a tent. —HOWARD SMILEY COLLECTION

Howard F. Smiley, the co-pilot of the B-26 that attempted a wheels down landing in the "Million Dollar Valley,". This photograph was taken on the morning after the emergency landings, January 17, 1942, and shows the "nose popped open like a baked potato," behind him.—HOWARD SMILEY COLLECTION

Alexander and Purdy remained with the middle bomber crew for the night. On the following day, Tuesday, January 20, "Baker made several trips with the bomber crews to Toobally Lakes. On Wednesday . . . Purdy and myself with the remaining men made another trip to the north ship and on instructions from Major Cork, destroyed secret papers and any injured secret instruments, we then returned to the middle Bomber . . . and were met by Baker who had just landed and all left for Toobally Lakes. Another Canadian Airways Fairchild on skis came in to the Toobally Lakes and with the Junkers was just able to take the remaining personnel . . . to Watson Lake. Purdy and I remained . . . at the cabin." Alexander and Purdy were picked up and flown to Watson lake the following day.

An account by the other BCPP constable to accompany Baker during the rescue, Jack Purdy, is in a book he published in 1992.[7] At the time of the rescue, Purdy was stationed at the McDame Creek detachment, a small, remote community about 60 miles (95 km) south of Watson Lake on the Dease River. Purdy had called Canadian Airways to fly his sick wife to Watson Lake, so that she could be flown out to hospital in Vancouver on the regular Yukon Southern run. Before he had time to return to his detachment, he was asked to accompany Baker, air engineer Frank Coulter and Alexander to assist with the rescue. Purdy's description is essentially similar to Alexander's.

Another contemporary report consists of cables between Watson Lake, Elmendorf Air Base and Ladd Field in Alaska. They make for difficult analysis because they usually have truncated texts and are hard to put in sequence. All are heavily stamped "Confidential" and "Restricted."[8] The first one, dated January 17, and signed "GAFFNEY CO LADDFIELD," refers to a cable from Watson Lake on the 16th reporting the three B-26s were missing well beyond their fuel endurance, and requests authority to involve Yukon Southern and Pan American Airways in a search. The second one, dated January 17, addressed simply to Washington, D.C., and signed DAVIDSON/LADD, reports that "the three B dash Twenty Six reported missing have been located down in brush at Watson Lake end." Presumably this refers to the astro-fixes received. In any event, there is a summary report dated January 30, 1942, that gives all the information in brief. After listing the serial numbers of the aircraft, and names of pilots, it provides the details:

Constable Keith O. Alexander of the BC Provincial Police who, with Constable Jack Purdy, played a major role in the rescue of the bomber crews. —CHARLIE ESTLIN COLLECTION

Lat. 59º 52' N, Long. 126º 03' W at 1615 PST, Jan. 16, 1942. Flight became lost in poor weather, and with darkness setting in, all airplanes landed in snow covered valley. Pilot of 40-1459 [E. Avery] reported one engine lost due to shortage of fuel while landing; 40-1501 and 40-1459 landed with wheels up; 40-1464 with wheels down. No salvage of military or personal equipment, except secret equipment, was accomplished due to inaccessibility. Celestial bearings were radioed from 2 of the wrecked airplanes - which were located by U.S. Army aircraft enroute to Alaska on Jan. 18, 1942.

[Signed] Robert O. Cork

Lieut. Colonel, Air Corps,

Commanding

There is one more interesting document: a document that demonstrates the urgency with which the American military was sending aircraft up to defend Alaska against an anticipated attack by aircraft from Japanese aircraft carriers. It was an untidy scramble—a loss of almost 40 per cent of aircraft on the ferry flight:

Lt. Col. Walter Smith, GHQ, telephoned 4:55 2/19/42, giving Capt. Weber the following information:

P-40s.
There were 25 of them; 5 of them cracked up—one at Portland, one at Sand Point, one at Medford, and two at Fort Nelson. Were from the 11th Pursuit Interceptor Squadron.

B-26s.
There were 13 of them had trouble—one at White Horse, one at Watson Lake, and three of them at Fort Nelson. Apparently one of them had been fixed up, because 9 of them were reported serviceable. Were from the 77th Bomb.[9]

Accounts by other people who were in the area at the time correspond comfortably with Alexander's. First, we have Jack Baker, who was Yukon Southern's radio operator and dispatcher at Watson Lake. His recollection is that the USAAF undoubtedly found the downed aircraft. According to him, Russ Baker, who was in Watson Lake at the time, was asked to go and see if he could land at the site of the downed aircraft and bring the crews in.[10]

Gordon Cameron, an engineer with the British-Yukon Navigation Company/White Pass in Whitehorse at the time, recalls: "It didn't take long to find them because actually they were right on Amber Two from the airways [the directional radio beam between Ft. Nelson and Watson Lake]. I'm pretty sure they were found and brought out within two or

P-40s.
There were 25 of them;
5 of them cracked up—one at
Portland, one at Sand Point,
one at Medford, and two at
Fort Nelson.

three days." Then comes the familiar postscript: "Russ Baker was a real BS-er. I know because I worked with him."[11]

Then, in 1969, Stan Bridcut, owner of Watson Lake Air Services, who had had frequent inquiries over the years about where the remains of the bombers were, landed at the site: first to pinpoint the coordinates; and second to take a photograph of one of the surviving airframes. His description is as follows: "They [the bombers] weren't too far back from the Smith River, on the east side, about 3,500 to 4,000 feet [1 070-1 220 m], in a sort of meadow-type clearing. It wasn't high in the mountains—less than a thousand feet [300 m] above the Watson Lake airfield—and it wasn't a gully. I landed there in the wintertime, on skis, with my Super Cub. It didn't give me any problems in the Super Cub." He conceded that it might have been a different story in a Junkers W-34. He also confirmed that all the instruments and engines had been taken out, but the airframes were in good shape. "The one I landed by was right in the open."[12]

The last account of this episode comes from the co-pilot of the third bomber to make an emergency landing in the valley. Lieutenant Howard F. Smiley, who now lives in Florida, generously provided an account written in 1990. This account clearly demonstrates the urgency with which the US military pushed to get aircraft up to defend Alaska against potential attacks by the Japanese immediately after Pearl Harbor. Smiley's first pilot was Lieutenant William J. Dancer and, according to Smiley, they picked up their brand-new B-26 bomber at the Sacramento Air Depot, taking off to begin their flight to Alaska on January 5, 1942. "[At that time], as co-pilot and observer [in a B-26], I had a total of ten hours, no landings or take offs. My first pilot, who outranked me by five weeks, was a little better off with a little more time and about two landings and take offs."

Smiley's account also illustrates what an admirable job the young and relatively inexperienced crews accomplished in an environment that must have been almost totally alien to most of them.

They arrived in Edmonton on January 15, and set off for Whitehorse, the following day:

On the evening of the 15th., our CO, Major Cork, gathered the pilots into his room for a briefing. Among other things he explained that there were no aeronautical maps to take us beyond Edmonton to Whitehorse, Yukon Territory, our next stop. This was to be a flight of some 1000 miles [1 600 km].

. . Baker was a real BS-er. I know because I worked with him.

The Martin B-26s were often called "Flying Prostitutes" because they had no visible means of support; they only had a 66-foot [20 m] wingspan. Later models had three more feet [one metre] added to each wing

Howard Smiley

Then Major Cork introduced us to a couple of Canadian bush pilots who, on 8½" × 11" sheets of paper had made pencil sketch maps showing a lake here, a river there, etc. This was all very nice of them, but in a run of 1000 miles we were to see actually hundreds of lakes and [several] rivers! They left us with a cheery, "You can't miss it [Whitehorse]."[13]

Because "each plane was carrying a full crew including a celestial navigator with his sextant," this particular flight of three bombers, experienced no difficulty up to and beyond Fort Nelson: "The sun was out and the navigators could take their sun lines." Then "we ran into a snowstorm and had to drop down and try to find our way with pilotage, a tricky thing to do in the Canadian Rockies." Before long the light was fading and they were running out of fuel; so they made the sensible decision to find a "shallow valley and try for a good forced landing. A suitable shallow valley was quickly found and the other two planes bellied in with no injuries."

Smiley recalls that the spot they picked for a landing was quite level "and in the gathering darkness the surface appeared smooth with little tuffs of grass sticking up above the snow. What we did not realize (due to lack of experience in mountain flying and not being briefed in the matter) was that the snow is deeper on the valley floor and what looked like tuffs of grass were actually the tops of bushes sitting in 4′ to 5′ [1.2-1.5 m] of snow." He continues his account of the landing:

It was then our turn. As we were on the final approach, our speed was excessive (we would bring these early speed demons in at about 140-150 mph [225-240 km/h]; they would stall out at about 125 mph [200 km/h]) and so to slow the plane down a bit, Dancer called for wheels and I lowered the landing gear. . . . As we hit, the plane swung 90° to the left, the nose wheel collapsed and the nose dug in the ground, popping open like a baked potato. Dancer went out through the windshield with head injuries. I was knocked out in my seat with my feet entangled in the controls. The rest of the crew was in good shape.

After the crew had administered first-aid to the two pilots, they "whipped out the wing covers and made a fine shelter under the left wing. Fortunately we had emergency gear which was sufficient for the duration—gear which included arctic type wear, sleeping bags for all and food rations for two weeks, so we settled down for a long stay. Both Dancer and I could get around in good shape."

Two days after the landing, January 18, Smiley records that it

dawned clear and cold (about 0°). Along toward noon, as we were in our cozy shelter, we suddenly heard a low humming noise off in the distance. We dashed outside and looking toward the sound [south] we saw several little specks and one larger speck going from left to right just over the trees on the horizon. These specks were the P-40Es and their escort on their way from Fort

. . . we ran into a snowstorm and had to drop down and find our way with pilotage, a tricky thing to do in the Canadian Rockies.

Nelson to Watson Lake. Our crews, as well as the other crews had prepared for just such an event. Almost immediately, flares and tracer bullets from the plane's guns started to blaze away, a real Fourth of July! We watched to see if the planes had seen our signals, suddenly the whole flight slowly turned to the right and flew over our positions. . . . As the planes passed over us, we all stood outside so that they could count us and see that there was no serious injury amongst us.

On the following day, January 19, Smiley records that a single-engine monoplane on skis, with two pilots, landed at the site. "While the two pilots remained with the ship a Canadian Mountie* got out to check the condition of the personnel of our three planes and found that only Dancer and I would possibly need a little more medical attention. He loaded us into the skiplane and then returned to the three planes to see what more help he could be to them." Smiley and Dancer were flown to Watson Lake. From there, they were flown by the USAAF to Ladd Field, Fairbanks, Alaska. Two days later Smiley was pronounced fit and a week later he was back flying what he called "our beloved beast, the straight B-26," and was on his way to the Aleutians.[14]

When Baker was angling for a BC Forest Service contract in 1945-46, he dealt with, and became firm friends with, William Cy Phillips. Phillips later became forester in charge of fire suppression, as well as a booster for Russ Baker. John Condit recorded Cy Phillips' opinion: "It always seemed to me Russ told a true story but embellished it, made it a little better. . . ."[15] In this case he appears to have carried "embellishment" a long way. To begin with, Baker claimed not only to have been heavily involved in the search for the downed bombers but, because of his superior local knowledge, to have found them 50 miles (80 km) away from the fix he had been given; and that, after he had found them, he went back to Watson and suggested that the two policemen with a dog team should accompany him "to the nearest point, from which the police could mush in and bring out the crews." Then after the policemen had inspected the area on his second trip and said, in effect, that it couldn't be done, Baker once more flew back to Watson. Yet neither Alexander nor Purdy mention this second trip and none of the seven people active in the area at the time who wrote or were interviewed about the episode has any recollection of Baker being involved in the search at all.

Secondly, Baker claimed that when he found the bombers, they were "fairly high up in the mountains, lying in a gully." This is a pretty fair stretch from other descriptions that they were in a wide valley at the

* The second person in the front was not a pilot: it was air engineer Frank Coulter; and there were two policemen, both constables with the BCPP.

4000-foot (1 220-m) level, which, as Stan Bridcut pointed out, is only about a thousand feet (300 m) above Watson Lake airfield.

Thirdly, and somewhat of a quibble: according to Baker's own written account, the second position report received by radio from the downed bombers advised that "some of the men were in very bad condition" and that "their food supplies were low." Yet, after arriving over the site of the downed bombers, circling repeatedly before deciding the landing was unsuitable, he flew over to Toobally Lakes to spend the night in a trapper's cabin. The following morning, when he changed his mind and decided to land, the first thing he did was to give "the crew our emergency rations and other food stuffs that we had brought to drop to them if a landing was found impossible." Logic surely suggests, knowing that the crews on the ground were in serious trouble and short of food, he should have dropped the food and supplies the previous afternoon?

Fourthly, Baker's reluctance to land at the site is puzzling. The line between over-caution and reasonable circumspection is, of course, a tricky one; but in this case he knew beforehand from radio reports, and could see for himself when he arrived, that two of the bombers had landed wheels up with virtually no damage except to the propellers. The pilot of the third one tried it with wheels down; the inevitable result in deep snow was that he cracked up. As well, the B-26 was known as a "hot" aircraft: that is, having what in those days was an almost excessive landing speed of more than 100 mph (160 km/h); whereas Baker's Junkers had a landing speed of approximately 50 mph (80 km/h)—in addition to which it was on skis. However, this is coming perilously close to armchair quarter-backing. Whatever the indications, Baker could not have been sure of what was under the temptingly smooth snow. It required considerable courage to commit himself to that first landing.

Finally, Pierre Berton added a "gee whiz" journalistic spin to things: "Twenty-four American flyers trapped in Million Dollar Valley and not a pilot willing to chance a landing in the wilderness? Baker would chance it, not once but six times and get a medal for it."[16] One is reminded of Mark Twain's complaint when newspapers reported that he had died: "The report of my death was an exaggeration." For Berton's words clearly indicate that other pilots had been asked, had taken one look at the site and said, "No way!" Whereas, in fact, there seems to be no evidence that any of the experienced bush pilots in the area at the time (those flying for

. . . not a pilot willing to chance a landing in the wilderness? Baker would. . . .

Northern Airways out of Carcross, those for the BYN/White Pass out of Whitehorse, or those flying the line for Canadian Airways/CPA) was ever asked to help either to search for the bombers or to evacuate the crews. Furthermore, after the first landing, while Baker was flying the injured bomber-crew members to Watson Lake for treatment, Alexander recorded that the two policemen and Frank Coulter, as well as bomber-crew members, stamped out and marked with spruce boughs, "a 2,000 ft. [610-m] runway."[17] Consequently, there was little or no risk involved in the remaining five landings.

In short, Baker, who was certainly a capable pilot, simply found himself in the right place at the right time. He was not chosen to help because he was a star—he didn't achieve that image until after he met Pierre Berton on the "Headless Valley" sortie in 1947 when, in John Condit's definitive comment, "Two men who delighted in making a marvel out of the ordinary had put their talents together."[18] Nevertheless, setting aside all the unnecessary hype—both Baker's and Berton's—it is clear that Baker did a very creditable job of rescuing the bomber crews.

Chapter Nine

Million Dollar Valley— The Clean-Up and The Kudos

"That particular day, five B-26s crashed in the north. Three of them at Million Dollar Valley,*[1] *one at Watson Lake and one at Whitehorse."*

GORDON CAMERON

S EVERAL OF THOSE other pilots who were claimed by Berton to have refused to "chance" it, while Baker did six times, were called in to help shuttle the rescued bomber crews from Toobally Lakes to Watson Lake, and to effect a salvage operation late in February or early in March 1942 (no one can recall the exact dates). Among them was Herman Peterson. He had just joined Northern Airways, based at Carcross, and was sent in as a helper and co-pilot with pilot Alec Dame to salvage as much as possible from the bombers. Peterson doesn't recall any problem with landings and take-offs in the Fokker Super Universal (CF-AJC) they were flying (but this, of course, was after the first landing had been made and a runway stamped out and marked). The weather had returned to its seasonal norm: -30° to -50°F (-35° to -45°C), which made it tough going because they had to strip the bombers of all equipment, as well as the engines, which were flown out to Toobally Lakes. From there, everything was moved to Watson Lake in a BYN/White Pass aircraft, a twin-engined Curtiss Condor biplane, CF-BQN, flown by Les Cook.[2]

Gordon Cameron, an engineer with BYN/White Pass in Whitehorse, recalls that the day the three bombers made their emergency landings was a bad one for the USAAF:

* By this time, the site had been ironically designated "Million Dollar Valley."

This BYN/White Pass Curtiss Condor, CF-BQN, flown by Les Cook, was used to ferry salvaged equipment from the downed bombers from Toobally Lakes to Whitehorse. —ROYAL BC MUSEUM

Gordon Cameron, an engineer for the BYN-White Pass company, who was in Whitehorse when the B-26s went down near Smith River. He is standing in front of a rare bird, the Curtiss Kingbird, CF-BVG.

Cameron posed in the nose-cone of the B-26 that crashed on the runway at Whitehorse. —GORDON CAMERON COLLECTION

That particular day, five B-26s crashed in the north. Three of them at Million Dollar Valley, one at Watson Lake and one at Whitehorse. The one at Whitehorse was taking off; they'd just graded part of the runway—it was fairly narrow—and, just before the guy was about to rotate, he caught the right-hand gear on the snow. The wing peeled back and one of the blades of those hollow Curtiss propellers came through, smashed the elbow of the co-pilot, then hit the engineer, who was working the throttles between the pilot and the co-pilot. It went into his rib cage and up and broke his shoulder blade. But he was up and running around the hospital in a couple of days; whereas the co-pilot was finished because there was no elbow left.

The one at Watson Lake was coming in just at dusk and he undershot a bit and at the last second he realized that the trees lining up the runway out on the lake and the runway itself were at different levels. He pulled the nose up too late. The wheels hit the embankment; he bounced into the air and then dove in on his nose. I think one crewman broke a leg. I remember it because a CPA plane came into Whitehorse on a sched run, and they had to turn it around [to Watson Lake] with a nurse on and it flew back to pick up these fellows.

For the salvage, a week or two later, they flew out of Whitehorse in BKV, which was a big Bellanca, and a Fairchild [American?] Pilgrim and they hauled the material out from the downed aircraft. They had a strip at Toobally Lake, and they brought the stuff out: the gun turrets and that sort of stuff which ended up on the floor of the hangar in Whitehorse. They flew out a little tractor—I think it belonged to Happy LePage—to make the strip on Toobally. The Bellanca, BKV, Mackenzie Air Service [by then CPA], flew a lot of the stuff out too.[3]

And finally, a description by Lloyd Ryder, another engineer working for Canadian Airways/CPA at the time:

I don't know how the rescue went, but I went in a Pilgrim with Harvey Johnson, Canadian Airways at that time.[4] They dismantled a Caterpillar here in Whitehorse . . . and they flew that in to Toobally Lakes with a DC-3. Then we went to Toobally, Les Cook was the pilot this time, and we flew it in the old Pilgrim in three pieces over to the crash site. I think it was in the first part of March.

We had a problem because we couldn't get the big part of the Cat in, and we had to load it right at the back between the doors, with the doors open and tied with rope. Well that put the C of G [centre of gravity] so far back—the help we had, we put everybody right up as close to the pilot as possible. The pilot sat up there all by himself in the Pilgrim.[5]

The Cat was used at the site to improve the strip so that heavier loads could be carried and to help move the salvaged engines to it. "Ironically," Ryder adds, "[the bomber pilots] were told in Edmonton if they had any problems, don't land on any lakes. There was Toobally Lake which was only about 25 miles away from the crash site and they could have landed there." Presumably the advice was not to try a wheels-down landing on a snow-covered lake because, as the third bomber pilot demonstrated, this would inevitably result in a crash when the nosewheel dug into the snow. Had they all done belly landings at Toobally, all three aircraft could have been salvaged.

As a brief postscript to the clean-up, in the mid-1960s David Tallichet, an ex-Boeing B-17 pilot in the Second World War, and restorer of post-war planes at Chino Airport in California, located the three B-26s and flew home to plan for their retrieval. In 1971, he led a group of Californians to Million Dollar Valley. They flew into the site from the Smith River airstrip in a helicopter. The wings and the airframes were still remarkably well preserved. They separated them and flew them out with an Okanagan Helicopters' Sikorsky S-58. The remains of all three bombers were then driven down to Fort Nelson by truck, loaded onto Pacific Great Eastern Railway flatcars, and eventually moved all the way down to California.[6]

Because the fuselage of 40-1464—the one Smiley was in—was in the best shape (except for the nose) and had its landing gear intact it was eventually restored with a new nose section to flying condition and flown by Kermit Weeks in the early 1990s.[7] At present it is on display at Kermit Weeks' "Fantasy of Flight" Aviation Museum.

The kudos from the Million Dollar Valley episode came nearly six years later when Russ Baker was awarded the United States Air Medal. Interestingly, the citation makes no mention of the search. In part, it reads:

Mr. Baker unhesitatingly volunteered his services and ski-equipped aircraft for rescue purposes. With full knowledge of terrain conditions which made landing and take-off extremely hazardous, Mr. Baker demonstrated exceptional daring and pilotage ability in evacuating twenty-four U.S. Air Force personnel and classified equipment. The professional knowledge, resourcefulness, and outstanding courage displayed by Mr. Baker in the accomplishment of a dangerous and difficult task reflect great credit upon himself and is in keeping with the highest traditions of the pioneers of civil aviation in the Canadian Northwest.[8]

There are several indications that influential people north of the border had been lobbying for this award. A letter to Baker, dated March 26, 1945, from Burton Lewis, managing editor of Canadian Aviation, begins: "Not that it is anything much to cheer about, but I have at last received some word from Washington. Our correspondent there writes: 'Col Cork [the senior USAAF officer at Watson Lake in 1942] has recommended Baker for the Air Medal . . .; but there is, as always, a hitch.'" The hitch was that the recommendation should have come within two years of the event; now it would be necessary to gain Congressional approval to bypass this regulation.[9]

On October 31, 1947, under the letterhead of the American Chinese Trading Company in Seattle, Eber W. Badcom wrote to Warren G.

. . . several indications that influential people north of the border were lobbying for this award.

Magnuson, Chairman of the US Senate Committee on Interstate and Foreign Commerce, urging him to seek a Congressional exemption from the two-year limitation, "after learning of Russ Baker's acts from a mutual friend of Mr. Baker's and mine" and went on to recommend financial compensation as well. He emphasized the importance of the award and the financial compensation "because Mr. Baker is at this time striving to establish an airline. . . ." Finally, he attached a copy of Baker's own account of the rescue.[10] Senator Magnuson responded on January 2, 1948, to say that the exemption was granted (Baker was informed of the award in February 1948). However, Magnuson added, "If Mr. Baker was acting as an employee of the Canadian Pacific Airlines at the time of the rescue, it is necessary that a request for payment for his services be initiated by the company."[11] At this, Baker quickly lost interest in the compensation and there is no further mention of it in the files.

No doubt the wave of beneficial publicity generated by Pierre Berton's account of the "Headless Valley Expedition" in 1947, described in the next chapter, helped to promote the granting of this award, which brought with it another surge of favourable publicity. Later yet, it transpired that not only was the medal awarded nearly six years after the event but "Approximately 1,250,000 Air Medals were awarded during the period December 7, 1941 and June 30, 1947. . . ."[12]

According to John Condit, Baker "typed out the story of his feat" at the urging of a friend, Michael J. McCormick Sr., in the back of the latter's Kamloops everything-for-the-cowboy store. Condit describes McCormick as a drinking partner when Baker was flying a forestry contract out of Kamloops in 1946, shortly after the incorporation of Central BC Airways—"a publicity-type man" who "celebrated [Baker] in local interviews and articles." The photocopy of Baker's report in Condit's files is headed: "Typed out at my request," with McCormick's initials on it.[13]

Considerable space has been devoted to this episode because, for Russ Baker, it was a pivotal event and a powerfully beneficial one. The award with its favourable publicity coming just as he and Walter Gilbert were, with some deviousness, lobbying the BC Forest Service for contracts and setting up their new company, Central BC Airways, while still working for Canadian Pacific Airlines, virtually jump-started this new venture.

As well, it created not only a legend, but also an unfortunate legacy, and there is irony involved. Berton's portrayal of Baker as a hugely power-

Because Baker is at this time striving to establish an airline.

Game Warden Charlie Estlin who found, at the abandoned
Police Detachment at Lower Post, a copy of the report Keith Alexander
wrote just after the rescue of the crews.—CHARLIE ESTLIN COLLECTION

Herman Peterson of Northern Airways in Carcross was heavily involved in the
first salvage operation in March, 1942. This was his first operation for Northern
and he flew as a helper and co-pilot with Alec Dame in a Fokker Universal.
—HERMAN PETERSON COLLECTION, ATLIN HISTORICAL SOCIETY, 9723

In 1969, Stan Bridcut, of Watson Lake Air Services, landed in "Million Dollar Valley" to examine what was left of the three B-26s, and to take these two photographs of the bomber that landed between the other two.—STAN BRIDCUT COLLECTION

ful, surpassingly skilful pilot of almost mythical bravery, willing to take risks fighting ferocious weather on an almost daily basis—a myth to which Baker became a willing accessory—is, on good authority, some way from the truth. In fact as Gordon Ballentine recorded earlier, "I discovered Russ to be just as cautious as I. . . ."

Another, highly experienced pilot, Sheldon Luck, recalled that "McConachie used to call him [Baker] the sunshine pilot because he was so cautious about the weather."[14] A hoary old adage in bush flying is that "there are old pilots and bold pilots, but no old, bold pilots." Nearly all of the earlier generation of successful bush pilots proved this. They minimized the risks by not flying in dubious or plain bad weather. People like Punch Dickins, Walter Gilbert and Herbert Hollick-Kenyon were all intelligent and cautious pilots—hence their long and successful careers.

Baker falls into this category. Unfortunately, though, he did not preach what he practised. Instead, when Pierre Berton was creating his romantic portrayal, Baker not only bought into it, but enthusiastically contributed to it. The legacy, created by this and other similar dramatizations of bush flying in the Canadian north, has been an unfortunate one because it has endured even to the present, and many young pilots seeking to emulate that macho image have exceeded their experience and abilities and come to grief as a consequence. As recently as 1996, the headline to a *Globe and Mail* newspaper article about an accident was "Bush-pilot culture slammed in report"; and below that a sub-heading, "Bush-pilot bravado blasted in Safety Report"[15] The accident in question involved two de Havilland amphibian turbo Otters that took off more or less together from Kitimat, heading down the coast to Campbell River. They followed the coast; one pilot stayed down over the water and landed safely at the company's dock. The pilot of the other aircraft, despite the prevailing low cloud and fog, decided to cut across country the few remaining miles to the airport. He flew into a small 1,700-foot (500-m) mountain. The pilot and eight out of the ten people on board were killed.

The Air Transportation Safety Board's report recorded that "Over an eleven-year period (01 January 1984 to 31 December 1994), there were 70 accidents involving commercially operated aircraft not conducting low-level special operations, where the aircraft were flown into terrain, water, or obstacles, under control, while the crew had no awareness of the impending disaster."[16] In its lengthy report, the Board, while acknowledg-

BUSH PILOT CULTURE SLAMMED IN REPORT

The federal Transportation Safety Board has heavily criticized the Canadian bush-pilot culture for its deadly overconfidence and the federal Transport Department for doing little to curb it.

Pilots of small aircraft, especially commercial operators, are boldly flying into bad weather conditions and crashing with fatal consequences, because of inadequate training and lax government regulations, says the safety board in a new report.

Globe and Mail
October 1996

ing the difficulty posed by competitive pilots, criticized Transport Canada for lax monitoring of existing VFR weather minimums.

The legacy of the fearless bush pilot, in no small measure a journalistic creation, lives on. Fortunately, the spirit of the dedicated bush pilot, serving the people of the north was, and still is, a solid and truthful reflection of the air crews who flew and are flying in the bush. This is the part of the bush-pilot legacy that deserves emulation and respect.

Chapter Ten

Climbing the Ladder:
Central BC Airways

Understandably, when the company was incorporated on July 8, 1945, there was no mention in the registry of Gilbert's or Baker's names.

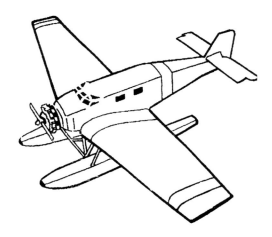

DURING THE TWO YEARS after the Smith River rescue, Baker's desire to be his own boss seems to have grown. At any rate, in a long letter now in the Canadian Airlines archives, under the heading "Grief in Brief," Baker records a litany of complaints against head office in Vancouver. After detailing specific examples of his complaints, he virtually demands that

All phases of the Fort St. James-Prince George operation, apart from the Main Line should be left entirely in our hands as considerable confusion has occurred by Vancouver quoting on trips to points of which they have no knowledge and consequently misquoting. . . .

In any event I think that these matters should be left entirely in my hands. If the Company do not think me capable of running this operation then I should certainly be replaced. If the appointment of Asst. Supt. means anything then sufficient confidence should be placed in me to allow me to run this operation in the manner that I see fit so long as it is in no way detrimental [*sic*] to the policy of the CPA.[1]

These are strong if not quite rebellious words and suggest that he was by then thinking seriously that he had both the reputation and the ability to run his own company. He eventually did so in a manner familiar to bush-flying operators. He worked on customers of his employer and lined up business before going independent. These were principally mining and forestry people with whom he had been operating for some time and

YOUNG AIRLINE MOVES INTO BIG LEAGUES

Vancouver (CP)—Central B.C. Airways Limited, one plane and a dream back in 1946, Saturday announced a "much expanded service" moving it into the big leagues of Canadian aviation. Under the name of Pacific Western Airlines Ltd., a 20-plane fleet "will compete for the position of Canada's third largest airline." Company headquarters will be moved from Kamloops to Vancouver.

Victoria Daily Colonist
May 31, 1953

WALTER E. GILBERT, president of Central B.C. Airways Ltd., who has been east arranging delivery of two Cessna Cranes for local operations.

F. R. "RUSS" BAKER, managing director of Central B.C. Airways Ltd.

who clearly favoured him. It's not always very ethical, perhaps, but widely practised in all business and professional spheres.

While working for Canadian Pacific, both Walter Gilbert and Russ Baker had done a good deal of flying for the BC Forest Service. Gilbert had a reputation going back to the early 1930s as an outstanding bush pilot; as well, he had a pleasant personality. Consequently, when the forestry people were looking into a more substantial use of aircraft, most importantly for fire patrol and suppression, these were the two pilots they favoured. First, however, the Forest Service had to decide whether it was going to set up its own air service or contract it to an existing company.

John Condit suggests that Gilbert and Baker were motivated by C. D. Howe's 1944 decree that the CPR would be required to divest itself of all air activities within a year of the end of the war—which would leave them out of a job. No doubt that was a reasonable anxiety, but to continue to work for CPA while negotiating, first to relieve CPA of the Forestry Service contracts it had held up until then and later to set up a company of their own in direct competition, comes pretty close to crossing the ethical line.

While the Forest Service was still deliberating, it asked Gilbert to advise them what aircraft it should purchase if it decided to form its own air service. Gilbert recommended twin-engines for safety. Eventually, the decision was made to contract the work out; but, because Gilbert and Baker still had only a potential company, with no aircraft, negotiations became complex—especially because CPA had once again put in bids for the contract. In the interim, Walter Gilbert—while angling for a potential job as chief pilot if the Forest Service decided to run its own show—was posted to Prince George by CPA to organize the first experimental forestry contracts in 1945. Gilbert was to fly out of Prince George and Baker out of Fort St. James. All this while the two of them were busy setting up their own company, to be called Central BC Airways.

Understandably, when the company was incorporated on July 8, 1945, there was no mention in the registry of Gilbert's or Baker's names. Instead, two of Baker's friends held the top jobs: Frank Cooke, a former Fort St. James provincial policeman, was named president, and the Fort St. James grocer, Lawrence Dickinson, who had done business with Baker for some years, was secretary-treasurer. Neither of the real principals resigned from CPA until the end of 1945.[2]

The first experimental contract awarded to CPA was, the Forest Service found, both too little and too late, and Gilbert proposed that his company, Central BC Airways, would provide both sufficient aircraft and better service. He forwarded an outline of Central BC Airways' plans for forest patrols to the deputy minister of forests in December 1945. If it won the 1946 contract, CBCA would acquire war-surplus Cessna Cranes on wheels to patrol south-central BC forests, as well as Bellanca Skyrocket floatplanes, with a 2,000-lb [900 kg] payload for use on the northern BC coast.

Gilbert went on to request an initial two-year contract to help in the raising of financing for the proposed purchases; he also requested a recommendation to put before the Air Transport Board. In response, he got a very enthusiastic endorsement. There was, however, still the problem of financing. This was partly solved when Russ, like McConachie before him, met a wealthy mining promoter: in this case, Karl Springer, whom Jim Spilsbury, president of Queen Charlotte Airlines, described sardonically as Baker's "Sugar Daddy."[3] Springer eventually agreed to put up $150,000, but only after the company had been registered and had signed a Forest Service contract. Later, Baker claimed that Springer's financing was granted only on the understanding that he, Baker, would be running the company.

With this, and other smaller loans raised mostly in Fort St. James, Vanderhoof and Prince George, as well as a generous swatch of endorsements from various individuals and agencies, Gilbert and Baker applied for the necessary charter to a hearing of the Air Transport Board held in Prince George in March 1946. CPA had objected on the generalized principle that there was no requirement for another company at the time, but did not send a representative. As well as CBCA, three other companies were granted charters in that spring: Kamloops Air Services, Port Alberni Airways and Queen Charlotte Airlines. The Kamloops company became a competitor for the forestry contract and, in the years ahead, Jim Spilsbury's Queen Charlotte Airlines became a bitter competitor. Eventually, Baker bought out both of them.

Walter Gilbert, whose title was president and general superintendent (Baker was operations manager), laid out CBCA's plans to buy war-surplus Cessna Cranes and two brand-new Bellanca Skyrockets. The licence to operate a non-scheduled charter air service was granted in April 1946. On

THESE MEN "KEEP THEM FLYING"

CAPTAIN A. ("PAT") CAREY flies a JUNKERS Freighter for Central Airways, at Fort St. James. (He is a little late appearing in this series but has been so busy, shuttling back and forth across the North, that we couldn't catch up to him to get a picture, until "freeze-up.") "Pat's" total of flying experience in these parts adds into the thousands of hours. He is establishing a permanent home at Fort St. James.

Central Airways LTD.
BRITISH COLUMBIA
FREIGHT · PRINCE GEORGE, B.C. · PASSENGER

OPERATING BASES: FORT ST. JAMES, B.C.
PRINCE GEORGE, B.C.

Ask Franchise For Air Line

Granting of a franchise to the Central B.C. Airways Ltd. to operate in Central and Northern British Columbia, is being asked of the Air Transport Board, Ottawa, by the city Board of Trade.

Board members enthusiastically received a letter from A. McB. Young, stating that the air line company, incorporated in July, would have its headquarters here and operate bases at Prince George and Fort St. James.

Two of the directors of the company, which has one plane at present, are Lawrence Dikinson and Frank Cooke.

The board also approved letters written by the president, William Bexon, urging federal authorities to grant permission and materials necessary for Douglas and John Thomas to proceed with the construction here of a cold storage locker plant, "which would be of benefit to the community."

* Pat Carey was still flying an Otter out of Stewart 30 years later—until he left it jammed in a cleft in the rocks of a sidehill not far from the Granduc mine.

May 3, the new company was informed that it had been awarded the forestry contract, this ensuring Karl Springer's financial participation.

Central BC Airways did not fly off to instant success and prosperity. There were two or three rocky years ahead. The first contract was a generous one: it involved an area stretching 200 miles (320 km) north of Fort St. James, east to the Alberta border and took in the Kamloops and Nelson forest regions to the south. It allowed for 500 flying hours and a minimum payment of $30,000. There was also a stipulation that all aircraft had to be equipped for two-way radio communications. Nonetheless, the Bellancas failed to materialize and the Cessnas began operations without radios.[4]

Evidently, the Forest Service was indulgent and, gradually, CBCA dug itself out of its difficulties. In place of the promised Bellancas, it was able to lease a Norseman that Pat Carey flew in the Stewart area, mainly for mining exploration.* As well, CPA abandoned its eight-times-a-year mail contract in what is now the Williston Lake area and CBCA took this over. Still, the first season ended with a deficit of $10,000. Karl Springer was not encouraged.[5]

Then CBCA had a stroke of luck. At the beginning of February, 1947, Baker was chartered to fly a journalist, Pierre Berton, into the Northwest Territories: a trip authorized by the publisher of the *Vancouver Sun* to undertake what he called an expedition to the Nahanni Valley. Berton, a highly accomplished journalist, had a particular talent for dramatizing events and glamorizing individuals.

Vague, unsubstantiated rumours had been circulating—rumours probably emanating from prospectors who had spent too long in the bush and then enjoyed the creative benefits of alcohol for the first time in many months. There were tales of a tropical micro-climate embracing something like a Shangri-La in the Nahanni Valley, replete with palm trees and exotic animals. Another tale was of the discovery of the headless corpse of a prospector, offering titillating possibilities of an unknown tribe of head-hunters. It all made splendid copy and was promptly transformed by journalists like Berton into the "Legend of Headless Valley."

Berton and a *Vancouver Sun* photographer, Art Jones, set off with Baker in his Junkers W-34 from Prince George on February 1, but flew only as far as Fort St. James on the first leg. Here, Berton took advantage of a break, while they waited for weather, to write a long article about the career of

Russ Baker, as told by Russ. It claimed nearly 10,000 hours of bush flying and more than 2,000 mercy flights. Moreover, it is made to appear that virtually every one of these mercy flights was made in conditions of dire peril:

Maimed loggers, dying Indians, expectant mothers, flu-ridden children, fever-stricken prospectors have all buffeted northern gales to safety on his plane.

Sunday afternoon we flew up from Prince George to this tiny trapping settlement in just 40 minutes. Germansen Landing is another 50 minutes away but in 1938, buffeting snow, rain, hail and wind squalls, it took Baker 7½ hours to make the trip from Germansen to Prince George.[6]

He got through because he had to. On board were a man and a woman, one suffering from double pneumonia, the other stricken with appendicitis.

"It seems like every time I go on one of these mercy flights I strike it tough," Russ said.[7]

There is more—much more—in the same vein, as Berton describes his own adventures on the journey. Flight engineer Ed Hanratty joined the "expedition" in Fort St. James. On the next leg, to Finlay Forks, they "battled a 40-mile-an-hour [60 km/h] blizzard into this trading post at the headwaters of the Peace River and our plane bumped savagely on the rocky ice of the Finlay River."[8]

They struggled on in their attempts to reach Fort Liard, from which they would explore the valley. In fairness, one should point out that on February 3, the lowest temperature ever recorded in North America, -81°F, was logged in Snag, Yukon; and on the leg from Finlay Forks to Telegraph Creek a week later, Berton claimed they flew in temperatures of 70 below. A journalist like Berton and a normally cautious pilot like Baker were prepared to take what most people and pilots would regard as absurd risks to maintain the momentum of the "expedition." Their luck held. Writing from Fort Nelson on February 11, Berton recorded that

It seemed almost as if the ancient superstition* was true as the engine of our Junkers aircraft turned slowly over in the frozen cold, at the start of the next-to-last lap of our adventure assignment into the Headless Valley area.

The motor coughed and a cylinder blew wide open. Although it has caused another frustrating delay in what has become an uphill battle to reach the valley, legendary home of headhunters and prehistoric monsters,[9] it was actually a miracle in disguise. . . . It might have blown out as we battled freezing temperatures between here and Deer River, when we raced with the stork to bring a pregnant trapper's wife to a doctor's care. It might have blown out as we skimmed the saw-toothed mountains of the Nahanni ranges. . . . "Now you know what bush flying is really like," said Russ Baker.[10]

When they were starting out, on January 31, Walter Gilbert, who had flown into and through the Nahanni Valley in the 1930s, and knew that all was hokum, sent Baker an ironic telegram: "FLASH, TROPICAL

* Presumably Berton is suggesting that the curse of misfortune to befall anyone entering the Nahanni Valley also applies to those heading for it.

One of the early Ansons obtained for Central BC Airways' first Forestry contract, and behind it a DC-4 used on the DEW Line airlift that did much to stabilize PWA.—CANADIAN AIRLINES ARCHIVES

Left to right: Pierre Berton, Russ Baker and photographer Art Jones, at the start of the "Expedition" in February 1947 that, in a very real sense, brought fame and fortune to both Berton and Baker.—NATIONAL ARCHIVES OF CANADA, PA-102384

Russ Baker greeting
a powerful friend and
supporter, the "Minister of
Everything," C. D. Howe.
—CANADA'S AVIATION HALL OF FAME

Baker in a pensive mood, perhaps listening to a lecture on fiscal responsibility by Karl Springer.—CANADA'S AVIATION HALL OF FAME

Two successful airline presidents and their wives relaxing in Hawaii. *Left to right*: Madge Baker, Russ Baker, Grant McConachie, Margaret McConachie.
—NATIONAL ARCHIVES OF CANADA, PA-102410

Russ Baker's last resting place, on a knoll overlooking Stuart Lake at Fort St. James. He died in 1958. —BOB TURNER

The community of Fort St. James commemorated its aviation history with a Junkers Day in 1991. On July 12, after a parade of floats with an aviation motif, a 1/3-scale model of a Junkers W-34, mounted on a pedestal in the town's waterfront Cottonwood Park, was unveiled and dedicated. Three veteran pilots, all of whom had been based in Fort St. James, pose in front of the memorial. Left to right, Ernie Harrison, Pat Carey, Sheldon Luck.—BOB TURNER

VALLEY ISSUING FROST WARNINGS. SMUDGE POTS INDICATED IN ORANGE GROVES."[11]

One of the last dispatches, published on February 15, carries the headline: "Headless Valley: No Cursed Land, Just Icy Waste," and followed with, "Oh credulous and gullible world! Your far-off valley on the lost horizon of the North, the Shangri-La you wanted so much to believe in, the vale that set your soul aflame with the fire of adventure, exists only in your own imagination"[12]—and much of that, one is tempted to add, in Berton's calculated rhetoric.

At all events the Nahanni Valley venture turned out to be the mother lode for both Pierre Berton and Russ Baker. As John Condit observes: "Berton celebrated Russ Baker, his pilot, day after day in stories that hit front pages across the continent, then went on celebrating the pilot in broadcasts, books and articles until the time he came to write an eulogy upon Baker's death. Two men who delighted in making a marvel of the ordinary had put their talents together."[13]

Just such an eulogy, headed, "Tribute to Russ Baker", substantiates Condit's assertion:

This was the plane [Fox Moth] that launched him on his career. Its performance was so poor that he told me he never once saw the tops of mountains but had to fly between them; it just wouldn't climb that high.

He operated out of Fort St. James and his beat was that furious ocean of jagged peaks that stretches off to the west—a land of canyons and glaciers and granite walls often shrouded in fog.

When he was carrying a payload Mr. Baker could not afford the extra weight of snowshoes, sleeping bag or emergency rations.

The noseplate was cracked and he was often blinded by flying oil which cut off his vision. He had neither engine nor prop cover and on freezing winter days he used to have to borrow blankets, drape them over the engine, and build a bonfire beneath it to warm it for takeoff.[14]

This represents an interesting blend of erroneous information and charged language.

Firstly, Baker never was based in Fort St. James with the Fox Moth. In the summer of 1937, Ginger Coote sent him up to the Fort once in the company's Fox Moth, CF-API, to assess its business potential as a base. Thereafter, his logbook indicates that he made one circuit from Prince George of the eight-times-a-year mail runs (Prince George, Fort St. John, Ft. McLeod, Ft. Grahame, Finlay Forks, etc.) for McConachie's UAT in January 1938.[15] The following month he was hired by Canadian Airways, based at Fort St. James, and flew only a Fairchild 71 or a Junkers W-34—

both of which had ample capacity for survival gear—until he formed his own company, CBCA, in 1945.

Secondly, when it comes to an "ocean of jagged peaks," one is not sure whether to characterize this as a mixed metaphor or an oxymoron; then, with the addition of "furious" as a qualifying adjective, Berton endows oceans and mountains with human emotions: "full of anger or fierce passion," according to my dictionary.

Nevertheless, "The Nahanni articles did Central BC Airways a lot of good," said Karl Springer. "Of course, they were a lot of bullshit. Prospectors had been going in there for years."[16] However, while both Berton and Baker went on to success and celebrity, not all of Berton's hype pleased Baker. In a letter on CBCA letterhead from Fort St. James, dated March 3, 1948, Baker, having read a draft of a new book by Berton, has this to say:

Dear Pierre:
I have just received the rest of the book and also today I received your telegram.

First I would like to say that I would not consider having my name used in this book in its present form. I object strenuously to every line which I utter in the story being filled with curses. Second—I have been in touch with some of the people mentioned in the story and they object to the point of going to law if their names are used. Third—In many places the flying terms and descriptions are inaccurate. Four—The conversation as supposedly taking place between Madge and myself is totally different from the manner in which we converse with each other. . . .

. . . The original form in which you sent [the book] to me would do me a great amount of harm and make both Madge and myself look ridiculous in not only their eyes but also to the rest of the flying world. After all remember that I have two children growing up and I do not want them to read the book in its present form and think that their father was two stages lower than a truck driver. . . .[17]

Evidently this book was never completed; but clearly, things were smoothed over because the public display of mutual admiration endured until Baker died.

Meanwhile, CBCA continued to improve its position. By 1948, Springer was ready to contribute nearly $21,000 for a de Havilland Beaver, CF-FHB, the very first one constructed—but not new when CBCA acquired it. The Beaver was quite remarkably superior to any other bush plane on the market at the time. Its short take-off capability left pilots starry-eyed. With the Beaver, Baker moved down to Kamloops for the 1949 forestry contract, renting a house high on a bluff overlooking the city.

Another small company, Kamloops Air Services, run by ex-RCAF pilot Harry Bray, had been established in its namesake town in 1946. Bray oper-

*Of course,
they were a lot of Bullshit.*

Company Obtains First Monoplane

Capt. Russ Baker skimmed across Prince George on Tuesday evening in the first of three Cessna Crane twin-engined cabin monoplanes being obtained by Central B.C. Airways Ltd. in non-scheduled charter operations out of here and Fort St. James.

Another plane is being secured from Vancouver and a third from Moose Jaw in the near future.

Ed Hanratty is the first local man to be engaged for ground crew by the company and will be stationed at the local base being established at the lower end of the golf course.

First job taken by Russ Baker was aerial reconnaissance for the B.C. Forest Service in combatting an outbreak of spot fires

ated with two Republican Seabees and had prospered during the big Fraser Valley flood in 1948. By 1949, though, he was struggling. At the same time Baker was not making much profit by just flying the forestry contract, so he set out to take Bray out of the picture. Bray describes the unequal contest: "Russ would sit up in his eyrie and wait for my Seabee to go groaning up the North Thompson. Then he'd get Al Williamson [journalist] or a fellow by the name of Charlie, who was a taxi driver and had a little lodge, to phone for an immediate charter. And I would be gone by this time and I couldn't give them immediate service, so they'd wire the Air Transport Board that at 10 o'clock on June 17 he had asked for service from Kamloops Air Service and had been denied." However, Charlie recanted and blew the whistle on the game when the Air Transport Board held a hearing on a CBCA application for a charter licence out of Kamloops. The application was denied.[18]

Before long, however, in 1948, Baker offered to buy Bray out. Bray resisted for a while but eventually gave up. He was forced to sell for $10,000 and a guaranteed job for six months at $200 a month. Bray's last word on the affair reflects so many other comments on Baker. "It was a very bitter experience. But I did find Russ was a good man to work for. I hated his guts, but you couldn't help liking him. He was bullshit from one end to the other."[19]

But the real loser was Walter Gilbert. From the beginning, Baker had resented the fact that Walter was the president and general superintendent, while he, Baker, had the lesser title of operations manager. Consequently, he set out to undermine Gilbert. Before long, Karl Springer's anxiety about the financial situation manifested itself in accumulating complaints about extravagant expense accounts. Although, at a board meeting in Prince George on May 31, 1947, "Accounts receivable for the preceding November showed $2,000 advanced to Russ and $250 to Walter,"[20] Baker succeeded in persuading Springer that Gilbert was the free spender. At the next board meeting in Vancouver on June 11, Gilbert was shocked to hear that the first order of business was a motion to accept his resignation. He had no option but to tender it.

In the beginning, Russ Baker had desperately needed Gilbert's reputation with the Forest Service to secure the necessary contracts stipulated by Springer before Springer would invest the substantial financing needed to start the company. Thus did Baker reward Walter Gilbert. It was only after

Gilbert was dumped and Springer had taken over as president, that Springer realized who really was the big spender. "Russ never inspired any financial confidence," he said. "I was a pretty good brake on Russ. I always had hold of the purse strings. . . . At one time I had half a million in it, and it used to worry me a hell of a lot. Oh, no, that was a fundamental mistake on my part—to go into it at all."[21]

With this unfavourable assessment, we will leave Russ Baker's Central BC Airways and return to it in the next chapter, when he is engaged in tactics similar to those described above.

Chapter Eleven

Jim Spilsbury
and the Battle of Alcan

*"At long last, on January 4, 1944,
we left on our first revenue flight."*

JIM SPILSBURY

A. JAMES (JIM) SPILSBURY—aviator, artist, author, self-taught radio manufacturer, legend of the West Coast—was one of the most intriguing figures to emerge from the Depression years and become a leading figure in BC's aviation history. His is an appealing story. It is, to begin with, unconventional, but more significantly perhaps it is a romantic tale of rags to riches, of unlikely success that led to ultimate sadness. It is very difficult to avoid images of a hero battling more than one villain; consequently, an objective approach requires an act of discipline.

The story begins on Savary Island where Jim Spilsbury spent most of his youth, graduating from high school in 1918. Living on an island, he had spent a great deal of time messing about on boats, and his parents decided that the merchant marine offered the most likely path to a sustained career. He was apprenticed as an officer. Unfortunately, he found it a lonely existence because the only officer on the ship he sailed in who would speak to him—who in fact befriended him—was the wireless operator; and, because the deckhands were all Chinese who could speak only a word or two of English, Spilsbury spent much of his time during the voyage in his company. Then, after six months, he persuaded his family to buy him out of his apprenticeship.

However, the time he spent in the wireless operator's cabin was to bear fruit in the long run. It instilled into the young Spilsbury an abiding interest in radio. When he returned to Savary, he took the standard job of a young man on the coast: he worked in a logging camp, operating a steam donkey engine in the woods. He earned his steam ticket and made good money, which he invested in parts to build a radio of his own. He appears to have trained himself in this relatively new technology and was soon building radios to sell, as well as repairing radios for other people. The end result was that he took up the business full time.

During this period, the British Columbia coast was well populated with logging camps and canneries, but that population suffered from isolation. The only way in or out was by small boat or coastal steamship. A working radio gave people a significant relief from the sense of isolation; but Spilsbury's problem was getting into this potential market: boats were both expensive to buy and slow to make their way through the myriad of inlets along the coast. The problem of the boat was solved by a sort of loose lease-purchase agreement for a very old cod-fishing boat with a nine-horsepower engine.

With this boat, the *Mary*, in 1935, at the height of the Great Depression, Spilsbury made a modest living. "Mind you," he said, "this only lasted for forty days of the year, then it was back to chopping wood and digging wells."[1] Next, the deal fell through when the owner repossessed the cod boat. By now, though, the entrepreneurial spirit had taken hold of Spilsbury and he found another boat, one far superior to the old cod-fishing boat; fortuitously, he was able to arrange the same easy payments: a dollar a day. He registered it with the designation of his ham radio licence: the *Five B.R.* This time he was really off to a modestly successful career.

The increasing use of radio telephones along the coast ensured that Spilsbury had plenty of business; indeed, he found by 1937 that he had more than he could handle. He was being criticized by disgruntled customers who were having to wait too long to be served. When the Second World War began he tried to enlist in the Air Force; but at that time they were only accepting university graduates as aircrew. All the while business was growing—not only maintenance but in the manufacture of radios—so his next initiative was to take a partner. Through the network of ham radio operators to which he belonged, he found Jim Hepburn.

CIVILIAN AIRCRAFT GROUNDED IN B.C. BY ORDER IN COUNCIL

An order-in-council gazetted Saturday in Ottawa bans all flights over British Columbia and its waters by civilian aircraft not engaged in training pilots or operating on regularly scheduled passenger flights, except with the express permission of the civilian inspector of aviation.

Previously a 200-mile [320 km] zone inland from the coastline had been declared a prohibited area, and the ban on civil flying applied to this region. The whole province and the contiguous waters now are regarded as prohibited areas.

Charter aircraft come under the ban. Few others are affected because there are practically no civilian aircraft being flown for private transport apart from charter planes.

Whitehorse Star
January 30, 1942

This was a big step up and, with the help of a modest inheritance his wife had come into, the expanded firm, now called Spilsbury & Hepburn Ltd., opened a small office-cum-workshop at the foot of Cardero Street on the Coal Harbour waterfront in Vancouver in April 1941. This brought with it another increase in workload.

The possibility of an alternative to the trusty *Five B.R.* first came to Spilsbury in 1942 when he was flown up to a lumber camp after missing the Union coastal steamer. The boss of the logging company, in a hurry to have a new radio installed, paid for his fare on a CPA de Havilland Rapide. The contrast between the time it took him to reach destinations on the coast by air versus the water opened his eyes. Just as he was appreciating this, wartime restrictions removed his fuel allowance and he had to tie up the *Five B.R.* The only alternative then was to travel on Union Steamships' coastal service, which was already taxed to capacity.

By this time, Spilsbury and Hepburn had taken on responsibility for maintaining a chain of radiophones installed up the coast of the mainland and Vancouver Island. They were operated by members of the small communities who were to report enemy aircraft incursions. The lack of transport meant that Spilsbury's company could not fulfill its responsibility.

Relief came from a somewhat flamboyant, not to say unreliable, cousin of Spilsbury's, Rupert Spilsbury, who had been serving as a flying instructor on the Prairies, and then as pilot for the Trans-Atlantic Ferry Command. Now he was working as a test pilot for the CPA maintenance facility in Vancouver. In his off hours, which seemed to be generous, Rupert would go down to the office on Cardero Street and shoot a dramatic line about his flying experiences. It was he who suggested to Spilsbury that the obvious answer to their transportation problem was to buy an aircraft. There were two obvious objections: if they couldn't get gasoline for the boat, why would they get it for an airplane, and who was going to fly it?

Rupert, who apparently favoured doing something and then thinking about it later, brushed these objections aside. He pointed out that the aircraft would use far less fuel than the boat to reach their destinations; furthermore, because he had a good deal of free time in his present job, he could fly it for them on a part-time basis. As well, he pointed out that because of the wartime restrictions, there were numerous suitable aircraft available at reasonable prices. In short order, apparently, Rupert found an advertisement for just such an aircraft, a Waco, complete with wheels, skis and floats.

The reasonable price was $2,500. The first difficulty was that the aircraft was in Montreal. However, the owner was anxious to sell and he eventually agreed not only to deliver the Waco to Vancouver but to accept $500 down and the balance over two years. The next problem was an obvious one: how to gain the necessary permission to operate in the face of restrictions that kept all but TCA and CPA from flying—CPA with a very limited amount of bush flying along the coast? It was, according to Spilsbury, a classic battle with bureaucracy. He had to get permission from the Department of Transport, the Air Force, the Oil Controller, and back to the DoT again.

The obvious lever was the contract to maintain the Aircraft Detection Stations along the coast; this was manifestly a national security task and, eventually, all the different permits were granted, as well as a permit for unlimited gasoline. There followed weeks of waiting for the plane. Eventually they received a telegram from Princeton advising them that the owner had left the aircraft there and returned to Montreal. Rupert picked up the Waco and flew it down to Vancouver.

At long last, on January 4, 1944, they left on their first revenue flight to Salmon Arm (near Seymour Inlet) with a complete radio-telephone station. This first trip was entirely successful. It had taken 50 minutes of flying to accomplish what would have taken four days by boat. Their elation quickly subsided when they found a figure well known in BC aviation circles waiting for them on the dock. It was Carter Guest, regional inspector for the DoT. He had heard nothing about this aircraft or its permits and the first thing he did was to demand the Certificate of Airworthiness. Spilsbury had understood that the aircraft could carry four passengers and 1,000 pounds (435 kg) of freight; instead, the C of A revealed that it could carry far less on floats. Guest threatened to ground them if there were any more violations, as well as pull Rupert's commercial licence. More ominously yet, they were advised that when the C of A expired the following September, there would be a full inspection.

Nevertheless, they began to use the Waco with increasing frequency and very much to their advantage. When Rupert was unavailable to fly it, they hired Bill Peters, who was flying part time for CPA. They had made a quantum leap in the extent of territory they could cover and the amount

Guest threatened to ground them if there were any more violations. . . .

"Rupert [Spilsbury] was the pilot. We landed on the river, and there was all kinds of people there. Bill Cameron and Siple—-Siple was involved in the Wright installation [on a Canso]. He was going to get it done in two weeks and we were going to go home. They're all standing there waving on this spit that comes out right in front of Fairchild Aircraft on the river in Montreal. We made our approach right over the end of spit, touched down—-made a pretty nice landing and skidded along. I always used to pull the cable that released the co-pilot's seat and drop down onto the floor. Well I did that and, by the time I hit the floor, I'm standing in water. We were right up on a great big pile of rock."

Curly Nairn

of work they could accomplish. The improvement to their business had been so marked they now had seven full-time employees working for them. These were heady times for Spilsbury & Hepburn, who still specialized in radio equipment and repair—but this was about to change.

This change came about when they were asked by a logging company if the Waco could be chartered to do some timber cruising from the air. The charter was very successful, and others soon followed. Unfortunately, one of them, a request from lumber baron H. R. MacMillan, who wanted to go to Prince Rupert, turned sour. The weather was down and the pilot turned back. MacMillan was angered because he was made to pay at the full rate. Later it became clear that Spilsbury had made a formidable enemy.

From now on, they began to make more money from charters with the Waco than from their radio business. Oddly enough, the DoT did not challenge this initiative but, the day the C of A expired, Carter Guest and Norm Terry, from the Inspection Department, were waiting for them. There followed a painful scene for Spilsbury. Norm Terry, the engineering inspector, walked up to the Waco, took a very sharp, long-bladed knife out of his pocket, went under the wing, stabbed his long blade into it and made a big slash. Terry made many such slashes both in the wings and the fuselage and left them with a thoroughly discouraging list of problems to be rectified—nothing less than a major overhaul of the entire aircraft and the engine.

This was a long and painful crisis for the company. The best estimate for this work, $4,800, was beyond their means, but was eventually solved by two initiatives: one practical, the other purely fortuitous. Spilsbury contacted one of his friends on the ham radio circuit. Jack Tindall had been running a general store at Refuge Cove, and Spilsbury managed to persuade him to sell the store and buy into Spilsbury & Hepburn. The second initiative almost defies credibility. Spilsbury belatedly discovered that the man they had hired a year earlier as a general handyman, Charles Banting, was a highly qualified air engineer. Too close a friendship with John Barleycorn had sidelined his aviation career; now, suddenly, he revealed for the first time his qualifications and suggested that if he were put in charge, he could get the machine flying within a month or so. He did just that.

The Waco went back to work up and down the coast, catching up with the backlog of radio business, but now increasingly tending to earn more on charters than on the radio side. Things at last began to go Spilsbury's way—until some of the enlightened aviation legislation enacted by C. D. Howe to control the cut-throat competition that, before the war, had begun to cost lives—was brought to his attention. Spilsbury learned from an official of the Air Transport Board that, now the war was over, their special permit no longer applied; thus, if they were going to continue the charter flying, they would have to apply for a Class 4 charter licence, which they did.

This might not have been too much of a problem if CPA had not decided to contest the application. What happened next smacks of divine intervention. There was a set 30-day interval after the application had been filed and before the hearing to allow any other interested party to intercede. On the 29th day a telegram arrived from CPA to say that it was intervening. However, CPA was obliged under the act to provide a copy of its brief to Spilsbury & Hepburn. This document arrived at the last minute before the hearing.

The package appeared to contain all the necessary information but, as well, there was a great deal of additional information—information about CPA's intervention strategy during the hearing, which was held on September 2, 1945. Clearly this had been accidentally included by a secretary, and contained some very damaging evidence of illegal charters by Spilsbury and Hepburn that would obviously kill their charter application. This presented a crisis of conscience for Spilsbury. Should he return it or take advantage of the unexpected godsend? In the end: "We decided to be noble about it," Spilsbury concludes. "If we sent it back, that poor secretary would be found out and lose her job, and we didn't want that. So we dropped the entire file into the furnace."[2]

As a consequence, CPA's lawyer was driven to vague generalizations at the hearing and, some months later, Spilsbury & Hepburn was granted a licence authorizing the company to fly from a fixed base in Vancouver "to any point or area that can be safely served, but more particularly along the coast line of the Province of British Columbia."[3] They decided to call themselves Queen Charlotte Airlines.

There followed a period of heavy flying for Bill Peters in the Waco, but the opportunity for many more revenue hours was apparent, and they began to think in terms of scheduled flights to the Queen Charlotte Islands with stops on the way. Spilsbury recognized that he would need a

We decided to be noble about it . . . if we sent it back that poor secretary . . . would lose her job.

larger aircraft, with more passenger and freight capacity—and with instrument flight capability. The opportunity, with potential funding from a wealthy businessman, to acquire three Grumman Goose, twin-engined amphibians, was scotched when the businessman's son advised him they were obsolete.*

Instead of the Grumman Goose, they found a practically new war-surplus Cessna Crane for sale in Calgary for $2,000. The original intention had been to use the engines as spares for the Waco, but the machine was in such good condition that they decided to install passenger seats and use it for QCA's scheduled run. When it was ready, Bill Peters set off for the inaugural run to Masset on October 4, 1945. When he got back, the DoT, represented by Carter Guest, was waiting for him. First, they couldn't do scheduled runs on a charter licence; they would require a scheduled flight licence. Second, the aircraft had no Certificate of Airworthiness. Third, Carter Guest lifted Bill Peters' licence.

The first priority, obviously enough, was to get another pilot to fly the Waco. Spilsbury hired an ex-service pilot, John Hatch, and he turned out to be a welcome asset, both in flying and in customer relations. There was, nevertheless, much more potential business than they could handle with one plane and one pilot.

Cousin Rupert was responsible for the next move. One of Rupert's friends from his Trans-Atlantic Ferry days was Wally Siple, who had taken up the business of buying war-surplus aircraft and finding a market for them. He had bought 24 Supermarine Stranraer flying boats constructed by Vickers in Montreal in the 1930s. They were being flown down to South America. One of the pilots was Rupert, with Hank Elway as his engineer.[4] The Stranraer could carry a two-ton payload and all 24 of them were parked at Jericho Beach, in Vancouver; they were destined for sale in South America and Rupert persuaded Spilsbury to jump in while they were still available.

The problems of financing the purchases they were contemplating were solved by persuading a consortium of lumber companies to put up the funds. However, under the then existing air regulations, the ex-RCAF Stranraers would require a number of modifications before they could be given a civilian Certificate of Airworthiness. Consequently, when Spilsbury approached Carter Guest for an opinion, he was given what he described as a very positive negative.[5]

. . . Guest lifted Bill Peters' licence

* Ironically, the Goose turned out to be a very successful aircraft: claimed by the businessman's son to be obsolete in 1945, it was still in service in 1988.

Fortunately, Wally Siple was a natural wheeler-dealer. He reassured Spilsbury that he could get the Stranraer licensed—and it turned out that he could. He was friendly with the daughter of the director of aircraft inspection in Ottawa—a daughter who was also a fully qualified aeronautical engineer; thus, only weeks after Carter Guest had issued his warning, the first Stranraer, CF-BYI, was ready to start work as a commercial airliner.[6]

Spilsbury's move into scheduled airline operation was noted in the Vancouver Province, January 4, 1946, under the heading, "Twice-a-Week Hops to Rupert":

Twice-weekly air passenger service to Prince Rupert is planned shortly by Queen Charlotte Airlines Ltd., incorporated this week for $250,000.

This firm is an associate company of Spilsbury & Hepburn Ltd. A. J. Spilsbury is president of both concerns.

A Spilsbury & Hepburn 15-passenger flying boat now makes a weekly return hop to Prince Rupert via the Queen Charlottes.[7]

The last paragraph appears to contradict the first one, anticipating the inaugural flight by two months.

In fact, they set off for the inaugural run to Prince Rupert via the Charlottes on March 6, 1946, and, after overcoming a number of small nervous crises, and some typical coastal weather, reached Rupert on March 7. According to Spilsbury, because the weather was down, they spent the night in Coal Harbour; but the local newspaper reported that "the first stop was made at O'Brien Bay in Johnstone Straits where that night was spent."[8] Public reaction, once again according to Spilsbury, was very favorable: "We couldn't believe it. The mayor and town council were there with signs—Prince Rupert Welcomes Flight Number One—they made a huge fuss of us."[9] However the *Daily News* seemed a good deal less bullish, observing that it would be a non-scheduled service, "probably once-a-week"; and ended the article with "Mr. Spilsbury . . . [hoped to] obtain the use of the Seal Cove air base, temporarily at least." Fortunately for Spilsbury's peace of mind, the newspaper report of March 11, 1946, under the heading "Regular Air Service Now Commencing," was much more favourable, reporting a once-a—week flight into Rupert and a second aircraft that will "operate from Vancouver to the Islands, crossing to Prince Rupert when business warrants."[10] For QCA had promptly ordered another Stranraer and begun to hire more pilots immediately after the inaugural Stranraer flight to Rupert.

THE SOVEREIGN STATE OF ALCAN

On an early spring day in 1952, some unexpected news arrived at an isolated Indian village on the banks of the Cheslatta River in northwest B.C. A helicopter owned by the Aluminum Company of Canada delivered the Indian agent from Vanderhoof to tell the people that soon their village and land would be underwater.

Telkwa Foundation Newsletter
Spring 1983

From the start, though, the company was woefully underfinanced and, because of this, it assembled aircraft of various types simply because they were available at the right price. By the end of the 1940s, QCA could justifiably claim that it was the third-largest airline in Canada after TCA and CPA. At the same time, people began to refer ironically to QCA as "Queer Collection of Aircraft." A partial list includes Waco, Norseman, Cessna 180, Stinson, Bellanca, Fairchild Husky, Stagger-Wing Beech, Stranraer, Canso, Dragon Rapide, Cessna Crane, Anson and, by 1953, DC-3. Such diversity resulted in complexity of operation. Air engineers had a tough time keeping up with all the types; worse still, maintaining an adequate store of spare parts was both expensive and very difficult to keep track of.

The same problem obtained with the pilots, who were called on to move from one type of aircraft to another with some frequency; and who were, in any case mostly, ex-service pilots with little or no previous experience in the rough and tumble of flying the coast VFR.* This was a particularly difficult situation when it came to running scheduled routes and led in turn to pushing the weather and a disturbing number of accidents. Nevertheless, the company continued to expand—but the Post Office had reverted to its prewar policy with QCA: it offered the airline next to nothing for carrying the mail. The fight to get a reasonable airmail contract was both lengthy and debilitating.

And then, beginning in 1949, what should have been a bonanza turned out in the end to be QCA's nemesis. This was the Aluminum Company of Canada's Kitimat-Kemano aluminum smelter and powerplant project. It was an expansive project, but not everyone greeted it with enthusiasm. Many were concerned about its environmental impacts, especially along the borders of Tweedsmuir Park. Dams were to be built on Whitesail Lake, Des Lake, the east end of Tahtsa Lake and at the Canyon dam site on the Nechako River. This would, in effect, reverse the flow of water in the watershed and create a 335-square-mile (920-km2) reservoir, the water from which would be released through a 10-mile (16-km) tunnel through the mountains from the west end of Tahtsa Lake, which in turn dropped it 2,600 feet (790 m) into the powerhouse turbine generators at Kemano. The powerhouse itself was to be constructed in a giant cave excavated from the base of a mountain. The power generated would then be transmitted to the aluminum smelting plant to be erected at Kitimat.

. . . a "queer Collection of Aircraft."

* Visual Flight Rules, meaning eye contact with the ground or water at all times.

It was promoted, with some justification, as the largest industrial project ever undertaken in British Columbia. At first blush, this looked like the answer to any aviation company's prayer because the construction period would be extensive and would require constant air support, both for passengers and freight.

By then, C. D. Howe had rescinded his draconian measure to ban all airlines except TCA after the war; instead, he now promulgated a number of regulations that would serve to limit the kind of ferocious competition that had not only delayed progress but cost many lives in the 1930s. On the face of it, this was enlightened legislation. It would provide operators with protected areas and limit the constant round of price-cutting that had made aviation a grim exercise in survival—a situation exacerbated by the Post Office Department's determination to deny airmail contracts—and preferably, when they did award contracts, to make a profit from those struggling companies.

All in all it looked like a profitable watershed for both Alcan and QCA. In the end, sadly, QCA's metaphorical dam—the new air regulations—gave way, because, in practice, those regulations turned out to be smoke and mirrors when large corporations such as Alcan were involved. While Spilsbury's own account of this period may tend to sound like the exaggerations of an embittered loser, there is ample evidence to support his contention that "C. D. Howe and Co. owned the whole of that part of the country. They had so much political clout, they could do just about what they liked, and they did."[11]

And if some of what follows sounds like another exaggeration, it should be remembered that a long, dreary Depression had been followed by a war that, whatever its evils, had restored the Canadian economy to a period of prosperity and full employment. As well, in 1950 the frontier ethic was still very much in evidence. Environmentalism in British Columbia was still a lonely voice. The province was brimming with natural resources crying out to be developed—resources so vast that they could never be depleted. Too many trees could never be cut down; too many minerals could never be recovered; too many fish could never be caught. Consequently, when Alcan made its proposal both federal and provincial governments looked on the Kitimat-Kemano area, and the lakes to the east of them, as inaccessible and, for the time being, unproductive. The prospect of a

All in all, it looked like a profitable watershed for both Alcan and QCA.

The Consolidated Cansos, another war-surplus acquisition, were the workhorses of the fleet in QCA's latter days.—ROYAL BC MUSEUM

The Supermarine Stranraer became the backbone of Queen Charlotte Airlines "queer collection of aircraft."
—GEOFFREY ROWE COLLECTION

The Morrison-Knudsen
construction camp,
Kemano, 1951.—G. HUNTER,
NATIONAL FILM BOARD PA111577

R. Carter Guest was the Department
of Transport Inspector of Air Regulations
for BC and the Yukon. Jim Spilsbury was
convinced that, because of wartime
restrictions, there were so few
commercial aircraft operating in BC,
Carter Guest spent the majority of his
time harrassing QCA.

Map of the Alcan Kemano-Kitimat Project.

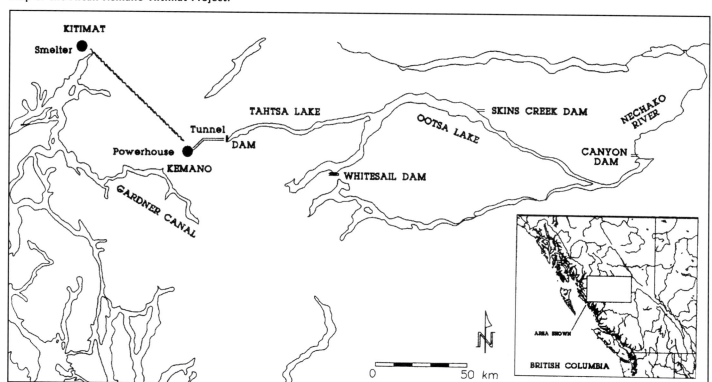

A recent photograph of Jim Spilsbury, wireless wizard, airline president and talented artist.—JIM SPILSBURY COLLECTION

AIRCRAFT
CHARTER-SERVICE

WACO
SEAPLANE

100 MILES
PER HOUR

•

•

PILOT & THREE
PASSENGERS

RADIO
EQUIPPED

◆ **IT PAYS TO FLY** ◆

Freight - Passengers - Timber Cruising
Trappers Supplies - Hunting Parties
Fishing Parties - Photographic Surveys

CHARTER RATES
$45.00 per hour - 45c per mile

Vancouver To _____
Per Passenger - $ (ESTIMATE)
ABOVE RATES DO NOT INCLUDE GOV'T. TAX

SPILSBURY & HEPBURN LTD.

P. O. Box 285   VANCOUVER, B.C.
PHONES: MARINE 2724 - NITE: BA. 0489-R - BA. 8145-M

An early poster, before Jim Spilsbury's enterprise expanded into Queen Charlotte Airlines, the third largest airline in Canada.
—ROYAL BC MUSEUM

QUEEN CHARLOTTE AIRLINES LTD.
AT POINT OF MAILING

Mr. J.E. Kyte,
Queen Charlotte Airlines Ltd.,
VANCOUVER - AMF B.C.

VIA AIR MAIL

John Kite was for several years the chief dispatcher for QCA.—ROYAL BC MUSEUM

giant industrial development there was as tempting to political leaders as a succulent bone to a hungry dog.

Furthermore, the incumbent federal Minister of Trade and Commerce, C. D. Howe, had built up, under the umbrella of wartime national emergencies, unprecedented personal power. In the dying days of Mackenzie King's long incumbency, and the early days of the newly anointed caretaker prime minister, Louis St. Laurent, Howe's authority became almost unlimited. He had quickly exploited postwar reconstruction, followed by the Korean War and the Cold War, as emergencies to maintain such individual power "without," as Richard Overstall observes, "being unduly concerned with the democratic process."[12] As well, he had become closely involved with Alcan during the war when he had been Minister of Munitions and Supply (augmented in 1944 by the Department of Reconstruction). During this period, he had engineered very substantial subsidies and tax depreciations for Alcan as emergency war measures.

As Richard Overstall records in his article, "The Sovereign State of Alcan," "Howe went even further for Alcan. In 1950 he went on a selling trip to the U.S. attempting, but failing, to negotiate a billion-dollar contract for the company with the American government's strategic stockpiling agency. When the Liberals were defeated in the 1957 election 'C. D.' . . . was soon rewarded for his work with an appointment to Alcan's Board of Directors."[13]

The concessions to Alcan listed in Overstall's article make startling reading. "The water rights and flooded land in the Nechako and Nanika watersheds were a provincial responsibility. They were conceded to Alcan by...the Byron Johnson government. Both mineral and timber rights within the flooded area were given to the company—rights it wanted, not to use the resources, but to keep other users away. Thus the timber was never harvested but allowed to drown in the rising waters of the reservoir. No stumpage fees were paid to the government." At the same time, the federal government ignored pleas from the International Salmon Fisheries Commission to order construction of a $500,000 cold water release tunnel around the Kenney Dam on the Nechako. "Summertime flows of cooling water are needed to allow sockeye salmon to migrate up the Nechako to their spawning grounds. Perhaps as a reward for this inaction, the fisheries minister at the time, James Sinclair, was made a director of Alcan after he

"Actually, Baker didn't do very much flying. He never had the hours that he claimed. Grant McConachie was a great self-promoter, too, but he was a nice guy."

Jim Spilsbury, QCA

retired from politics." And finally, the native communities in the area were summarily, and without any consultation, told to move out.[14]

In the light of this, it is interesting to see, in the long list of whereas clauses in the contract signed between Alcan and the Government of British Columbia, dated December 20, 1950, this one: "WHEREAS the construction of such an aluminum plant at or near the site of the said water power would accomplish, without investment by or risk to the GOVERNMENT, the development of power, the establishment of a permanent industry, and the beginning of a new centre of population. . . ."[15]

In reality, Alcan was given very generous financial concessions by the government on behalf of taxpayers, and there was considerable risk to the environment—particularly to the Nechako sockeye run.

But the part of the Alcan project we are concerned with was Alcan's ability to circumvent the air regulations; and this brings us back to Russ Baker, whom we left basking in the glow of Berton's rhetoric after the Headless Valley caper. He had been making some headway. Probably because of the reputation Berton had broadcast for him far and wide, Baker immediately became a favourite of Morrison-Knudsen, the company contracted by Alcan to undertake the construction phase of the project. The difficulty was that the Alcan project really needed a regular, Class 2 scheduled service from Vancouver up the coast to Kitimat. Baker's Central BC Airways was limited to charter flying, while Spilsbury's Queen Charlotte Airlines had the necessary Class 2 licence to provide this service.

Typically, Russ Baker later claimed that the first survey flying for this project was done by CBCA. As John Condit records: "In its 1955 annual report (after it had taken over QCA), PWA asserted that in 1949 it had 'made history with the original survey flying for the huge Aluminum Company development.' That history had already been made." QCA pilot Hughie Hughes—who later became a well-known helicopter pilot with Okanagan Helicopters—had done it in a Norseman in 1948.[16]

Baker's initial move was to hire Dick Laidman, a pilot who had moved around from one venture to another after the war. Baker promised him the title of chief pilot if he would join CBCA and open up a base at Burns Lake, a small town that had suddenly come alive with construction activity. Laidman demanded the recently acquired de Havilland Beaver and got it. Laidman's next task was to persuade V. A. Roberts, the assistant Alcan

YOUNG AIRLINE MOVES INTO BIG LEAGUES

Vancouver (CP)—Central. B.C. Airways Limited, one plane and a dream back in 1946. Saturday announced a "much expanded service" moving it into the big leagues of Canadian aviation.

Under the name of Pacific Western Airlines Ltd., a 20-plane fleet will "compete for the position of Canada's third largest airline." Company headquarters will be moved from Kamloops to Vancouver

Victoria Daily Colonist
May 31, 1953

project manager and brother-in-law of H. W. Morrison, president of Morrison-Knudsen, that he needed CBCA's services. Roberts was not a flying enthusiast, but an initial trip over the dam sites made him an instant convert. As a direct consequence, CBCA was able to sign a contract with Morrison-Knudsen to base aircraft, on three-hour call, at Prince George, Burns Lake, Kemano Bay and at the west end of Tahtsa Lake.[17]

While the legality of this contract was questionable, it was still only for charter flying with smaller aircraft such as the Beaver and the Norseman; and it still precluded direct flights from Vancouver to Kitimat or Kemano. Russ Baker set out to change that. The result was an ongoing battle of paper between CBCA and Alcan on the one hand, and the Air Transport Board on the other. The rhetoric grew stronger as the conflict went on. It was, in any case an unequal fight. The Air Transport Board was trying to maintain some semblance of impartiality, but most of its instructions were equivocal. One cannot escape the conviction that they were being leaned on to favour Alcan's wishes.[18]

Before then, though, the battle had really been joined. Eric Cowden, who joined QCA as an apprentice air engineer in 1948 and left to join the up-and-coming Okanagan Helicopters in 1952, recalls that, before he left, base engineers of both QCA and CBCA had instructions not to provide avgas to the opposition. "Of course," he chuckled, "we all ignored it: you never knew when one of our machines might be stuck needing gas at one of their bases."[19]

Then, in 1953, Morrison-Knudsen signed another contract with CBCA (which had recently changed its name to Pacific Western Airlines),[20] allowing the company to fly direct along the coast from Vancouver. The Air Transport Board finally put its foot down, or appeared to. In a letter signed by John R. Belcher, the board's acting secretary, to Baker, dated June 30, 1953, he was advised:

I am therefore directed to inform you that upon the termination of the present contract on June 30th all flights between Vancouver, Kitimat, Kemano and Kildala Arm on the basis of that contract must cease. . . . I am also to say that the employment of other carriers to carry out charter work between Vancouver and Kitimat, Kemano and Kildala Arm on your behalf will result in steps being taken by the Board to protect Class 2 carriers against such action.[21]

Baker, of course, went back to Alcan. He wrote to T. C. Lockwood, general traffic manager. "The point which is of prime importance to you of course is the fact that your Company and its contractors are not getting

Base engineers had instructions not to provide avgas to the opposition.

the service you require and this undoubtedly results in considerable unnecessary expense on your part. We would like to be able to give you better service and it is my opinion that Alcan M/K and other contractors working on the Project should have the right to charter as required both large and small aircraft from any qualified operator."[22] This was the doctrine of open skies and free enterprise with a vengeance.

Alcan's response, in this case via Morrison-Knudsen, is a typical example of the pressure Alcan was putting on the board. It was a long letter of complaint by C. E. Elliot, the company's controller, to Ralph Campney in July 1953. Campney at the time was a Liberal MP, shortly to be Solicitor-General and later Minister of Defence. Interestingly, this letter was addressed not to his parliamentary office but to his company, Messrs. Campney, Owen, Murphy & Owen. The letter ended with: "We were under the impression that the Dominion of Canada was operating on a free-enterprise basis, but are we to understand that the Department of Transport shall dictate to us and tell us who shall carry our personnel and whom we shall have the authority to do business with?"

Apart from the arrogance of this letter, what Elliot is complaining about is precisely the reason the regulations were formulated in the first place: to remove the cut-throat "free enterprise" that had caused so many problems in the pre-war years. The letter ends with, "We know that you are in a position that you could assist us in getting this matter straightened out. . . ." There was more of this sort of correspondence, from Alcan, PWA, and QCA, much more; but according to John Condit, Spilsbury and his lawyer made a crucial error.

Esmond Lando, Spilsbury's lawyer, persuaded Spilsbury to agree to withhold objections to PWA's application to be allowed to fly aircraft into "Alcan installations at Kitimat and Kemano on the coast. This was on the strict understanding that Russ had no privilege to fly up and down the coast. . . . The ATB showed itself more concerned with the needs of the Alcan project than with Esmond Lando's generosity."[23]

"It became clear," the ATB's letter explained, "that during the construction period there was a special need demanding great flexibility of service and availability of various types of aircraft at short notice and at various points." This, of course, can be looked at in two ways: either it was a remarkable example of something for which bureaucracy is seldom renowned—flexibility—or it can be seen as leaning heavily towards C. D.

A QCA publicity brochure showing various scenes of activity, as well as a page of silhouettes of the "Queer Collection of Aircraft."—BRITISH COLUMBIA ARCHIVES

this is the story of Q.C.A....

Since the beginning of time, every age has had its pioneers—the men who pave the way for the development of new industries and the exploitation of new commercial fields. In the wake of these pioneers, the first and foremost important need which arises is that of communication and transportation — a direct contact with the big cities and sources of supply.

The pattern which the industrial development of British Columbia has taken over the past ten or fifteen years created just such a need — Queen Charlotte Airlines — a modern, fully equipped transportation unit — has "grown up" with British Columbia and established itself as a vital link for the people in the outlying areas of the province.

With the purchase back in 1943, of the little Waco seaplane shown in the upper left-hand corner, Queen Charlotte Airlines was "in business" — it would have been hard to realize then that Q.C.A. was destined to grow with British Columbia and in such a short space of time rank as Canada's third largest scheduled airline.

In these years since 1943, many equipment changes have taken place—today, 28-passenger DC-3 airliners give frequent service to the mainland and Island cities and the drone of the twin-engined Canso amphibians or large flying boats has

1943

1945

1946

1947

become a familiar sound to the people of mining and logging camps and the isolated communities all along our coastline.

During these ten years, every endeavour has been directed towards the constant improvement in quality and frequency of Q.C.A. service.

One of the first requirements of any scheduled airline is a staff of highly specialized and efficient personnel. Q.C.A.'s staff have been carefully selected for their particular qualifications, for the job they have to do — they have years of experience in the airline business and their combined skill and knowledge are at your service.

Each one knows his job and does it well — the pilots, the crewmen, the ground personnel, the office staff, the administrators — each one in his own capacity contributes to the comfort and reliability of your flight. These are the men and women who make Q.C.A. it is their story which we would like to tell.

1948

1951

1953

Engines, radio units, electrical components and instruments are changed and the entire aircraft is thoroughly examined.

Such repetitive work, while costly, is the only means of maintaining a high standard

Shop tooling and manufacturing procedures are constantly reviewed for betterment.

An average of fifty maintenance personnel are employed within the company's network of bases, many of whom are government-

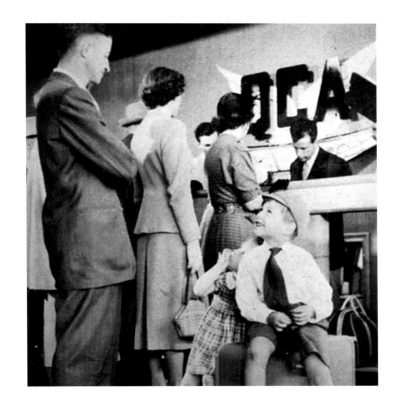

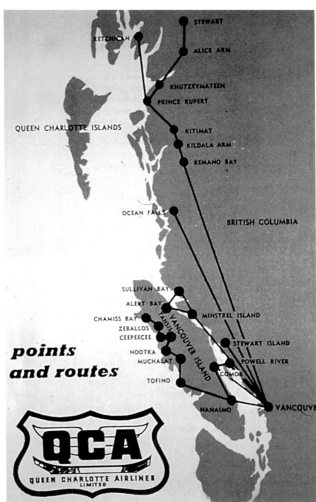

points and routes

STEWART
KETCHICAN
ALICE ARM
KHUTZEYMATEEN
PRINCE RUPERT
QUEEN CHARLOTTE ISLANDS
KITIMAT
KILDALA ARM
KEMANO BAY
OCEAN FALLS
BRITISH COLUMBIA
SULLIVAN BAY
ALERT BAY
MINSTREL ISLAND
CHAMISS BAY
ZEBALLOS
CEEPEECEE
NOOTKA
STEWART ISLAND
MUCHALAT
POWELL RIVER
VANCOUVER ISLAND
COMOX
TOFINO
NANAIMO
VANCOUVER

QCA
QUEEN CHARLOTTE AIRLINES
LIMITED

Howe's penchant for overcoming what he saw as obstacles by declaring an emergency. In any event, this was a giant foot in the door for PWA. Baker took full advantage of it. He could now use his Kemano charter base to fly in men and materials from Vancouver and, before long, make a mockery of the charter category.

However, it was not all a one-way street. Not all QCA's problems were caused by Baker. In 1952, the newspapers reported that "Queen Charlotte Airlines, Canada's third largest, has cut its aircrew and maintenance staff as much as 35 per cent because of the 11-day strike of coast woodworkers."[24] QCA still relied for the majority of its revenue on the logging camps up and down the coast and when there were disruptions, it hit them hard. The following year turned out to be another slow one in the logging industry and QCA was awarded "an 'emergency' subsidy of $125,000,"[25] with yet another subsidy of $100,000 in 1954. Not surprisingly, Baker reacted vigorously, reiterating PWA's willingness to provide an unsubsidized service along the coast.

Perhaps, though, during this period—and this is speculative—Baker had become overconfident and stepped beyond the bounds of the Air Transport Board's tolerance. For, in November 1953, the Vancouver Sun ran an article under the heading, "Air Firm To Defy Gov't Board." Baker claimed to have found a threat by the Board in response to his own demand that there should be no restrictions on the Kitimat flights. The board's response was: "That's our business to decide. It will also be our business to decide whether Pacific Western will be permitted to fly a coach service to Winnipeg." Baker termed this "'a dictatorial threat' . . . against PWA for criticizing Board policies regarding the Kitimat service." He went on to say that "if the Board refused PWA's application . . . he would have to consider launching the [Winnipeg] service without such authority."[26]

Then again, a month later, another newspaper headline read: "'Police State' Charge Hurled As Airline Opposes Board." Evidently the chief inspector for the board, Leslie Knight, had, "Instead of calling a hearing [to investigate reports of rate cutting], interviewed people at their place of business while accompanied by a uniformed RCMP officer." The company being questioned was described as a "travel agency": Coastal Air Services; and PWA successfully petitioned for a BC Supreme Court injunction of restraint against Knight.[27] A few days later the injunction had been lifted and, before long, the Air Transport Board shut down Coastal Air Services.

Baker termed this "a dictatorial threat,". . .

With his added fleet and additional responsibilities, Mr. Baker admitted he was concerned over the duplication of PWA and QCA services. In mid-1955 arrangements were completed for the purchase of QCA and with the financial aid of Karl J. Springer, noted Canadian mining executive, the deal was put through. Shortly afterwards the assets of Associated Airways of Edmonton were added and PWA emerged as the third largest airline in Canada.

Vancouver Province
May 23, 1956

Consequently, it is not too far-fetched to speculate that Baker had become a little too self-assured, not to say arrogant, in his disputes with the Air Transport Board; and both its bureaucrats and the incumbent Transport Minister, Lionel Chevrier, reacted accordingly by awarding the subsidies to QCA.

However, even with assistance of the subsidies, Spilsbury was gradually worn down. PWA had been granted a low-interest loan of $230,000 by the federal government's Industrial Development Bank that enabled Baker to add Bob Gay's Associated group of aviation companies, with its valuable charter bases, to his growing list of takeovers. Baker had succeeded in making a friend of the very wealthy and powerful H. R. MacMillan after taking him into Coldfish Lake for fishing and hunting expeditions. It was MacMillan who interceded for him and greased the wheels for the loan.

Meanwhile, QCA was in trouble, not only because of Baker's aggressive depredations, but because its own operation was chalking up a disturbing roster of accidents. Some were undoubtedly caused by faulty procedures; others were pretty close to sheer bad luck. Bill McLeod, then QCA's base manager in Prince Rupert, and his wife, Joan, who was dispatcher, provided the following description of one such mishap.

McLeod had forgotten the exact date (it was July 29, 1949), but the Rapide that QCA was operating on the Prince Rupert-Queen Charlotte Islands route was being flown by Roy Berryman. This one, CF-BND, had been loaded up with three women passengers, one of whom was pregnant, and some freight the night before. The weather turned sour, so they cancelled, took the passengers to a hotel for the night and, because the machine had been refuelled and the freight loaded the day before, got away to an early start in the morning.

After a while, Joan, as dispatcher, became anxious because she had had no word from Berryman. Eventually, when he failed to arrive in the Charlottes, and did not return, she raised the alarm:

I got onto CPA and got them into the air with a great deal of difficulty—not because of a local pilot but because he had to check with Vancouver who immediately asked, "What are they going to pay you?" There was a sort of chorus of "Who gives a damn?" and they took off. As it happened Bill [McLeod] was coming back from Masset, and I got through to him in the air. It was he who spotted the aircraft down on Digby Island.[28]

What they learned later was that, while he was still over Digby Island, a mile or two from Prince Rupert, and still only at about 500 feet (150 m),

Berryman lost first one engine, and then, just after he had turned back, he lost the other. He had no option but to go into the trees. He managed to steer between two substantial ones, which always helped in this situation by taking the main impact and slowing the fuselage and cabin section down—as well as lessening the risk of fire.

After Bill McLeod had spotted the remains of the Rapide it took three hours to land at Seal Cove, round up the RCMP launch, cross to Digby Island and then walk in through deep bush to get to the site. The rescuers were relieved to find no one injured; but the machine was a total write-off. However, this was another publicized accident, made all the more depressing when they worked out why it had happened. When they checked the fuel tanks, both were dry. The tanks had been filled the day before and, if there had been a leak, it would have been very evident on the relatively tranquil waters of Seal Cove. The suspicion arose that the tanks may have been siphoned—and this turned out to be the case. According to the police, a local native had been boasting about how well his kicker worked on avgas. He had almost certainly tied up alongside the Rapide, whose fuel tanks were conveniently in the lower wing. The police were pretty sure that he had drained the Rapide's tanks overnight, leaving just enough gas to take off and reach Digby Island. In the end, though, they couldn't prove anything.[29]

One could, of course, take the strictly rigid approach and say that the pilot should in any case have checked the tanks again before taking off that morning. In reality, though, it was a very unpredictable and unfortunate accident that did not help QCA's reputation. While the newspapers headlined the actual crash, not surprisingly they did not follow up with the cause of the accident.

But it was a much more serious accident in October 1951 that really signalled the beginning of the end for QCA because it gave Russ Baker so much ammunition. Huge, black, front-page headlines on October 18 announced that "NANAIMO AIR CRASH KILLS 23," followed by a sub-headline, "Kemano Workers Die as Q.C.A. Plane Hits Mount Benson," and went on to describe it as "the worst air disaster in the history of Vancouver Island."[30] This was the most damaging kind of publicity. Although a coroner's inquest two days later returned an open verdict—the Canso was not overloaded and it had a fuel reserve of four hours when

. . . he had drained the Rapide's tanks overnight . . .

it crashed—it appears to have been another example of the bush pilot bravado syndrome.

The pilot, Doug McQueen, with no instrument rating, had taken off in indifferent weather, too late to reach Vancouver before dark. The crash occurred at 6:55 p.m. in fog and near darkness. This was a devastating blow for QCA. There were no signs of any mechanical malfunction, so the obvious conclusion was that McQueen had been flying VFR in the dark—which was illegal—and in foggy weather. He had drifted off course to the west, and mistaken the lights of Nanaimo for Vancouver. He turned even farther west before swinging east to approach what he thought was Vancouver airport and crashed into Mount Benson at the 1,600-foot (490-m) level. The Canso immediately burst into flames and all on board died.

While Spilsbury did finally receive a mail subsidy, it was too little too late. Then Russ Baker's company was granted equivalent status to fly direct from Vancouver into Kitimat with a Canso he had acquired before this dispensation because he was so confident it would be approved. C. D. Howe's "enlightened" legislation to prevent cut-throat competition was now being blandly contravened—with, of course, the full support of Howe himself.

The end came when Baker proposed an amalgamation of QCA and PWA, with himself and Springer in charge of the resulting union. Naturally, Spilsbury refused. By now, though, both Alcan and the federal government were working hand-in-hand to give Alcan's favourite, Baker, a monopoly of business on the coast. A fascinating glimpse of how C. D. Howe exercised his powers at the time is provided by correspondence in Canadian Airlines Archives. Baker had been determined to take over QCA and had written to Howe for help. Howe's reply, in a letter dated September 30, 1954, was as follows:

Dear Mr. Baker,

Thanks for your letter of September 27th informing me of your negotiation with Queen Charlotte Airlines. I am sorry indeed that a consolidation of Pacific Western and Queen Charlotte Airlines has not been possible up to now. It would seem to be very much in the interests of West Coast aviation if this consolidation could take place.

You will appreciate my position and realize that I do not enter directly into aviation matters of this kind. I have, however, taken one or two steps behind the scenes that may be helpful to your situation.

Please regard this letter as entirely confidential.

Yours sincerely,

(Signed) C. D. Howe[31]

Please regard this letter as entirely confidential. (Signed) C.D. Howe

This letter was followed up by another after the takeover—one that illustrates the remarkable flexibility of Howe's principles when it became a question of the air regulations he himself had formulated:

Dear Russell:

I have read with interest your new schedule of rates to West Coast points and congratulate you on being able to effect a substantial reduction in these rates.

While monopoly may be objectionable as a general principle, it certainly improves the efficiency of air transportation. I am glad your public is reaping the benefit.[32]

In short, monopoly is objectionable, but not, as with TCA, if Howe mandated it; nor, as with PWA, if from behind the scenes he worked to orchestrate it.

Spilsbury persevered for another year but then, in June 1955, he finally conceded defeat. According to Condit, PWA bought out QCA for $850,000;[33] according to Spilsbury, "in July of 1955 the airline was sold. The final price was $1.4 million, of which my share was just over $400,000." In an interview with a reporter at the time, Spilsbury is quoted as saying, "We've all agreed not to release the price, I can only say that it's a very good figure."[34] In *The Accidental Airline*, Spilsbury goes on to add that, "after the takeover Baker had all the QCA files taken out behind the hangar and burned."[35]

Not unnaturally, Spilsbury remains embittered by his eventual defeat; but his had been a remarkable achievement, and the people who worked for him found him both a man of his word and an admirable boss. Bill McLeod described him as "a really great guy to work for." Another employee, air engineer Curly Nairn, who worked for Siple when Siple bought all the war-surplus Stranraers—intending to sell them in South America but left with many of them on his hands"*—had moved over to QCA in 1944 and worked for that company for 11 years. He describes his reaction when PWA took over:

I worked for PWA for six months, but I didn't like working for them. I didn't like Baker and there was a lot of drinking going on. They made me a kind of a chief mechanic there, and I saw my supervisor sober about a week before Christmas, and I never saw him again until I turned in my notice about March. Never saw him because he was always drunk. That's the way they operated. Whereas, QCA ran a good operation—they had people like the operations manager Eric Bendall. They were good. They had a system and a maintenance schedule and they stuck by it, and PWA came along and they threw it all out.[36]

Spilsbury's accomplishment in creating what came to be the third-largest airline in Canada was so unconventional it has a touch of the

". . . All this time, with the Norseman on the ground for an engine change, and the Husky having a strut repaired, Howard Hughes had been out in our Norseman doing all the work. There was a Union Steamships strike on, so everybody was yelling for their liquor and Howard had a hell of a time trying to keep up with things.

Curly Nairn

* Nairn also recalls that, "After I left him [Siple], he moved them all over to the Island at Pat Bay, and the hangar burned down."

B.C. Airways Takes in Four Companies

VANCOUVER (CP)—Central B.C. Airways Limited, one plane and a dream back in 1946, today announced a "much expanded service" moving it into the big leagues of Canadian aviation.

Under the name of Pacific Western Airlines Ltd. a 20-plane fleet "will compete for the position of Canada's third largest airline."

Company headquarters will be moved from Kamloops to Vancouver.

Announcement of the company's growth into an organization which will "now serve all of British Columbia and the West Coast" was made by former bush pilot Russ Baker, vice-president and general manager.

Mr. Baker at the same time announced amalgamation into Pacific Western of a group of small companies including Associated Air Taxi Ltd., Vancouver; Associated Aero Services Ltd., Associated Air Taxi and Port Alberni Airways Limited.

romantic about it—particularly when compared to the other two principal success stories in aviation of that era: Grant McConachie and Russ Baker, both of whom had advantages Spilsbury didn't enjoy—in Baker's case, particularly the firm support of C. D. Howe and H. R. MacMillan. While Howe had quietly indicated his support, MacMillan had personally intervened to assure the granting of the low-interest loan of $234,000 to PWA from the federal government's Industrial Development Bank—a loan that eventually made it possible for Baker to buy out Spilsbury.

On the other side of the coin, QCA had a disturbing number of accidents, some of which could be attributed to the cut-throat competition the company was exposed to, but others because of an inexperienced approach to airline flying. Sadly, as Curly Nairn attests, by the time Spilsbury had overcome the problems of operational inefficiency, and was running a safe and efficient airline, it was too late. The combination of Alcan, Russ Baker and their good friend C. D. Howe defeated him.

For all that, Spilsbury and QCA left behind a lasting legacy on the coast. Routes were established and aviation became the norm for travel all the way from the Portland Canal on the Alaska border to Vancouver and Victoria. Aviation replaced the coastal steamers as the main means of travel all along the remote coast, and Spilsbury's crews in no small measure pioneered the way. Spilsbury himself went on to write several delightful books, including The Accidental Airline, co-authored with Howard White, that describes his flying years with wit and insight.

It is fitting to give the late John Condit—who was commissioned to write the definitive history of PWA—the last word in this context. He described Russ Baker's actions as "piracy."

Part Four

MILESTONES

Chapter Twelve

Emancipation

"Coffee, tea or me?"

SHELLEY BERMAN

T HERE WERE OTHER LEADERS besides corporate presidents and politicians who deserve to be remembered: people who were the first to become involved. In the late 1930s and 1940s many changes were occurring in the aviation industry and society as a whole. Canadians were prospering in the post-war years; and, although for many Canadians the pace was still very slow, ideas and attitudes were changing.

Expanded commercial flying began to open the door slightly for women, and slowly minority groups were becoming part of the civil aviation scene. Chinese-Canadians, despite their distinctly second-class status, had demonstrated great courage and ability in the Armed Forces during the war years; consequently, by 1946 they had made considerable progress. The Vancouver *Daily Province*, under the headline, "Young Chinese Launch Own Flying Club Here," reported that although its "official title was 'The Chinese Aero Club of B.C.,' it is better known under the unofficial label of 'Flying Dragons.'"

Evidently most were ex-servicemen or ex-airline mechanics, but seven were young women. "Already under pilot instruction are Mr. Low, his sister Ann, William Chun, James Der, Lyon Joh, Lillian Mahull, Gim Wong, May Wong and James Wing. While some members are flying purely for pleasure, the ultimate goal of the club is to train both pilots and ground crew for eventual participation in airline work in China."[1]

Another Chinese airman who started his career at about the same time, Hong Mah, became something of a celebrity as a bush pilot. By 1956, "Hong had been employed by Pacific Western Airlines and was senior member of the airlines' bush-pilot crew when he died at the age of 43."[2] The newspaper article goes on to cite typically hair-raising stories of Hong's experiences: "Like the time a crazed sled dog attacked him while he was flying a Beaver aircraft at 5,000 feet [1 500 m].... When the plane landed, the dog was unconscious and Hong had deep fang wounds in his arms, hands and throat. He had used a wrench to fell the dog, which had slipped its chain in the cargo hold of the plane."

The article was an obituary and there were several similar incidents, dramatized by the journalist, but all with some foundation because Hong Mah had an enviable reputation as a competent bush pilot. Sadly, he died in an unexplained accident in 1967, terminating an 18-minute flight from the small mill settlement of Georgetown to his home base at Prince Rupert by crashing into the side of a mountain.

As for Canadian women, there were still very few opportunities in business or in aviation, both of which were still male-dominated. Nevertheless the women made better progress than the Asians or the native peoples: they were allowed to vote at the end of the First World War; whereas the Chinese did not earn that right until just after the Second World War, and the native peoples not until 1960.

And although Alys Bryant had flown in British Columbia as early as 1910, and other women were active in aviation in the late 1930s, their role as leaders was limited. This, of course, had nothing to do with ability; it was the consequence of social attitudes at the time. The prevailing mood in the 1930s was still that man was the provider and woman the home-keeper. In addition, there was the myth that it required considerable strength to fly an aircraft, and that women were physically weak; whereas, in fact, although the responses to the controls in 1930s aircraft were somewhat slower than on later models, the controls were no heavier to operate and could easily have been handled by all but the frailest person, man or woman.

Surprisingly, this myth was still prevalent for a very long time—into the 1980s, in fact, when Pierre Berton, in one of his more extravagant eulogies to Russ Baker as a bush pilot, described his great strength and wrote of downdrafts in the mountains as "Niagaras of air, pouring off the ridges. . . ." He went on to write that "Baker wrestled his aircraft through the turbulence like a horseman on a bronco. He had the physique of a boxer and the strength of an ox and needed both in that tempest-tossed

If a woman showed an interest in flying, male pilots accepted her as 'one of the boys,' and she was accorded any assistance they could provide. In the early years when women began to fly, all the women were trained, and well trained, by male instructors. The discrimination against women flying came from society generally, but rarely from male pilots.

Daring Lady Flyers
Joyce Spring

CITY WOMEN FLYERS SPENT DAY IN AIR

'Dawn to Dusk' Relay Complete Success.

A large number of spectators visited the Sea Island airport on Sunday to watch Vancouver's women flyers doing their "dawn to dusk" relay. Miss Tosca Trasolini started all-day flight at 6:59 a.m. and other members of the "Flying Seven" carried on at half-hour intervals. Airport attendants and mere male flyers had some moment of anxiety during the early morning, when there was a fairly heavy ground fog, but the girl pilots made their landing and take-offs without any trouble.

Vancouver Province
June 1936

land."[3] In another, similar but earlier eulogy, Berton used a different analogy: Russ Baker "was the strongest man I ever saw. He had a chest like a barrel and the biceps of a blacksmith. He needed them for the fifteen years he spent wrestling with a joystick, alone in that turbulent sky."[4]

Not all women acquiesced to this male-oriented social decree. One of the leading dissenters was Margaret Fane, who was born in Edmonton and learned to fly there on a variety of aircraft. She earned her Private Licence, No. 1317, in 1933 and her Commercial Licence, No. A1236, in July of 1935, the first woman pilot west of Toronto to do so. Earlier that year she had visited Los Angeles and, among others, met Amelia Earhart, a member of the American group of 99 women pilots. There was talk of Canadians joining this club. Instead, Fane returned to Canada and helped inaugurate the Flying Seven.[5]

The seven young women were: Margaret Fane and Elianne Roberge, who later earned her commercial licence, along with Jean Pike, Tosca Trasolini, Betsy Flaherty, Alma Gilbert and Rolie Moore, all with private licences.

The impetus for the formation of the Flying Seven, according to journalists, was that the "girls" had been rebuffed at an air show:

It all began, this protest business, at an air show in Vancouver this summer sponsored by the Junior Board of Trade. Many famous flyers and flying machines were there, but somehow the girls weren't allowed to go on the field to examine them.
"Can you imagine it?" smiles pretty Tosca Trasolini. "We were just as interested in the different machines as a lot of men around the place, but they stopped us at the gate. Told us we couldn't go in. But don't worry, we made it! I had to get hold of a little ribbon allowing you admittance, and I got inside. I looked over all the aeroplanes and then passed the ribbon on to the other six girls outside and they came in one by one."[6]

The actual protest took the form of an endurance flight staged from dawn to dusk. One by one, the Flying Seven took off to replace each other during the day, and this initiative demonstrated their competence as pilots and brought them country-wide publicity.

It is intriguing nowadays to read the descriptions in the media. They were written up by newspapers across Canada, and their venture was looked upon as an engaging stunt. To all appearances they went along with this approach; at any rate, one of them seemed not to have objected to being photographed in the cockpit of a Fleet trainer with an open compact, touching up her makeup; and no one seemed to mind, publicly at least, when the photograph was published in a newspaper over the cutline, "Powder Puff Pilots." Similarly another, later, caption to a photograph of Margaret Fane described her as a "Daring Young Doll in Her Flying Machine."[7] This lack of resentment, however, may have been a response to another attitude in the 1930s: if women did intrude on a conventionally male domain, society condemned them if they abandoned their "femininity."

Fane worked for Ginger Coote's Bridge River & Cariboo Airways as a dispatcher and, occasionally to stand in as co-pilot while Ginger caught up on sleep:

One time I remember when Art Spandier and Ted Dobbin went up to put a radio in at Gun Lake. They went up in a Waco and Ginger and I went up in a Norseman. We had all the equipment in it, and he had been out the night before . . . and when we got in the air, he said, "You can take over; I'm going to have a nap." Well, I took over and flew for him and, when we got there, I couldn't wake him up. I had to because I hadn't landed a Norseman on floats, so I kept jiggling this thing. Finally, I set the stabilizer and went back and shook him and he came back and landed it—no problem.[8]

Apart from these occasional flights, she did not fly commercially. In 1939, Fane worked as a dispatcher and radio operator for Ginger Coote Airways during the Zeballos gold rush period, then went on to a number of administrative jobs with CPA. Nonetheless, she appears to have been the first woman to fly aircraft commercially, at least occasionally, in British Columbia, and she was one of the pioneer women working in the aviation industry.[9]

Women pilots made a significant break through the barriers of social prejudice and misconceptions during the Second World War, when many of them became ferry pilots, delivering aircraft from factories to their destined military units; and they quickly proved that they could handle any of the aircraft then being manufactured, up to and including multi-engined bombers. As well, women worked in other areas of aviation, particularly in manufacturing and maintenance.

Nevertheless, the rather breathless rhetoric about women pilots was still very much in evidence after the war. A newspaper article in 1948 is a good illustration: "Grandma would have had a heart attack! At the very least she might have swooned over her petit-point. Her granddaughters cavorting about the wide blue yonder earning such tags as 'female sky pilots' or 'air jockeys' would not have amused her." The article concerned a number of women learning to fly at the Victoria Flying Club. Among

Margaret Fane Rutledge photographed in the cockpit of a Fleet Trainer, Vancouver, 1937.—MARGARET RUTLEDGE COLLECTION

them was 19-year-old Phyllis Drysdale: "Club executives claim she is the youngest girl in Canada to have a commercial licence."[10] In short, as late as 1948, the simple fact that women could and did fly as pilots was still newsworthy.

However, dropping back a decade to 1938, a new dimension—stewardesses—was added to the budding Canadian airline industry and, in particular, to TCA aircrews. The idea of having "attractive and personable young ladies to serve as hostesses aboard the company's planes" was dreamed up by a shrewd traffic official of United Air Lines in the early 1930s. United's executives were sceptical and hesitant, but eventually "eight stewardesses were made crew members on sections of the San Francisco-New York Airway. To the surprise and delight of all concerned, they were immediately popular—so much so, in fact, that more girls were employed."[11]

The TCA stewardesses, while they never flew the aircraft, of course, were the first women in British Columbia to fly commercially on a regular basis and consequently deserve recognition as leaders. As in United Air Lines, the qualifications for this new category were immutable. To be a stewardess one had, first of all, to be single, young and attractive; secondly, one had to be a trained nurse. There were more rigid specifications: "not less than 5 feet [152 cm] or more than 5 feet 5 inches [165 cm] tall; not under 95 pounds [43 kg] or over 125 pounds [57 kg], and not less than 21 years or over 26 years of age."[12]

Today, the first qualification, single and attractive, would cause an uproar, but the tactic was interesting and just as effective here as in the United States.

The first two stewardesses to join TCA were Lucille Garner and Pat Maxwell. According to a newspaper interview, both "took preliminary training with United Air Lines, and the UAL stewardess manual became their bible. In April, 1939, when TCA started its transcontinental passenger service, Garner became chief stewardess with Maxwell as her assistant and they were sent to Winnipeg to give 14 girls three weeks training. The senior stewardesses each brought half the class to Vancouver for orientation on a mail flight and the cross-Canada service became a reality."[13]

Interviews with four women who worked through the terminology evolution from "stewardesses" to the more acceptable "flight attendants" provide a crisp summary of social change from 1939 to the present. One

The Third Column

Air-Borne Ladies

By Old-Timer

A POPULAR s o n g twenty-five years ago warned the girls: "You can't walk back from an aeroplane ride."

That didn't deter them here.

Just as Edmonton men blazed new trails in Canadian civilian flying, Edmonton girls blazed sky-trails of their own.

Powder-puff pilots were well-known here even before mail was being flown across the Canadian Rockies. Among them were Evelyn Hudson and Margaret Fane. The latter was the first woman in Alberta to qualify for a commercial pilot's licence.

of the first of these young women (we will deal with the other three later) was Eleanore Moore. Born in Revelstoke, B.C., She was educated in Kerrisdale, a suburb of Vancouver, and trained at Vancouver General Hospital as a nurse, graduating in 1938. She describes how she came to join TCA in 1939:[14]

A friend of mine had an uncle with some influence, and she suggested I should go for a job as a stewardess on TCA. You had to be a nurse then for the job. To begin with, I wasn't very keen; but I was getting a little tired of the hospital—I was on night duty—so finally I said yes.

I went out to the airport and saw Billy Wells, and he hired me. We had just a little bit of training in Seattle with Lucille Garner. She was the first one hired, and she was the chief stewardess—and there were two other girls who started with me: Jean Vallance and Peggy Sherrick.

Moore made her first trip on October 17, 1939, in CF-TCJ, a Lockheed 14-H2 (Super Electra), with George Lothian as captain and eight passengers. They logged eight hours and 50 minutes—Vancouver to Lethbridge—with two stops on the way, presumably for weather.

The Lethbridge trip [she recalled], took quite a long time because we could only go a little over 10,000 feet [3 000 m] and we were often held up because of weather. Most of the passengers we carried were VIPs. One person who travelled a lot was H. R. MacMillan. We waited often in Lethbridge for weather before coming back. Trips were fairly long, and one trip we made was quite a dangerous one. George Lothian was the captain, and we had a lot of icing and we had to turn back. I remember the passengers—I was unaware of the problem—they were worried because we'd turned back [to Vancouver]. So I went up to the cockpit to ask George Lothian what was the matter, and he was quite annoyed. He said, "Go on back and stay there"—or perhaps it was a little more forceful: "Go and sit down and shut up." But the passengers were all asking me what was the matter and, of course, I couldn't tell them. That only happened to me once, but I heard about several other times when icing occurred.

If we went above 10,000 feet [3 000 m], everyone had to go on oxygen. I flew with Maurice [McGregor] quite a bit. We didn't really do very much during a trip. We just gave the passengers tea and coffee and different kinds of sandwiches. After that, we just sat in the back of the plane—and then the idea was that we were supposed to point out to passengers towns and villages we were passing over; but we were never sure of where we were.

Asked if she had ever had problems with unwanted advances from passengers, or general harassment, Eleanore replied that she never did because the ones carried were nearly all well-known people—mostly older and sedate. There were very few women and children travelling then. "We didn't have any alcohol on board, of course, and I don't remember anyone getting on with any signs of drink—though I guess some of them who were probably a bit scared had a couple before boarding. I think having a young woman along reassured them."

We had to be very careful about our appearance, and we weren't allowed to marry. But it was a very satisfying position; we certainly didn't have to work very hard. We had to be very careful about our appearance, and we weren't allowed to marry. But it was a very satisfying position; we certainly didn't have to work very hard.

Eleanore Moore's Logbook

Eleanore Moore Begg in her first
Trans-Canada Air Lines' uniform.
—ELEANORE BEGG COLLECTION

Three young stewardesses anyone
would be happy to fly with. Left to
right: Peggy Sherrick, Jean Vallance
and Eleanore Moore in Winnipeg,
1939.—ELEANORE BEGG COLLECTION

Eleanore and Roy Begg in Vancouver, 1996.
—BOB TURNER

DATE	AIRCRAFT TYPE AND REGISTRATION	TIME IN AIR			REMARKS	Trip no.	1st leg	2nd	3rd	Total hrs.
		1st Pilot	2nd Pilot	Passenger						
		Time carried forward:—								
17/10/39	Lockheed-TCS. #33	Lothian	Foley	8	Delay in QL—	1/16	2.10	2.41	4.32	8.83
18/10/39	Lockheed-TCM #35	Lothian	Foley	8	Return UR. acct icing	2/18	3.09			3.09
19/10/39	" TCS #41	Lothian	Foley	8		2/18	2.22	2.43	1.48	6.13
4/10/39	" TCI #31	McGregor	Albult Kenyon	9	No stop QR. acct wx.	1/23	4.27	3.01		7.28
25/10/39	" TCM #35	McGregor	Albult Kenyon	3		2/25	2.34	2.01	1.47	5.82
31/10/39	" TCG #29	Leigh	Rood Bradley	8		1/30	2.17	2.10	2.32	6.59
31/10/39	" TCJ #32	Bowker	Barnes	3		4/31	.53			.53
31/10/39	" TCS #32	Bowker	Barnes	6		5/31	.46			.46
1/11/39	" TCS #32	Leigh	Bradly Rood	9		2/1	2.32	1.57	1.53	5.42
7/11/39	" TC.	Rankin	Segrim		Termination UR acct wx—	1/6	2.05	2.—		4.05
7/11/39	" TCJ #32	Rankin	Jones	3	Trip originated QL—	2/6	1.56	1.49		2.05
11/11/39	" TCI #31	Segrim	Baker	7		1/10	4.23		3.09	7.32
12/11/39	"	Segrim	Baker	9		2/12	2.45	1.40	1.50	6.35
14/11/39	" TCQ #39	Lothian	Foley	13	Miss Ketchum & me from QL—	1/13				8.05
14/11/39	" TCO #37	Brady	Anders	2		6/14	.53			.53
15/11/39	" TCO #37	Brady	Anders	4		5/15	.45			.45
15/11/39	" TCN #36	Lothian	Foley	6	Non-sched-UR QL— Mr & pa to wgt	2/15				2.35
17/11/39	" TCP. #40	Rood	Crosby	10	Beautiful Trip—	1/16	2.45			2.45
18/11/39	" TCQ #39	Brady	Anders	3		6/18	.55			.55
	TOTAL TIME:—									81.15

The first page of Eleanore Moore's log book.—ELEANORE BEGG COLLECTION

Nina Youngman Morrison standing beside the Canso in 1955. It was her responsibility to take the hose and wash the aircraft down after her last flight each day on the Prince Rupert to Sandspit route. CPA was still landing on the water at Seal Cove. The pilot would lower the wheels and taxi up the ramp.
—BILL GREEN, NINA MORRISON COLLECTION

A CPA Canso at Prince Rupert Airport on Digby Island. This one looks as if it could do with a wash.—CANADIAN AIRLINES ARCHIVES

The idealized stewardess.

*For the airlines,
feminine glamour was
still de rigour
well into the 1960s.*

—CANADIAN PACIFIC AIRLINES PUBLICITY POSTERS

A CPA crew on the passenger loading steps in 1956. *Top*: Ray Van Houl, Harry Harding; *bottom*: Mary Kerr, Nina Morrison.
—NINA MORRISON COLLECTION

This, no doubt, was just what management had foreseen. Flying was still considered to be risky, if no longer very dangerous; but with the prevailing social standards of the time, no man would want an attractive young woman to see that he was scared—particularly if the young woman obviously was not.

The other route Moore flew frequently was the Vancouver–Seattle run, three trips a day—two return, and then staying at the Olympic Hotel overnight and returning to Vancouver the following day.

It was fun. The pilots were all young. We all liked them; most of them seemed to be such nice-looking young men. Unfortunately, they were all married, which was kind of too bad. We certainly had lots of fun travelling with them. . . . On the Lethbridge route, we made one trip and stayed overnight, and I'd usually have afternoons there; I only made one long trip. I went to Lethbridge and they were short of stewardesses and they sent me on to Winnipeg, where we stayed the night; and then I finally ended up in Montreal. Of course that was with different crews and we had quite a few stops: we'd stop in Kapuskasing, Armstrong and other places.

Most bush pilots, because of the implications of regimentation, were distinctly unenthusiastic about the prospect of wearing a uniform when they became airline pilots—one which consisted, as a rule, of white shirt and tie, a semi-military navy-blue tunic and trousers, and a military style peaked cap, with the airline's insignia for a badge. Rank was indicated by bars of silver or gold on their epaulettes. The women interviewed, on the other hand, evinced no such reluctance; they seem to have been relatively enthusiastic about their uniforms. In Moore's case, the winter uniform was a navy suit with a white ribbed wool sweater—"a small, straight-necked sweater"—and a cap similar to the Air Force side cap, with an insignia on it. In the summer, a field-grey uniform was worn, with an "attractive blue blouse"; and, of course, stewardesses wore skirts in those days.

They had to be very careful about appearance: grooming was all important and makeup was strictly monitored; but perhaps the most onerous constraint by modern standards was that they were not allowed to marry. Yet the insistence on single status does not appear to have been a bone of contention in the early days, presumably because young women did not expect to have to work after marriage, except as homemakers.

The food, mostly sandwiches, was all brought on prepared, in little cardboard boxes. The tea and coffee were in Thermos flasks. People did, of course, get airsick, and the bags had to be used quite frequently. When passengers boarded, the stewardess would wait for them at the door of the

. . . no man would want an attractive young woman to see that he was scared. . . .

aircraft. The ticket agent was always at the bottom of the steps. There was very little formality about loading: only a handful of passengers, only one door in the terminal, and only one plane; so, when the time came, passengers were told the plane was ready, and they walked out to it. The seats were comfortable and the cabin rather small—one aisle with one seat on either side. The stewardesses used to have to step over the main wing spar. They sat on a little jump-seat at the back. There was a small lavatory with a tiny washbasin and a chemical toilet.

Moore was with TCA for only a little under a year. She sometimes wished she had stayed with them longer, but then she got married and had to resign. It was wartime and her fiancé, Roy Begg, was in the Air Force, so most of the time they were coming or going and met when they could. When they married, Roy only had five days' leave.

Moore made her last flight on July 22, 1940, coincidentally with the same captain as her first, George Lothian. Her husband, Roy Begg, went on to a distinguished career in the RCAF, one of the highlights of which was an audience with the Queen.

It was almost as though the pilots were your brothers.

Despite what we would now regard as onerous restrictions, Moore obviously enjoyed her experience as a stewardess. "We didn't have to work very hard—no safety talk to the passengers—but we passed out oxygen masks which often had to be used when flying over the mountains, and made sure that seatbelts were fastened." She had "good fun," and "it was a very satisfying position." At that time, there was still a strong element of the romantic about flying, if not actually glamour, and clearly the TCA crews enjoyed a pleasant rapport. As well, there was the intangible compensation of knowing that one was a pioneer. Pat Maxwell commented on the changes over the next 40 years. With the advent of the larger aircraft, the sense of camaraderie wasn't the same: "It was almost as though the pilots were your brothers. Often today, the cabin crews don't even know the cockpit crew."[15]

When the second generation of stewardesses began to fly, working conditions for them had changed very little, but their careers illustrate a considerable swing in social attitudes towards women during the next 40 years. In 1955, 15 years after Eleanore Moore retired from TCA to get married, Nina Morrison began flying as a stewardess with Canadian Pacific Air Lines. On September 29, 1995, just before her retirement from CPA's successor, Canadian Airlines International, the CBC's Peter Gzowski interviewed her and two other veteran CPA stewardesses, Judy Woodward and Heather Ellis, on his Morningside CBC radio program and Nina has since met with the author several times. While not an aggressive women's rights proponent, she served on numerous committees during her career to improve working conditions and modify some of the more frustrating discriminations.

In his introduction to the interview, Gzowski congratulated himself for calling them flight attendants rather than stewardesses. His first question was, "You were all stewardesses when you started, I take it?"

"That's right," Morrison responded promptly. "When we started the word stewardess was *de rigueur*, but we got that changed pretty quick." [Nevertheless, that title had been in use for more than 30 years before it was changed.]

"What about 'stew'?"

"I think that was probably the worst word in the English language—it had such awful connotations. It was like Continental Airlines' saying— one of their wonderful slogans. . . ."

"I'm Sally; fly me to Peru?"

There was a chorus of "Yeah!"

On the day after this interview, Nina Morrison was scheduled to fly her last flight before retirement.

My last flight is part of a two-day pairing and I will be coming back on Friday off my last flight from the place I started 40 years and four months ago: Prince Rupert—where the sun is always shining. We're on a 737, a far cry from what I started on—which was a Canso flying boat [amphibian]. We had one, and I was a party of one, and I did everything, right down to washing the aeroplane after it came out of the water. In white coveralls and a hose in my hand—I was quite a scene.[16]

By the time of this interview, though, Morrison had progressed through the hierarchy of name changes and ranks: from Stewardess to Air Hostess, to Flight Attendant to Purser, to Flight Attendant-in-Charge and finally to Customer Service Director.

Responding to the suggestion that, in the 1950s, stewardesses "were, you know, sexy?" Morrison agreed. "I think that that was a time when the airlines did sell sex on the airline, and I say that because we couldn't be married, and we couldn't have children."

It makes odd reading nowadays to realize the severity of the restrictions placed on stewardesses as recently as the 1960s. When Heather Ellis

FLIGHT ATTENDANT'S SONG

I want to be a flight attendant; I can save you all.
Look to me for your instructions when the
   plane begins to fall.

Once I wanted to be a nun,
Until I found out what it takes from you.
Now I've settled on flight attendant, and I
   know my heart is true.

I'll never want to touch down, never want to
   see the ground;
I'll never get lonely because I'll always fly away.
I want to point out exits in a calm reassuring
   way.

Being a nun is such a selfish thing, When you
   think of the comfort you can bring

Each day as a flight attendant.
You'll all be like children to me, and my affec-
   tion will be real,
For the duration of the flight, anyway.

Here's your blanket, here's your mail; And
   when the flight is over, I bid you fond adieu.
Then 300 other people get on and my affection
   starts anew.

I'll fly out every day, knowing hazard takes its
   flight. I'll be so strong; I'll be pushing out
   the emergency doors, and pushing everyone
   out into the water,
Each of you holding on to your seat cushions,
   Your personal flotation device.

I'll be the last to leave the plane, when even
   the pilot's safe; I'll push off and swim away
   as the plane bursts into flames.

My knotted scarf will stay in place, and the
   waves will wash my brave face; and I will
   have saved you all.

I want to be a flight attendant.
I want to be the one who'll pull your mask
   down in case of fire. I want to fly for ever
   and my arms will never tire.

Canadian Airlines Archives

. . . the pilots could be "Grossly overweight."

joined CPA in 1969, she had to sign that she would not get married and that she would retire when she was 30. "At that time," she commented, "you weren't even supposed to admit you had a boyfriend—you kept him submerged somewhere." When things changed shortly after, and stewardesses were told that they could marry, at least 20 marriages occurred within a week; and, because most of them were already married, they no longer needed to have two phone lines: one for the airline so that the unacknowledged husband or boyfriend wouldn't answer, and another for their friends. "There were a lot of people who 'came out,' so to speak, at that time; and then the next step was that they allowed people to have children—they allowed you to stay as a flight attendant and have children. Those were big changes for us because, before then, it was a single girl's profession. The men could all be married: they could all have children, but the women were required to be single."

The emancipation had taken time and considerable effort. Some stewardesses, and Nina Morrison was among the leaders, had to become mildly militant feminists before they succeeded. For example: "I was a flight attendant on a flight and I was in charge; but the minute they changed the aircraft due to a mechanical, and put on a little bit bigger aircraft, say from a 737 to a 727, then they would call a man out to be in charge—I couldn't do that job. Oh, you could write a book on this, chapter and verse."

There were many more restrictions: a height and weight requirement. Every six months, stewardesses would have to present themselves to be weighed; and if they were over their hiring weight by five or ten pounds, they were taken off the line until they lost the weight. This led in the United States to a class action suit against United Airlines and American Airlines in 1994 because their flight attendants were required to keep their weight; but the union produced photographs of pilots demonstrating that the pilots could be "grossly overweight." The flight attendants won this action.

Yet more regulations were in place in the early days governing makeup and hair styling. First nail polish was forbidden and make-up minimal; next they had to attend makeup classes. By 1964, a particular shade of lipstick was stipulated so that it would show from the front to the back of the aircraft. "I can remember," Ellis recalled, "running to my car, hiding so that nobody would see what they did to my face. So we went from one extreme to the other, and now they've sort of just let you be and let you do your own thing."

Peter Gzowski remarked that he knew some single flight attendants who deliberately wore wedding rings to discourage passengers who made aggressive overtures. This led to the next question, more about the early days, the so-called "glamour" days: the "coffee, tea or me days."

"Oh, yeah," Morrison replied, "that's when we were cleaning the stuff off the floor, emptying the dishes into garbage bags. You have a hundred people say that to you, and they all think it's the first time you've heard it. A TV comedian, Shelley Berman, coined that one."

The conversation turned to the serving of food and its quality—especially the serving of hot meals on flights of less than one hour. Nina commented: "I've been doing that for the last couple of months. I came off overseas just so that I could do my last flight from my home town, and that would be on a domestic operation, and we do serve a hot meal on a 55-minute sector, and it's a real rush; there's none of that coffee, tea or me stuff, then. It's get the food out and get it in."

By contrast, the meals served in the very early days sometimes consisted of a Peek Frean cookie and a paper cup of coffee on the Canso flying boat between Prince Rupert and Sandspit—it was less than an hour's flight but then only 18 people had to be served, compared to 130 or so on a Boeing 737.

Morrison summarized her experiences:

I think the biggest change in our industry lies in the age differences. Before 1975 over half of our flight-attendant group were under 39. Today, I'd say, three-quarters are well over 45, and I think that has been a great thing because you should see these women over 45: they've got that experience and that savoir faire that shows up most of the time, and I'm just glad that we don't have anything like the age thing any more. This has been a wonderful career for these women and for all of us: we can have families, we've got grandmothers—the youngest grandmothers in the world are flying around on airplanes. I'm very proud of that.

In later conversations the author had with Nina Morrison, it became clear that she had been in the vanguard of many of the changes and improvements she described in her interview with Gzowski. Although at the time of the conversations Canadian Airlines International was in a financial crisis—a genuine threat of dissolution—she was very loyal to the company and credited it with sensitivity to the many improvements in working conditions suggested by the numerous committees she had

. . . "coffee, tea or me days."

sat on. She had been very happy during her career and looked back on it with satisfaction.

There is little doubt that the stewardesses/flight attendants were leaders in a new and important aspect of aviation history; there is also little doubt that the job has changed radically from Eleanore Moore's comment that "[we] didn't have to work very hard." In fact, the workload changed as radically as did the social and ethical factors. Handling the hundreds of passengers in contemporary airliners, virtually all to be served beverages and, on many flights, full meals in a confined space, is very hard work with little if any time to sit down except on the longest stages. Inevitably, discontented, sometimes aggressive and abusive passengers have to be dealt with in an unusually difficult environment—with the not always remote possibility of a hijacking.

As well, many flight attendants have behaved with great courage, calming alarmed passengers in an emergency and shepherding them to safety out of crashed and sometimes burning aircraft. And now, of course, we do have women pilots on airliners—some of them captains of the aircraft.

Chapter Thirteen

Herman Peterson:
The Last of the Great Bush Pilots

*"He is one of our national treasures
as far as the old bush flying is concerned."*

BOB CAMERON

*L*EADERSHIP MANIFESTS ITSELF in many ways: it can be the judicious influence of a powerful politician, or a rise to eminence in industry; it can be simply the first to show the way in any endeavour, or the change brought about by a singularly intelligent and courageous individual. As well, it can be the setting of an example that almost stands on its own.

Russ Baker died in November 1958, and Pierre Berton headed one of his eulogies "Last of the Great Bush-Pilots." While Baker was a very accomplished bush pilot, it was perhaps a little premature to describe him as the last. There are at least two other candidates who deserve consideration. One is Carl Agar,* and the other Herman Peterson. Whereas Baker flew the bush for perhaps 12 years, after which he became an executive, this candidate's bush-flying career spanned a quarter of a century, during which he logged more than 15,000 hours. Unlike Baker, he had no ambition to expand and become an airline executive. Instead, he set a quiet example of courage and dedication to the people of northern BC and the southern Yukon that was an outstanding example for any aspiring young pilot. He was, and is, an aviation leader because over his long career he showed how things should be done and led the way for aviation to be so much a part of life in the north. Leaders inspire; they demonstrate how it should be done without necessarily seeking publicity, and that is what Herman Peterson accomplished.

* Co-founder of Okanagan Helicopters, who pioneered helicopter operations in BC.

When I began flying in eastern Canada in the mid-1950s, I heard other pilots clear across the country speaking of him with respect and admiration. Then, when I began flying in BC in the early 1960s, I was told on several occasions something like: "If you're up Atlin way, make sure you drop in on Herman Peterson—he's one of the real bush pilots!" What I eventually learned about him was that he loved what he was doing; and it would be no exaggeration to claim that the people in the northwest corner of the province loved the way he was doing it.

Herman Peterson was born in La Tuque, Quebec, on December 29, 1913. His desire to fly began at a very early age. He does not recall exactly when, but one initiation occurred when he was about 10 years old:

The first aeroplane I ever set foot in was a Vickers Vedette.

> The first aeroplane I ever set foot in was a Vickers Vedette. That was when Stuart Graham was flying around doing a forestry patrol.[1] I was out on a fishing trip with my Dad and it landed on a lake a few miles away. So I insisted we'd got to go and look at it. It was anchored out on the lake. The engineer took us out to it in a canoe, and I sat in it and pushed the controls.[2]

His flying career began in the summer of 1935, when he moved to Quebec City and lived in a tent with the Fecteau brothers, Joe and Art, at the old St. Louis airstrip.

> I didn't know how to fly, but I bought an aeroplane that needed a lot of work and fixed it up. My aeroplane was a Simmonds Spartan [CF-ABC] and Joe had been out to Chicoutimi to barnstorm with it; but it was a muddy field and he flipped the aircraft. So I bought it from him for $250, which was a lot of money at that time, and he and Art helped me to rebuild it and taught me to fly.

The next move was to become caretaker at the old Cap de la Madeleine airport, where he began his formal flying training with an instructor named Fletcher. Finally, he completed his training and earned his commercial pilot's licence in 1941, at Barker Field in Toronto. The instructors were Fred and Marion Gillies and Margaret Littlewood. By 1942, he also had his air engineer's licence and moved west to work for George Simmons' Northern Airways at Carcross, Yukon, in February of that year. In the interim, in 1939, he had married Doris Bachelder in La Tuque. From the first, Doris was a very active partner, particularly after they moved to Atlin and set up their own company in 1950. Doris travelled across the country to join him three weeks after Herman had moved to Carcross:

> I stayed a few days in Vancouver and then travelled up by the CPR boat, the Princess Nora, to Skagway, and then on up on the White Pass railway. I liked it in Carcross; it was primitive, but it was a challenge. The population was mostly natives, and then, when the Army came in from

the States, we had 1,400 black soldiers there at one time. Herman arrived in Whitehorse on February 11, 1942. I came up on the fourth of March.[3]

The two principal aviation operators in the Yukon and northwestern British Columbia at the time were George Simmons' Northern Airways, and White Pass Airways, operated by the British-Yukon Navigation Company, in turn a component of the White Pass and Yukon Route (that operated the railway, the sternwheelers on the Yukon River, and the Airways). Based in Whitehorse, the White Pass fleet included a Ford Trimotor and a Curtiss Condor.

Peterson began his long career in the north as business was picking up in the region. He started the new job at Northern Airways as a crewman on a Fokker Super Universal. Simmons also had a Waco[4] and Peterson flew that for eight years. Then Northern acquired four Fairchild 71s and they were flown on the Canol Pipeline project.

The Canol project was initiated at the same time as the Alaska Highway was being constructed, mainly to provide fuel for all the heavy equipment required for that construction, and to provide fuel to the airfields along the Northwest Staging Route. It involved an expansion of the existing oil fields at Norman Wells on the Mackenzie River, and the construction of a 600-mile-long (965-km) pipeline to a new refinery at Whitehorse. From Whitehorse, a smaller pipeline would be built alongside the new highway to Ladd Field, the Army Air Force base at Fairbanks. Supplying both projects—the Alaska Highway and the Canol Pipeline— became a profitable source of revenue for Northern Airways, as well as several other operators in the northwest.

However, when he started to work for Northern Airways, Peterson's first job, as a helper to the pilot, Alec Dame, was to remove all the equipment from the three B-26 bombers that had gone down in "Million Dollar Valley" a month before.

We worked on that for a couple of weeks, under canvas, in the wintertime when it was sometimes between 40 and 50 below. We took the engines, instruments, arms—everything that would come off them—all the equipment and ammunition. Alec Dame flew the old Fokker. Bob Goldie was flying a Pilgrim at the time; we were both on the same job. We hauled a Caterpillar 22 from Watson Lake to there in pieces with that Pilgrim.

During the salvage operation, Peterson saw the White Pass Condor for the first time. Les Cook was flying it. Operating on wheel-skis, he hauled equipment and supplies from TooTally Lakes to Watson Lake. When the

NORTHERN AIRWAYS PLANE LOCATED THIS MORNING PILOT, PASSENGER SAFE

There was consternation locally when it was announced over the radio last night that a Northern Airways Fairchild plane, with pilot Peterson and a passenger aboard was unreported after leaving Frances Lake for Carcross at 4:30 p.m. Wednesday. The passenger, we have since ascertained was Mr. Buss of the local D.O.T. department.

We are happy to report that at 6:30 this morning Capt. Jarvis of the C.P.A. on his way to Whitehorse sighted the Fairchild plane about half-way between Frances Lake and Watson Lake. Both Peterson and Buss were apparently safe and sound waving their arms to the passing C.P.A. plane as it flew overhead. What was the cause of the forced landing or to what extent the Fairchild plane has been injured was not known at the time of our going to press.

Whitehorse Star
September 10. 1948

airfield was constructed at Watson, Bob Coutts flew all the gas in from Whitehorse. "The Condor would take 11 barrels of gas, and they'd burn 11 barrels of fuel on that round trip."

While working for George Simmons, and after he left to found his own company, one of Peterson's enduring tasks was to fly the mail. The Post Office Department had finally, and reluctantly, begun to award airmail contracts; and the remote, northwest corner of the province was an obvious area needing the service. This gave Peterson the opportunity to develop the bush-flying techniques that made him a celebrity in the region:

I flew the mail from here to Telegraph Creek and Iskut Lake for 25 years. When George Simmons was still on, we used to have that mail run. Pat Callison and I used to fly it.

All the mail was weighed by the post office. It was a class 3 service, so we had passengers and express and all that; but I was pretty proud of that mail contract. I never let anyone down and I never lost a letter.

What I'd do—they'd hang you for flying that way now—if I was coming back empty in clear weather, I'd fly the treetops all the way back and study the ground; so before long, I could actually walk it if I had to because I knew it so well. I could fly in almost any weather. Also, you learned how to manage your fuel, because if you ran out when you were that low, you were in the trees. I flew it many times in snow—you know, quarter-mile visibility—and I could still make it. I knew every rock on the way.

We hauled the mail down to Tulsequah for the winter and the following summer and the following winter. We were late with one trip down there. I was going down twice a week.

During freeze-up and break-up, we had to go down on wheels because they kept the strips open for the aircraft from Juneau. Then, in a day or two, when I had to take the mail down to Telegraph, we'd take the wheels off and put the skis on; go down and back and then do the same thing in reverse. We had a block of wood to put all the bolts on. We could change those wheels and the backing plates and everything in about 30 minutes.

In his more than quarter-century of bush flying, Peterson inevitably experienced some close calls. The first occurred when he was flying the Canol Pipeline project:

Flying the Canol, we got to know the route pretty well and we worked in some pretty dirty weather. On one occasion, Pat Callison had left about an hour before I did—we were flying loads up to Sheldon Lake from Carcross—and who should I meet? It was snowing and I was on the right side of the Ross River. Pat was following the same river on his way home again and he didn't even see me. He was just across the creek from me; we were that close.

Another, more serious one occurred while flying with Spud Heustis from Carcross, in the central Yukon, to Nansen Creek. After taking off in the spring of the year, just after they had taken the skis off and put the wheels on, the engine started slowing down. Peterson opened the throttle and noticed the oil temperature starting to go up. The engine kept slowing down and slowing down; then, all of a sudden, it just stopped. They were at about 6,000 feet [1 800 m], on wheels in the spring of the year. "The Fairchild doesn't glide all that good, either, and we were about ten miles [16 km] from Braeburn Lake, maybe more, and I just made it. Straight glide in, came in over the trees and just made it. Landed on the ice, and the ice was still strong enough to hold it." They had no option but to sit and wait until somebody found them: fortunately, it wasn't a long wait. "Harvey Johnson was flying a Lodestar then on the mail run up here and he spotted us. Stan McMillan and Bob Cashaur flew the Anson up with another engine and all the spares we needed, the hoists and everything, and we changed the engine."

The next, by far the most potentially serious mishap, occurred, too, while he was still flying for George Simmons out of Carcross in the fall of 1948:

I had a problem in an old Fairchild 71, [CF-]BXD, one time—I was lucky to be alive. We moved a weather station down from Frances Lake to Watson Lake. We made about six trips down to Watson Lake, and all that stuff was being hauled from there over the road to Carcross. So, the last load, instead of taking it back to Watson Lake, we brought it with us and, about 45 minutes after we left Frances Lake, around Blackstone Creek at the head of the Liard, the rudder pedal started shaking.

The only passenger, sitting beside Peterson, was "a great, tall guy. The cables come down the side on the 71, and I thought he was pushing on them with his feet; but he wasn't." Next the rudder pedals started to shake more violently. "I remember the left pedal went right forward and it locked. I couldn't move it." They had just passed a lake about five minutes back. Fortunately, the rudder pedal didn't jam there: it was a deep lake and they would probably have drowned. Instead, there was a beaver swamp; they were in a hard left turn and Peterson couldn't do anything about it, but he did manage to influence the turn with ailerons to get into the beaver swamp. They just cleared the trees going in and hit the water at 90 miles an hour [150 km/h]. As they hit the water, Peterson pulled the stick back hard and put his arm up in front of his face. This left the aeroplane sitting in six feet of water—with both the wings torn off. "I wasn't hurt all that badly," Peterson recalls, "but I was cut—just a scalp wound. I found out later what I had hit: it was the compass, mounted just behind the windshield."

AIRPLANE ACCIDENT NARROWLY AVERTED IN ATLIN AIRFIELD

What could have resulted in a very bad plane accident was narrowly averted when one of Northern Airways' planes was taking off the Atlin Field. Pilot Shell Gunn was at the controls at the time travelling around fifty miles an hour on the take-off when one of the tires burst causing the plane to swerve and take a bee-line for the brush at the side of the field. After travelling on bad ground and stumps, etc. for around two hundred feet, the plane came to a standstill with the result that a wing was badly damaged, also the undercarriage and other parts. When the plane came to a stop the door could not be opened at once and Herb Flesher went through the window (they say like a streak of lightening) thinking the plane might set afire. The passengers on the outgoing plane were Mr. And Mrs. (Bud) Harbottle and baby; Herb Flesher, Mrs. Ernie Clark and Monty Lamont. We are happy to report no one was hurt although all badly scared. We are informed the pants two gentlemen were badly damaged, but such a small thing does not matter much as it's all good for the Dry Goods business.

Atlin New-Miner
November 7, 1941

*. . . I never did find out who
she was to this day.*

They had survived with no serious injuries, but they were still in an unenviable position—in a small beaver swamp, surrounded by trees. They stayed where they were because, as Peterson says, "we couldn't do much else." On the third morning, at about six o'clock, they heard an aeroplane. A CPA DC-3 was off its normal course looking for them. It was a chilly morning in September and they had a small fire going, with a pile of spruce boughs beside it to make smoke. When they heard the aeroplane, they piled the spruce boughs on the fire, but nothing happened immediately because it was cold. There wasn't enough heat to drive the smoke up; it just stayed in the trees. Then, about ten minutes later, they heard the DC-3 coming back again. Fortunately, by then the fire was putting up a good plume of smoke above the trees; and, while the crew in the cockpit didn't see it, a stewardess was looking out of a rear window and she spotted the column of smoke. "They found us. I never did find out who she was to this day."

It was not only a disconcerting but a puzzling accident; one that called for an investigation. Bill Dalzell, of BC-Yukon Air Service, went in with his Fairchild 71 and cut the rudder post out. There were three hinges on the rudder post and the bottom hinge broke. There was enough springiness to pull the rudder over to one side. The [control-cable] horn[5] caught on the rudder post, the other one went fully forward and locked it. The post was shipped back to Ottawa. "There was quite an investigation over that one," Peterson recalls. "They found it was a structural failure. The fix on that was to cut all the fabric out around the hinges and check for cracks." Someone had failed to secure the rudder when it was moored in the water. The lagoon at Carcross, where the aircraft was frequently moored, was subject to strong winds, and Herman was convinced that the rudder flapping free over an extended period had caused the hinge to crack.

Herman Peterson worked for Northern Airways for seven years; for the last three, just after the Second World War, things were very slow and George Simmons had a run of bad luck. According to Peterson:

By 1949, George had been in the business for 19 years. Doris and I went on holidays at that time, went back to Quebec, and while we were gone they rebuilt that Waco—it had 22 coats of dope on it, all hand-rubbed—it was better than new. They took a 300 Jacobs engine out of a Mark IV Anson; but the stack got overloaded with fuel; the thing caught fire, burned right out. That was in 1949, and George had more bad luck: his mother was ill and his sister went to visit Captain McDonald on the *Tutshi* [the lake boat]; she fell down the companionway and hurt herself badly from that fall. She didn't want to go into hospital, but finally they did get her to Whitehorse and they shipped her right down to Vancouver where she died from internal injuries.

This all happened while the Petersons were still on holiday; but Herman realized that things were going downhill. He was the only pilot for two years before George went out of business; and then George became his partner for a year when Herman moved down to Atlin in 1950 and started as Peterson Air Service with an Aeronca Sedan.

The move to Atlin seems to have been partly practical—there was virtually no flying activity out of Carcross at the time—and partly because he liked Atlin. The village, first called a city, was created by a gold rush at the turn of the century; and, because it was so much easier to reach than the Klondike, many of the "stampeders" heading for Dawson City in 1898 turned gratefully aside. The White Pass and Yukon route's railway was under construction when the rush to get to Pine Creek on the east shore of Atlin Lake began and it dealt a severe blow to the contractors doing the work. A significant percentage of the labourers didn't just drop tools and take off; they took the contractor's tools with them and headed for Pine Creek. "Not only did they leave by the hundreds, taking with them their picks and shovels . . . but they took anything else they could lay their hands on."[6]

The Atlin boom, like its larger counterpart in the Klondike, only lasted for two or three years and then began to peter out. By the time Herman and Doris Peterson moved down from Carcross, Atlin had gained a reputation as one of the most attractive of the small and isolated communities in the Canadian north. Its climate, considering its latitude, is remarkably benign and it had settled down to a sort of stability lacking in most mining ghost towns. For her book on its history, Allison Mitcham chose the title, *Atlin, the Last Utopia*,[7] and most people who have been there will understand why. It is set in a landscape so strikingly beautiful that it tempts an excursion into purple prose.

With the move from Carcross to Atlin went the mail contract. "The Post Office Department said they would give us a contract if we were uccessful in our bid for a licence. As soon as I got the licence, the first trip I made was hauling the mail into Telegraph Creek." Nevertheless, things were pretty slow for the first two or three years, and Peterson flew by himself. He had intended to start a guiding and hunting venture, but someone else took over the guiding licence for the territory from him and Herman did the flying—which is what he really wanted to do. One of the things that had bothered George Simmons was that the highway came

. . . a landscape so strikingly beautiful . . .

into Atlin in 1949. "George said, 'When the roads come in the flying goes out, and I said, "Gee, George, there's a lot more people in the country."

From the time he began operating at Atlin, Peterson parked his one aircraft, the Aeronca Sedan, over at the island, just off the beach, which served to shelter it from the sometimes dangerously strong winds that swept up Atlin Lake. He would use a boat and then taxi back to the beach to take on loads, reversing the process on landing. Herman's wife, Doris, recalls:

I used to line people up, use the pickup to collect freight and stay on the radio when I wasn't doing that. I wasn't too nervous about Herman because he always came back. I had a worry session when he went down between Stewart and Telegraph, but nothing too serious; and then, when he was flown back from Telegraph Creek, just about the whole community was down on the beach to greet him. People round here thought a lot of Herman.

This potentially dangerous incident occurred in 1953, when Peterson lost the Aeronca. He recounts what happened:

I lost the Aeronca Sedan in the third year, between Telegraph Creek and Stewart. It was my own fault. The weather was a little bit socked in; I reached Raspberry Pass—I could see over the summit of the pass and I could have got through, but I had a load on and I got a little bit of a downdraft. So then I started to turn and I couldn't make it; there was a wall on my left side, and I knew if I did a turn at that stage I was going to stall out. So I put the nose down and landed in the bottom of the creek. It took the bottom of the floats off; the thing stood up on its nose and just teetered there, then it flipped over onto its side. I didn't get a scratch.

. . . six days of hard walking . . .

He had crash-landed on the right-of-way for the old telegraph line, and he followed it all the way to Telegraph Creek. It took six days of hard walking. He was in pretty good shape but for his feet, which were badly blistered. He had 65 pounds [30 kg] of food on board, and he packed it all on his back. He could have made better time if he had left some of it behind.

They were just getting into dried foods then. Mostly packaged soups, which are good and light—you just need water: chicken noodle, chicken rice, that sort of thing. I stopped about three times a day to brew up a cup of tea and did pretty well on the food side.

I came out of that one unscathed. I lost the aeroplane, but that's all. I had a bunch of helicopter parts on for Okanagan [Helicopters] at Stewart. They were doing topo survey work. Don Poole was the pilot and Eric Cowden the engineer.

With help from the bank and from friends, Peterson managed to get by those tough early years: "I was in hock for those two or three very slow years." But it was a period of transition; the boom years of the mid-1950s were just beginning, and business began to pick up. Before long, he and Doris found themselves swamped with customers.

A 1930 aerial view of Atlin, BC, taken by Carter Guest, long-time Air Inspector for the BC-Yukon region. The small island in the foreground was used as a docking base and shelter against the wind by Herman Peterson.
—BRUCE GUEST COLLECTION

The Northern Airways Waco ZQC-6, CF-BDZ, that caught fire in Carcross just after a major overhaul and became a write-off.
—HAINES COLLECTION, YUKON ARCHIVES, 1926

Herman and Doris Peterson examining the Eastman
E-2 Sea Rover, CF-ASY, at Atlin. Jim Eastman, the American
designer of the aircraft, brought it to Atlin in 1933. He
became a prospector and mining promoter and used ASY with
few problems until his death in 1945. Ruggedly built, the
hull was strong enough for take-offs and landings on the ice
of Atlin Lake during the winters.
—PETERSON COLLECTION, ATLIN HISTORICAL SOCIETY, 9697

This time with his own aircraft and as president of Peterson
Airways in Atlin, 1952, Peterson stands in front of Fairchild, 71
CF-AWV.—PETERSON COLLECTION, ATLIN HISTORICAL SOCIETY, 9724

Peterson bought his first de Havilland Beaver in 1956. It was the big step up for his company—which he had renamed Coast Air Services Limited—because the Beaver outperformed any of the existing bush planes by such a substantial margin.—PETERSON COLLECTION, ATLIN HISTORICAL SOCIETY, 9695

The grizzled veteran bush pilot, in his 82nd year, at Atlin with his scratch-built Smith Mini-plane, a single-seat biplane that is fully aerobatic. In his mid-80s, Herman Peterson is still flying it, as well as his Luscombe.—BOB TURNER

I flew the old Fairchild 71: AWV was the registration. They were just a basic freighter; the old Fokker was just the same; they had a very poor aileron control on them. Our 71 was 4,000 pounds [1 815 kg] empty and 6,000 [2 720 kg] gross, with the old Wasp Junior in it. It carried 960 pounds [435 kg] of fuel. We could just about get off glassy water with a thousand pounds [450 kg] on it—myself and full tanks. I don't know whether it was legal or not, but I don't think anyone flew legally in those days. Atlin is about 2,190 feet [670 m] above sea level, and 900 pounds [410 kg] on a hot day was okay. The 71 could beat a Norseman out of a small lake.

While Peterson did not make his fortune, after surviving a shaky start he made a comfortable living in the 1950s and 1960s. After losing the Aeronca, he had the Fairchild and added a Cessna 180. As early as 1947, he had seen the de Havilland Beaver demonstrated at Carcross by Russ Bannock—de Havilland's demonstration pilot—who, of course, was trying to persuade George Simmons to buy one:

But George didn't have enough money to buy one then. The Beaver was duck soup after the other machines. It'd jump off the water and all the controls were in the right places. They had some problems to begin with. The first one—the one Russ Baker had—they had to change all the skin on it. I checked out on the one that Russ Bannock brought up in '47. We used the lagoon [at Carcross], and the water in the spring is pretty low—you could practically wade across it. We used to take the old Fairchild and get about five gallons of gas in one tank and take off round that lagoon on one float, then land on the river and work from there until the water came back up. With the Beaver in the same conditions, you could get off with four people aboard, no trouble. It was a fine aircraft.

However, Peterson couldn't raise enough money to buy a Beaver until 1956; then he bought another one in 1957, the year in which the company name was changed from Peterson Air Service to Coast Range Airways. Meanwhile, a new pilot flying for him lost the Cessna 180:

We lost the 180, down at Telegraph Creek—piled up and burned up, but it wasn't the pilot's fault. What happened was, there was a north wind blowing and at Telegraph Creek, where it goes down into the Stikine, the wind funnels there; it's just like a suction. So he got caught in that. He was a new pilot and I had checked him out in small lakes, high lakes, wind conditions and everything. He was good—first class, never took any chances. Anyway, he got caught in this downdraft and they hit on the top of the summit and burned.

One of Bob Ellis's pilots from Wrangell was up there flying a Cessna 180 on floats. He was working for the fisheries—a salmon count. They saw the fire, took off and went up to the summit to investigate. They were 500 feet [150 m] above the summit and they got sucked down right alongside the other one. The pilot had 3,500 hours, but he didn't have a chance: this was a freak wind.

The second machine went into the timber, upside down about a hundred yards along the valley from the first one. The pilot was knocked out. One of the passengers pulled him out. But the aeroplane didn't burn and they survived it. So they had a story to tell when they came out.

Besides the pilot, we lost two good guys: Dr. Engel, GSC [Geological Survey of Canada], and a CM & S [Consolidated Mining & Smelting] man. Two expensive men to lose. I was seriously thinking of getting out of it then. You get over it, but you never really get over it.

Nevertheless, Peterson did get over it and, by 1960, a de Havilland Otter was added to Coast Range Airways' fleet.

I met Punch Dickins when I went down to buy the Otter—he was the sales manager for de Havilland. The Otter [CF-SUB] had 1,600 hours total on it. The first Otters that came out didn't have a synchronized stabilizer on them—you had to wind the cheese-cutter [elevator trim wheel] about 60 turns; but the new ones had the stabilizer linked to the flaps and you only had to use two or three turns one way or the other. Anyway, they modified it for us; they took all the old radio out of it and put new radio in, painted it to our own colours. It was like a brand-new aircraft when we bought it. I guess it's still down on the coast somewhere. The colours were yellow and red—yellow fuselage, red rudders, red elevators and red wingtips. We had all our aircraft the same way.

The Otter was his favourite aircraft. He flew it for three years and says that its performance was so impressive he could use it in lakes that no one had considered using in the past. Then, in the mid-1960s, a new pilot joined Coast Range Airways, and this moved Peterson's company into a new and profitable technology. "We had Al Pelletier flying for us; he was with us for four years. He was my right-hand man: fly in dirty weather, work hard, never complain," recalled Herman, and Doris added, "Yes, we went home for Christmas twice when he was here and he took care of everything."

"He used to get a month's holiday every year," Herman went on, "and he went down to Okanagan [Helicopters] and got his chopper training. So we bought a chopper the third year he was here—we had a [Bell 47-] G4."

Alf Stringer[8] had one; we were the only other company with one in British Columbia. We got a G4 because it used 80/87 [octane avgas]; we didn't want to stock 100/130, which is what the turbocharged machine used. We ran all our aircraft on 80/87: the Otter, the Beavers and everything ran on the same fuel. But the chopper was good for our company; it created a lot of work for the aeroplanes.* We put in 1,200 hours in two summers with it. You had to haul everything up from the lake to the top of the hill with it. Art Swannell did the topo survey all the way from the BC boundary to the west. They had choppers and we supplied them with the Beavers— sometimes two Beavers on the job.

The next initiative was to move up to a turbine helicopter:

We bought a Jet Ranger. They had a little trouble with the turbines at first, so we had it optioned for three years, because we didn't want to bring something up here that was going to give us a whole lot of trouble. Finally, when Bell had sorted out the engine problem and we were just about to take delivery, we sold out to Trans North. [CF-]FXX was the registration.

By 1967, after 25 years of bush flying in a very remote area in aircraft that were, for the first 12 years, fast becoming obsolescent, Peterson decided it was time to retire. He sold all his commercial aircraft to Whitehorse-based Trans North Turbo Air, but continued to fly for pleasure:

* Fixed-wing aircraft did the long-haul servicing of base camps, including delivery of avgas for the helicopters—and then helicopters carried out the daily work routine of moving survey crews on and off the mountains from these base camps.

I decided to turn my commercial licence back in because otherwise there'd be all sorts of jobs and everyone would want me to fly. We were under Edmonton [the area of DoT jurisdiction] then. I called them and told them what I wanted to do, and they said, "Why would you want to do that?" I told them. They said, "Okay, but any time you want your commercial back, you can have it." They've still got it on file.

. . . remembering to do the small favours . . .

After he had turned in his licence, Peterson bought a Luscombe, which he keeps on a float in front of his home on Atlin Lake. He built a dock that can be winched to shore if the wind starts to blow. He modified the Luscombe with a 150-hp engine and replaced the existing EDO 1400 floats with 1650s. With the 1400s, handling on water in a crosswind was very difficult. With the new floats: "That made a real aeroplane out of it. It's just like a Beaver—just like a cork on the water. You can get a 40-mph [65-km/h] crosswind and you don't even have to open the throttle to steer the thing; just push the rudder. The only problem is that, with the extra weight and the big engine, you don't have much range."

Peterson has also assembled a Smith Mini-plane, a single-seat biplane that is fully aerobatic, for which he has constructed a hangar at the airport. Doris disapproves because, unlike the Luscombe, she cannot accompany him when he flies it. He started building it in 1962, between mail runs or when the weather was out, and first flew it in 1967. Now, in his mid-80s, he still flies both aircraft.

Atlin had an airstrip of sorts from the 1930s. "You had to keep clearing the rocks off it, and there was a big hump at one end." Then, in 1986, when the Department of Highways decided to upgrade it to airport status, the department was petitioned by many people in the northwest of BC and southern Yukon to name it after Herman. Consequently, it was officially designated Peterson Airport. A fitting tribute to one of the last of the great—and this time blessedly modest—bush pilots.

Herman Peterson's reputation was built on more than flying skills. He identified strongly with the people he was serving in the isolated communities, always, or nearly always, remembering to do the small favours— bringing, to a man, tobacco, some ammunition for his rifle or, perhaps, a mickey of his favourite medicine; and, for a woman, cooking utensils, sewing materials or a bottle of cough syrup; and, most importantly, remembering to check to see if there was any mail for people along the route before leaving on a trip—sometimes making significant detours from his intended destination to drop off mail. Such things sound insignificant until you live in genuinely isolated areas; then they become enormously important.

In this, of course, he had the energetic Doris to help. When he came back from a trip with numerous slips of paper asking for small items, Doris would take charge, jump in the pickup and not only do the shopping but package things and mark them for their recipients—making sure that he didn't take off without them. Once again, this sounds like a small thing, but after a heavy spell of flying, it is hard for a pilot to remember what he has promised, and difficult to find the time to do the shopping. Over many years, these cumulative small acts made a tremendous difference to the people and many hours of extra work.

Lyman Sands, who has lived long in Atlin—so long that he can remember as a ten-year-old boy seeing Jim Eastman's three Sea Rover flying boats flying into Atlin in formation in 1933[9]—and who first met Herman Peterson when he, Lyman, was still a teenage schoolboy, talks of him with the same mixture of respect and pride as most people in the northwest corner of BC and the southern Yukon do.

Asked for an opinion on Herman Peterson's reputation, he replied, "the highest—the highest you can get." Among many comments, he said that Herman "knew this country like the palm of his hand, and he could fly it in any kind of weather. Though he didn't take chances—they all have to take chances once in a while, but he took very few. He was and is a great pilot."

Sands has an engaging anecdote about Peterson's methods of providing service. Lyman was coroner at the time and he and a policeman had to charter Herman to go south of Atlin about 40 miles [65 km] to hold a coroner's inquiry.

It was a nice day; we were going to leave here at about two o'clock in the afternoon. We went down there with our briefcases and our fishing rods. Herman said, rather snappily, "What've you got the fishing rods for?" Well, we said we thought we could maybe stop at one of the lakes down there to do a little bit of fishing before we came back.

He said, "I haven't got time for fishing. I've got lots of planes, there're lots of flights to make and in the summertime I've got to make my money. I haven't got time to stop for fishing." Well anyway, we went down and held this short coroner's inquiry, and took off on our return trip. When we got up in the air, there's a lake down below us, and he said, "Well, we could stop there for a few minutes, and just see what it's like for fishing." So he landed and the policeman got out onto one of the floats and cast a few times and no luck. So we took off again, and Herman said, "There's another lake over there; we'll stop there." Well they were really biting. Pretty soon Herman was out on the float with his rod, and I don't think we got home until about ten o'clock that night.

. . . He had the energetic Doris to help.

The interview with Lyman Sands concluded with the words, "He's a terrific person, and a very inventive one."[10]

As well as looking after his two aircraft, the hangar and dock, Herman Peterson has become widely recognized for his skills at restoring violins and crafting his own ones. In his mid-80s, he is allowed to retain his private flying licence and flies frequently in the Luscombe and the Mini-plane. This testifies to the high regard in which he is held not only by the public but also by Transport Canada, not normally a sentimental organization.

Tahltan elder Charlie Callbraith, whose father had a ranch at Telegraph Creek, and whose memory goes back to 1920 and the beginning of aviation in the north, has some interesting recollections. As a young boy, he saw the three de Havilland DH4Bs of the US Army Air Service's First Alaska Air Expedition landing at Telegraph Creek on their way back from Nome.[11] Ten years later, when he was working for the provincial Public Works Department in Telegraph Creek, he witnessed the problems encountered by the two aircraft of Pacific International Airways that were on their way to join the search for Paddy Burke.[12]

Charlie describes Herman as "a real nice guy; everybody in this country thought he was a great fellow." He recalls visiting Atlin some years ago when Herman took Charlie and his wife down to the airstrip to show them his Smith Mini-plane. "He took us into his shed [hangar], and he said, 'Give me a hand; I'll take it out.' He pushed it out and, after he got it outside, he said, 'Oh, I'll take it up and fly it for you.' My sister was with us and she was scared—she went off into the trees. He dived right close to us. Gee, you'd think he was going right into us; then suddenly, up he'd go again."[13]

And finally one more opinion by Bob Cameron of Whitehorse, the operations manager of Trans North Air, based in Whitehorse, who has known Herman for many years:

He's one of our national treasures as far as the old bush flying is concerned. As a pilot, he obviously was a very competent professional bush pilot. He's had thousands of hours on the old 71s, and later in the Beavers. He is a very meticulous engineer, who took care of his own aircraft. He's a craftsman: anything he does, whether it's maintenance or building his home-built aircraft, or anything else. He does all his welding himself; he's a perfectionist. An absolute wealth of experience. Another neat thing about him, he took a lot of pictures in the old days, and did his own developing, which again he did to perfection; so he's left us with a tremendous collection of photographs from when he was flying out of Carcross. I think that people shouldn't forget his

. . . one of our national treasures as far as the old bush flying concerned.

wife, Doris, who's been a team player. They didn't have children and she devoted all her time to backing him up—doing the shopping for people in the bush, staying on the radio, generally looking after all the details.

Certainly Herman Peterson would have to be ranked as one of our great bush pilots.[14]

Before the mid-1950s, very few bush aircraft had any electronic navigational aids; they had to rely strictly on their eyes and on maps. They did not have ADF (Automatic Direction Finding), LORAN (Long Range Navigation), or the ultimate and most recent equipment, GPS (Global Positioning System), which by utilizing satellite technology can provide the pilot with a very accurate fix at any time; and the maps before then were far from reliable: large areas of white space surrounded by dotted lines would be marked as "unexplored," and many of the features that were mapped were not where they should be. At least half of Herman Peterson's flying was done during this period, and it was then that he amassed more than half the 15,000 hours he logged. As he points out, "After a few years I became so familiar with the country that I didn't need a map. In any case, a map's no good to you when it's snowing."

Fortunately, a year or two after Herman had moved to Atlin a period of prosperity began. Commodity prices were high, natural resources were plentiful: governments and corporations quickly appreciated the necessity for good, reliable maps so that these resources could be explored and exploited. There was what could almost be described as a scramble to survey the country; and bush-flying operators, both fixed-wing and helicopter, became essential. Simultaneously, prospectors, geologists and logging companies became very active, all needing transport into areas where there was none other than bush aircraft.

In a remote region like Atlin there were also the government officials in forestry, fish and wildlife, as well as police, doctors, nurses and a host of others who needed to get around the country. The bush pilot had become virtually indispensable. In short, the team of Herman and Doris Peterson were the right people in the right place at the right time. They will not soon be forgotten in the northwest.

. . . a map's no good to you when it's snowing

Epilogue

I NNUMERABLE JETSTREAMS have passed over the province since 1960 and, not surprisingly, there have been many changes, both on the ground and in the air. Now, more than ever before, intercity travel by air has become routine and the operating companies have grown much larger, as have the airports necessary to handle the increased passenger loads.

As something of an irony, though, we seem to have taken a step backward in time by the year 2000. First, there was one major monopoly airline, Trans-Canada Airlines.* An evolution followed over the next 40 years, and three major airlines emerged: Trans-Canada/Air Canada, Canadian Pacific Airlines and Pacific Western Airlines. In 1987, PWA bought out Canadian Pacific from the CPR, combining the two under the new name of Canadian Airlines International. A fourth budding contender for the status of major airline was Max Ward's Wardair and, because of the ambitious legacy left by both McConachie and Baker—a determination to sideline TCA/Air Canada and become the dominant airline in the country—Canadian Airlines now went after Wardair and bought it in 1990 to leave Canadian free to compete against Air Canada.

Some have attributed Canadian Airlines International's financial problems to this over eagerness; it paid an unrealistically high price to take over Wardair and, consequently, has been running in the red ever since, amassing an almost insuperable debt load. Now in 1999–2000, with the financial collapse of Canadian Airlines and its takeover by Air Canada, it appears that we will be returning to essentially the situation as it was in 1939: Air Canada as the dominant, monopoly, intercity, transcontinental carrier.

In Canada, because of its geography and relatively sparse population, the equally important arena of bush flying has experienced similar but less dramatic changes. During the 1930s, the considerable population of loggers and fishermen along the BC coast, for example, had to be served by sea, almost exclusively the vessels of the Canadian Pacific's Coast Steamship Service, the CNR's Coastal Steamships and the Union Steamship Company's vessels. By the end of the 1940s, first QCA and then PWA had appropriated the majority of this business.

* In both major airlines—TCA and CPA—"Air Lines" in the titles became "Airlines," an evolution rather than a mandated change; as well, Trans-Canada dropped the hyphen in its title.

Meanwhile, of course, aviation technology has made gigantic strides. The days of trailing antennas and medium- and low-frequency radio have given way to single-sideband and very high frequency radio channels, vastly improving air to ground communication. Now both radar and computers have made virtually hands-off piloting of airliners a reality; while in bush as well as airline flying the advent of satellite technology has made feasible the GPS (Global Positioning System), affording pilots an accurate and continuous record of their position. There have been many more technological advances—too many to list here.

However, when I began my stint as a bush pilot in 1954—following an interlude of eight years since flying four-engined aircraft in the RAF—few of these innovations had made their way into that arena. We were still using trailing antennas for sporadic radio communications; maps, particularly in the far north, still left much to the imagination, and living conditions were still distinctly primitive. On the positive side, there were still a number of the pilots and air engineers around who had flown the bush before the war. Some had been doing so all along; others had served in the air force and returned after the war. In either case, I was always fascinated by their accounts of the past, as well, of course, as their opinions of the principals dealt with in this book—conflicting opinions that first spurred a latent desire to find out more about them.

Unfortunately, at the time I had no aspirations to try to become a historian and I did nothing to record their comments; consequently, I cannot offer quotes. Nevertheless, I do remember the gist of their opinions, particularly about two of our prime chosen leaders, Grant McConachie and Russ Baker. One observation about McConachie went something like this: "That guy was the best con artist I ever saw. If he asked you to jump off a cliff, you felt real bad about not jumping off the expletive cliff to please him." With the benefit of hindsight, I suspect that this gift was hereditary, recalling that Uncle Harry McConachie was a very successful snake-oil salesman. In general, though, opinions represented a sort of reluctant admiration: "He was a nice guy, but you had to watch out or he'd exploit the hell out of you."

When it came to Russ Baker, though, opinions were far more diverse. He was seen as a manipulator by some, by others as a justifiably crafty operator. However, this was nearly always followed by a caveat expressed by most of the people who knew him: it consisted of the term for exagger-

If he asked you to jump off a cliff, you felt real bad about not jumping off the expletive cliff . . .

ation that has become hackneyed by overuse. I can recall many people saying, as Gordon Ballentine has, that it was a pity he was so full of bullshit because he didn't need to be: he was a good bush pilot.

Baker was still alive in those days, but I was flying in eastern Canada and the Arctic; and, in any case, he was very much in the executive suite by then and I wouldn't have met him in the bush. All this did finally come together more than 30 years later when, as a curator in what was then the BC Provincial Museum, I began to publish books on aviation history. Naturally my thoughts went back to those fascinating, brave, improbable, gifted and imaginative, sometimes arrogant and cantankerous people— but particularly to those paradoxical personalities: Grant McConachie and Russ Baker.

There is an old axiom that nice guys finish last. While Baker may have been admired, he seldom seems to have been described as likeable and he certainly did not finish last; whereas virtually everyone described McConachie as a really nice guy, and he, too, was unmistakably successful.

But then history seldom accommodates a simplistic formula, and I found the real people far more interesting than the traditional glamorized media depictions.

**At the end of the day two Queen Charlotte Islands'
Stranraers sit face-to-face at the dock in Sullivan Bay
being refuelled.**—PETERS COLLECTION, ROYAL BC MUSEUM

Endnotes

CHAPTER ONE

1 Shirley Render, *Double Cross: James A. Richardson and Canadian Airways*, 1999, p. 74.

2 R. E. G. Davies, *A History of the World's Airlines*, p. 109.

3 K. M. Molson, *Pioneering in Canadian Air Transport*, p. 184.

4 J. R. K. Main. *Voyageurs of the Air*, p. 28.

5 W. Kaye Lamb, *History of the Canadian Pacific Railway*, p. 356.

6 For a comprehensive account of this development, see, Peter Corley-Smith, *Bush Flying to Blind Flying*.

7 Molson, *Pioneering*, p. 98.

8 *Ibid*, p. 184.

9 Leslie Roberts, *C. D. The Life and Times of Clarence Decatur Howe*, p. 19.

10 *Ibid*.

11 *Ibid*., p. 20.

12 K. M Molson, Pioneering, p. 195.

13 E. W. Beatty, *Letterbook* 162, February 1937–March 1937, Canadian Pacific Railway Corporate Archives.

14 Molson, *Pioneering*, p.185.

15 *Ibid*, p. 186.

16 *Ibid*.

17 *Ibid*, pp. 197-98.

18 D.R. MacLaren, interviewed by P.M. Stoddart, 1978: British Columbia Archives, Accession No. 3217, Tape No. 2, Track no. 2.

CHAPTER TWO

1 Molson, *Pioneering*, p. 199.

2 *Ibid*, p. 210

3 C. A. Ashley, *A Study of Trans-Canada Air Lines: The First Twenty-Five Years*, pp. 14-15.

4 *Ibid*., pp. 14-15.

5 *Whitehorse Star*, May 29, 1942, p. 1. In the event, TCA did not establish a service on this route, presumably because it considered it uneconomical.

6 Lamb, *Canadian Pacific Railway*, p. 359.

7 E. W. Beatty, *Letterbook* 160, October 1936, Canadian Pacific Railway Archives.

8 A. R. Hunt, "TCA: The Formative Years," *CAHS Journal*, Vol. 18, No. 2, 1980, p. 49

9 Ashley, *A Study of Trans-Canada Air Lines*, p. 11.

10 Beatty, *Letterbook* 160.

11 Kenneth Munson, *Airliners from 1919 to the Present Day*, p. 163. Munson also records that in 1934, too, KLM entered a DC-2 in the England to Australia Air Race, and that it "came first in the transport class and second only (to the D.H. 88 Comet) in the overall speed class."

12 *Ibid*, p. 165.

13 Lockheed used the name Electra again when it introduced the four-engined L-188 airliner to compete against the very successful Vickers Viscount in the late 1950s.

14 Richardson, who was bidding for the airmail contract between Vancouver and Seattle, and well aware that it wasn't the most practical aircraft for that purpose, had acquired the Rapide at the insistence of the Post Office Department, in accord with the Empire Preference policy of the government.

15 Lewis Leigh, "Electra Debut," *CAHS Journal*, Vol. 29, No. 4, 1991, p. 117.

16 Munson, *Airliners*, p. 165.

17 Render, *Double Cross*, p. 202.

18 Clint Murchison, the Texas oil multi-millionaire; in Robert Bothwell and William Kilbourn, *C. D. Howe: A Biography*, p. 290.

19 H. W. Seagrim, "TCA Introduces the Super Electra and Lodestar," *CAHS Journal*, Vol. 29, No. 4 1991, p. 124.

20 *Ibid*.

21 *Ibid*, p. 125.

22 Jack Schofield, "A Jet Too Soon," *West Coast Aviator*, March 1999, pp. 12-17. The "even a bigger surprise down the road," of course, refers to the Diefenbaker government's abrupt and destructive cancellation of the Avro Arrow project, because the Jetliner wasn't scrapped until seven years after the first test flight.

23 Don Rogers, "Testing the Jetliner," *CAHS Journal*, Vol. 10, No. 1, Spring 1972, pp. 16-22.

24 Michael Cooper-Slipper, phone conversation, October 1999.

25 Schofield, "A Jet Too Soon", p. 16.

26 *Vancouver Province*, March 21, 1956, p. 5.

27 David H. Collins, *Wings Across Time: The Story of Air Canada*, p. 80. The H2, in 14-H2 (Super Electra) stood for two Hornet engines. The 1408 was equipped with two 900-hp Twin Wasp engines in place of the earlier version 750-hp Hornet engines.

28 J. T. Dyment, "Pratt & Whitney and Canada's National Airline," *CAHS Journal*, Vol. 26, No. 3, 1991, p. 90.

29 For a more comprehensive description of the operational problems encountered with the early Lockheed airliners, see Peter Corley-Smith, *Bush Flying to Blind Flying*, 1994. Herb Noble did not join TCA until shortly after the Second World War; however, he recalls many sessions in the hangar coffee room when veterans reminisced about the difficulties with the Hornet engines.

30 *Vancouver Sun*, March 29, 1939, p. 28.

31 Bothwell and Kilbourn, *C. D. Howe: A Biography*, p. 298.

32 Leslie Roberts, *The Life and Times . . .*, Chapter Thirteen.

33 Bothwell and Kilbourn, *C. D. Howe: A Biography*, p. 308.

34 Roberts, *The Life and Times . . .*, p. 143.

35 W. L. Morton, *The Kingdom of Canada*, p. 213.

36 *Ibid*, p. 215.

CHAPTER THREE

1 From Norris Crump's foreword in D. M. Bain, *Canadian Pacific Air Lines*, p. 5.

2 Ronald A. Keith, *Bush Pilot with a Briefcase*, p. 13.

3 However, since McConachie had flown Prince Leo Galitzine, with Galitzine's newly purchased Fokker Universal, G-CASE, from Winnipeg to Edmonton in January 1932, McConachie probably met the Princess before this.

4 Ellis, *Register of Civil Aircraft*. Previously I had published the claim that a diligent search of the *Register* had failed to reveal this aircraft. Thanks to a more diligent search by Ross Herrington of Regina and Bruce Gowans of Calgary, I am able to rectify this error.

5 *Edmonton Journal*, January 6, 1932, p. 11; via Bruce Gowans.

6 *Ibid*., February 16, 1932, p. 9; via Bruce Gowans.

7 "Argonaut of the Air," Canadian Broadcasting Corporation, radio program, Venture Series, May 3, 1964.

8 Gordon McCallum, "He Learned to Keep Steam Up," *Vancouver Province*, February 3, 1954, p. 6. McConachie later married Margaret MacLean.

9 BC Ministry of Lands and Surveys, File No. 1124077, Letter No. 0117659.

10 *The Albertan*, May 19, 1934; via Bruce Gowans

11 Keith, *Bush Pilot*, pp. 85-90.

12 He purchased it from the late mining magnate Harry Oakes for, he claimed, $2,500. Oakes, he said, had purchased it two years before for sightseeing trips over Niagara Falls. CBC tape, "Argonaut of the Air."

13 Jack Baker, interviewed by Karen Woodward, Fort St. John, December 2, 1975; BCARS tape No. 1893.

14 Shirlee Smith Matheson, *Flying the Frontiers*, Volume II.

15 Heath Twitchell, Jr., Lieut. Colonel, US Army. *The Decision to Build the Alaska Highway: How and Why it Was Done*, Report prepared for the Naval War College, April 4, 1977, p. 35.

16 Jack Petley, interviewed by R. D. Turner and Peter Corley-Smith, Penticton, November 14, 1994.

CHAPTER FOUR

1 *Vancouver Sun*, March 18, 1937.

2 Molson, *Pioneering*, p.199.

3 Interview by author and R. D. Turner, Fort St. James, July 13, 1991.

4 In fact, "President Murphy of the Board of Trade" had called a well-attended public meeting in Vancouver to recommend Northern Airways for the mail contract. (*Stewart Northern Argonaut*, April 7, 1938).

5 John Condit, *Wings Over the West*, p. 12, records that McConachie did purchase Bridge River & Cariboo Airways (the existing name of Ginger Coote's company).

6 Sheldon Luck Collection.

7 *Ibid*.

8 British Columbia Companies Register, File No. 13670.

9 M. L. McIntyre, "The Fleet Freighter," *CAHS Journal*, Vol. 7, No. 1, Spring 1959, p.3.

10 Apparently this was a flaw in the pitot head placement; McConachie had experienced the same failure twice in light rain on the delivery flight and forgot to advise Luck. The fog was evidently moist enough to cause another failure.

11 Sheldon Luck, interviewed in Oliver, BC, March 7, 1995.

12 CBC, "Argonaut of the Air."

13 Keith, *Bush Pilot*, p. 196.

14 See L. Milberry, *Aviation in Canada*, p. 58.

15 Walter Henry, "The Barkley-Grow T8P-1 in Canada," *CAHS Journal*, Vol. 16, No. 3, Fall 1978, pp. 74-81.

16 *Ibid*, p. 80.

17 CBC, "Argonaut of the Air."

18 *Ibid*.

19 Ellis, *Canadian Civil Aircraft Register*.

20 Keith, p. 200.

21 Ellis, *Canadian Civil Aircraft Register*.

22 This was the son of the Barney Phillips who had hired McConachie to put him into Two Brothers Lake and later provided the aircraft to found United Air Transport. He died in 1943 and the younger Phillips took his place, staying with McConachie for many years after.

23 CBC "Argonaut of the Air."

24 *Ibid.*

25 Keith, pp. 179-80.

26 In fact, the concept for aerial navigation was proposed a decade earlier than that. Arctic explorer Vilhjalmur Stefansson, in his book, *The Northward Course of Empire*, published in 1922, headed one of his chapters, "Transpolar Commerce by Air"; (quoted by William R. Hunt, *Stef: A Biography of Vilhjalmur Stefansson*).

27 *Whitehorse Star*, August 2, 1940, p. 1.

28 Richardson Collection, Manitoba Archives.

29 Cited in Molson, *Pioneering*, p. 235.

30 Gordon Ballentine Collection. Although Ballentine still has a copy of this letter, he cannot recall any specific reason for this statement; just that the two had been so competitive in Fort St. James that there was bound to be trouble if Baker were left there.

CHAPTER FIVE

1 *Vancouver Sun*, April 10, 1941, p. 1.

2 Munson, *Airliners*, p. 170.

3 Ellis, *Canadian Civil Aircraft Register*.

4 *Whitehorse Star*, June 6, 1941, p. 1.

5 *Ibid.*, August 1, 1941, p. 1

6 Keith, *Bush Pilot*, p. 236.

7 Lamb, *Canadian Pacific Railway*, p. 359.

8 *Ibid.*

9 Bain, *Canadian Pacific Air Lines*, p. 25.

10 Lamb, *Canadian Pacific Railway*, p. 357.

11 *Whitehorse Star*, April 24, 1946, p. 3.

12 Bain, *Canadian Pacific Air Lines*, p. 29.

13 Mansell Barron, interviewed in Kamloops, March 9, 1994.

14 Bain, *Canadian Pacific Air Lines*, records 15 DC-3s at the time.

15 *Vancouver Province*, June 1, 1948, p. 25.

16 Lamb, *Canadian Pacific Railway*, p. 364.

17 McConachie worked for the railways for only four years, so this would have represented a remarkably rapid series of promotions.

18 CBC, "Argonaut of the Air."

19 Keith, *Bush Pilot*, p. 255.

20 Eventually, Canadian Pacific Air Lines replaced the steam passenger liners with airliners for the luxury crossing of the Pacific. They were all, like the steamships, named "Empresses."

21 Keith, Bush Pilot, p. 225.

22 *Ibid.*, p. 266.

23 Lamb, *Canadian Pacific Railway*, p. 365.

24 Bain, *Canadian Pacific Air Lines*, p. 30; "between August 14, 1950, and March 30, 1955, nearly 40,000 military personnel were carried on 703 charter flights."

25 F. Maurice McGregor, interviewed by author and David N. Parker, Victoria, BC, May 22, 1985 (all McGregor quotes from this interview).

26 Bain, *Canadian Pacific Air Lines*, p. 31.

CHAPTER SIX

1 Robert D. Turner, *West of the Great Divide: An Illustrated History of the Canadian Pacific Railway in British Columbia 1880-1986*, p. 30.

2 *Ibid.*, pp. 5-6.

3 Lamb, *Canadian Pacific Railway*, p. 356.

4 C. Martin Sharp, *DH: A History of de Havilland*, p. 103.

5 Bain, *Canadian Pacific Air Lines*, p. 32.

6 Sharp, *DH: A History of de Havilland*, Appendix 13.

7 Bain, *Canadian Pacific Air Lines*, p. 30.

8 Keith, *Bush Pilot*, p. 284. Martin Sharp lists five CPA crew, five de Havilland men and one Smith's instruments engineer.

9 Bain, *Canadian Pacific Air Lines*, p. 84.

10 CPA carried 89 passengers on its longer routes, and up to 110 otherwise. W. C. (Cam) Cross, "Flying the Britannia with Canadian Pacific," *CAHS Journal*, Vol. 28, No, 1, Spring 1990, p. 24.

11 *Ibid.*

12 *Ibid.*, pp. 24-26 and 34.

13 Robert Francis, "The McConachie Story: World Airline Looks Homeward," *Saturday Night*, May 24, 1958, p. 15.

14 *Ibid.*

15 Keith, *Bush Pilot*, p. 297.

16 *Ibid.*, p. 298.

17 Bain, *Canadian Pacific Air Lines*, p. 33.

CHAPTER SEVEN

1 Condit, *Wings Over the West*, p. 8.

2 *Ibid.*

3 *Ibid.*, p. 9.

4 *Prince George Citizen*, February 2, 1939, p. 1.

5 Condit, *Wings*, p. 9 and 10

6 *Ibid.*

7 Baker's only available log book, Canada's Aviation Hall of Fame.

8 British Columbia Companies Register, No. 13678.

9 See Corley-Smith and Parker, *Helicopters: The British Columbia Story*, Chapter Five.

10 Interview by author and R. D. Turner, Fort St. James, July 13, 1991.

11 *Vancouver Province*, April 7, 1938.

12 British Columbia Companies Register, No. 13678, April 8, 1938.

13 Condit, *Wings*, p. 12.

14 *Vancouver Province*, February 5, 1938.

15 In fact, it was 18 years since Baker had flown the "Lone Moth."

16 *Victoria Colonist*, July 17, 1955, p.10.

17 This was the contract awarded without tender that Tommy Thompson, general manager of Canadian Airways, complained about bitterly.

18 *Whitehorse Star*, January 27, 1939, p. 1.

19 Sheldon Luck, interviewed in Penticton, March, 1993.

20 Ellis, *Canadian Civil Aircraft Register*.

21 1945 CPA Seniority List; Gordon Ballentine Collection.

22 Molson, *Pioneering*, p. 207.

23 Charlie Elliott, of Pacific Airways, was operating out of Fort St. James at the time with his Waco. He crashed at Tchentlo Lake in May. Elliott's engineer, William Martin, walked out over the mountains to Fort St. James and Baker flew out to rescue Elliott; but Elliott died in hospital a week later. Emil Bronlund was the Consolidated Mining & Smelting supervising geologist in Fort St. James. At the time, Bronlund was operating his own DH Hornet Moth.

24 Richardson Collection.

25 *Ibid.*

26 R. Carter Guest was the Department of Transport Inspector of Air Regulations for BC and the Yukon at the time.

27 The law firm would almost certainly be Williams, Manson, Brown & Harvey, which was practising in Prince Rupert at the time.

28 Sheldon Luck, interviewed in Penticton, March, 1993.

29 *Prince George Citizen*, July 14, 1938.

30 Condit, *Wings*, p. 16. Condit interviewed Emil Bronlund in 1978.

31 *Ibid.*

32 Overflow is a condition in which water or slush to a depth of several inches has flowed over the ice, lifting a crust of snow with it. It is often impossible to perceive this from the air.

33 Gordon Ballentine, "Winter of '39: Fort St. James," *CAHS Journal*, Vol. 22, No. 2, Summer 1984, pp. 47-50.

34 Canadian Airlines International Archives. Interestingly, the final paragraph of this memo is as follows: "I would ask you to keep this information as completely confidential and destroy this memo as when it was passed to me, it was not supposed to be forwarded and if the information were to get out it would cause me difficulty."

35 Condit, *Wings*.

36 *Ibid.*, p. 15.

37 It was certainly close: about three weeks. Baker, February 15, 1938; Ballentine, March 5, 1938. From the January 1945 CPA Seniority List, Gordon Ballentine Collection.

38 Gordon Ballentine Collection.

39 Ballentine, personal communication.

40 *Prince George Citizen*, October 22, 1942, p. 1.

CHAPTER EIGHT

1 Baker's untitled report of the episode, Canadian Airlines International Archives.

2 *Ibid.*

3 *Ibid.*

4 *Ibid.* It was common practice to stamp out a take-off runway after landing on a snow-covered lake.

5 Report, Re: "Three U.S. Medium Bombers—Lost Between Watson Lake & Fort Nelson, B.C."—Game Department, Fort Nelson Detachment, "D" Division, Peace River District, February 5, 1942. The report was submitted to Inspector T. Van Dyk, O.C. "D" Game Division, Prince George, BC.
   E. (Charlie) Estlin, formerly a policeman with the BCPP, and later a game warden, found this report among some other old documents at the abandoned detachment of Lower Post while on an inspection trip in the area.

6 In the small, one-man detachments, the policeman doubled as a game warden.

7 John W. (Jack) Purdy, *Was Justice Always Served?* Edited by Pat Meehan, 1992, pp. 18-22. Since no publisher is listed, this was presumably published by Purdy himself.

8 As well, there is a sticker on the first one: "This previously privileged information is released under a waiver signed by Sheila E. Widnall, Secretary of the Air Force, dated 23 January 1996. This waiver authorizes unrestricted release of aviation accident reports prior to 25 January 1956." One cable has hand written annotations, "Coded" and "Filed in safe."

9 All of the above gratefully received from the US Air Force Historical Research Agency, Maxwell AFB, Alabama.

10 Jack Baker, interviewed in Fort St. John, June 10, 1997.

[11] Gordon Cameron, interviewed in Calgary, July 10, 1997.

[12] Stan Bridcut, interviewed in Whitehorse, May 30, 1997.

[13] Courtesy Howard F. Smiley.

[14] In January 1943, Howard Smiley was rotated back from the Aleutians to the 3rd Air Force Training Command in the US and stationed at Avon Park, Florida. He ended his tour of active duty as Base Executive Officer, Lake Charles, La. Air Base in July 1945, and returned to the practice of law that he had left to join the Air Corps in 1940. In 1964, he resigned from the USAF Reserve as a Lieutenant-Colonel.

[15] Condit, *Wings*, p. 65.

[16] Pierre Berton, *Just Add Water and Stir*, p. 30.

[17] Alexander Report.

[18] Condit, *Wings*, p. 48.

CHAPTER NINE

[1] Howard Smiley complains of inflationary poetic licence. "We were always led to believe that the cost of the B-26 was $250,000 each, WWII prices."

[2] Herman Peterson, interviewed in Atlin, May 14, 1997.

[3] Gordon Cameron, interviewed in Calgary, July 10, 1997.

[4] The American Pilgrim, CF-BUA, was still registered to the British-Yukon Navigation Company at the time, but sold to Yukon Southern/Canadian Pacific later that year (Ellis, *Canadian Civil Aircraft Register*).

[5] Lloyd Ryder, interviewed in Whitehorse, July 10, 1997.

[6] From a photocopy of an *Air Combat* article provided by someone who found it in the effects of a deceased relative. Unfortunately, the copy does not include the date of the issue nor the author's name. However, courtesy of Howard Smiley, I learned that a similar article was published in *Air Classics Quarterly*, Spring 1976, and the author is Richard Shepard.

[7] Courtesy Howard Smiley.

[8] Harry S. Truman Library, File 357 (December 18, 1947), National Archives of Canada.

[9] Russ Baker Collection, National Archives of Canada.

[10] *Ibid.* It would be interesting to see this account, which must have differed considerably from the one previously quoted because Colonel Cork (who recommended Baker for the award) would know that Baker had never been involved in the search for the missing bombers.

[11] *Ibid.*

[12] Condit, *Wings*, p. 27.

[13] Canadian Airlines International Archives.

[14] Sheldon Luck, interviewed in Oliver, April 14, 1997 (but Luck is scarcely an unprejudiced witness; he accused Baker of recklessness for landing on the rough water of Stuart Lake when he first met him).

[15] *Globe and Mail*, September 7, 1996, p. A1.

[16] Transportation Safety Board of Canada Website, Accident Report #a95h0012, n.d.

CHAPTER TEN

[1] Canadian Airlines Archives.

[2] *Ibid.*, p. 4. Condit records Madge Baker's claim that she was the real founder of the company because she found the money for the lawyer's fee from her housekeeping budget. She vehemently repeated this to me in a personal conversation at the Junkers Day celebration at Fort St. James in July 1991.

[3] Jim Spilsbury, interviewed by author and Robert D. Turner, Horseshoe Bay, February 1994.

[4] Canadian Airlines Archives.

[5] Condit, *Wings*, p. 47.

[6] The implication is that this was continuous flying time; in which case one is tempted to suggest that Baker must have encountered the jet stream head on during this trip. Germansen Landing is 150 miles (240 km) from Prince George in a straight line. Allowing another 30 miles (50 km) for deviations around high ground, this would have meant a ground speed of approximately 24 mph (38 km/h), and a headwind in the neighbourhood of 70 mph (110 km/h). Moreover, the fuel endurance of the Junkers 34 was just under five hours (K. M. Molson, *Pioneering in Canadian Air Transport*, p. 293), so he must have had to land to refuel. The description in the *Prince George Citizen* (July 14, 1938) was a little more specific: ". . . bucking snow, hail . . . [etc.] for a total flying time of seven and a half hours."

[7] Pierre Berton, *Vancouver Sun*, February 3, 1947, p. 1.

[8] *Vancouver Sun*, February 8, 1947, p. 1.

[9] A new addition to the legend.

[10] *Vancouver Sun*, February 11, 1947.

[11] Condit, *Wings*, p. 50.

[12] *Vancouver Sun*, February 15, 1947, p. 1.

[13] Condit, *Wings*, p. 48.

[14] Pierre Berton, *Toronto Star*, November 22, 1958.

[15] In a typed summary, headed "CERTIFIED FLYING TIME, of Baker's hours from July 8, 1937 to February 8, 1938. It is certified under the signature of "R. L. 'Ginger' Coote, Vice-President United Air Transport Limited," and is in the Canadian Airlines Archives.

[16] Condit, *Wings*, p. 48.

[17] Canadian Airlines Archives.

[18] Condit, *Wings*, p. 67.

[19] *Ibid.*, p. 68.

20 *Ibid.*, p. 54.

21 *Ibid.*, p. 40.

CHAPTER ELEVEN

1 Howard White and Jim Spilsbury, *The Accidental Airline: Spilsbury's QCA*, pp. 16-17.

2 *Ibid.*, p. 58.

3 *Ibid.*, p. 59.

4 Hank Elway quickly joined QCA, and later, when he left that company, became one of the pioneer engineers for Okanagan Helicopters.

5 White and Spilsbury, *The Accidental Airline*, p. 66.

6 Almost all of the above is paraphrased from *The Accidental Airline*. For some curious reason, very little else has been written about the early development of this interesting venture.

7 The use of the word "hops"—instead of "flights"—in 1946 is an intriguing throwback to the very early days of flying, when most flights usually were little more than hops.

8 *Prince Rupert Daily News*, March 8, 1946, p. 1.

9 White and Spilsbury, *Accidental Airline*, p. 71.

10 *Daily News*, March 11, 1946, p 2.

11 Jim Spilsbury interviewed by author and R. D. Turner, Horseshoe Bay. February 2, 1994.

12 Richard Overstall, "The Sovereign State of Alcan," *Telkwa Foundation Newsletter*, Vol. 6, No. 1, Spring 1983, p. 2.

13 *Ibid.*, p. 3.

14 *Ibid.*

15 Canadian Airlines Archives.

16 Condit, *Wings*, pp. 71-72.

17 *Ibid.*, p. 78.

18 There is a stack of photocopies of this correspondence in the Canadian Airlines Archives more than two inches (6 cm) thick.

19 Personal communication.

20 May 28, 1953, British Columbia Companies Register, File No. 019459.

21 Canadian Airlines Archives.

22 *Ibid.*

23 Condit, *Wings*, p. 83.

24 *Victoria Daily Colonist*, June 26, 1952.

25 *Vancouver Sun*, March 20, 1954, p. 1.

26 *Ibid.*, November 2, 1953, p. 1.

27 *Vancouver Province*, December 1, 1953.

28 Joan McLeod, interviewed in Errington, BC, February, 1983.

29 Bill and Joan McLeod, interviewed by author and David N. Parker, Errington BC, September 1982.

30 *Victoria Daily Colonist*, October 31, 1951, p. 1.

31 Canadian Airlines Archives.

32 *Ibid.*

33 Condit, *Wings*, p. 107.

34 *Vancouver Sun*, June 3, 1955, pp. 1 & 2.

35 White and Spilsbury, *Accidental Airline*, pp. 241-42. Spilsbury confirmed this claim in an interview with the author in 1994.

36 Curly Nairn, interviewed by author and R. D. Turner, Kamloops, March 1994.

CHAPTER TWELVE

1 *Vancouver Daily Province*, March 1, 1946, p. 8.

2 *Vancouver Sun*, January 19, 1967, p. 33.

3 Condit, *Wings*, (quoted in the Foreword), p. vii.

4 Berton, *Just Add Water and Stir*, p. 29.

5 Margaret Rutledge (*née* Fane), interviewed by author and D. N. Parker, March 10, 1989.

6 Stuart Keate, "Seven Canadian Birdwomen," *Toronto Star Weekly*, January 16, 1937, p. 5.

7 *Richmond News Advertiser*, February 1, 1978, p. 14.

8 Margaret Rutledge (*née* Fane), interviewed by author and D. N. Parker, March 10, 1989.

9 Elianne Roberge was the only other member of the "Flying Seven" with a commercial licence before the Second World War, which she earned later in Montreal.

10 Eileen Learoyd, "Girl Pilots Take the Air," *Victoria Daily Colonist*, November 14, 1948, p. 3.

11 Dick Rummel, "Glamor Aloft," *Vancouver Sun*, May 4, 1940, p. 3.

12 *Ibid.*

13 Donna Anderson, "Stewardess from the Start," *Vancouver Sun*, May 17, 1974, p. 40.

14 Interview with Eleanore Begg (*née* Moore), taped at her Vancouver home on August 9, 1996.

15 *Vancouver Sun* interview, May 17, 1974, p. 40.

16 The Canso was an amphibian; it would land wheels-up on the water at Seal Cove, on the outskirts of Prince Rupert. The pilot could then lower the wheels and taxi up the inclined ramp to the hangar.

CHAPTER THIRTEEN

1 This must have been a Laurentide Air Services Ltd. aircraft; if so, it was probably a Viking rather than a Vedette. Stuart Graham later became the Department of Transport Inspector for Quebec and the Maritimes.

2 Herman Peterson, interviewed by author and R. D. Turner in Atlin, 1995.

3 Doris Peterson, interviewed by author and R. D. Turner in Atlin, 1995.

4 This was the aircraft George Simmons had bought in his attempt to beat out McConachie for the mail contract between Vancouver and Whitehorse.

5 The rudder control cables on the Fairchild 71 led down the inside of the fuselage, emerging to the outside through fairleads some four feet (1.2 m) from the tail section. They were attached to two horns protruding on either side of the rudder.

6 Roy Minter, *The White Pass: Gateway to the Klondike*, p. 229.

7 Lancelot Press, Hantsport, Nova Scotia, first published 1992.

8 By then, Alf Stringer was president of Vancouver Island Helicopters.

9 See Corley-Smith, *Bush Flying to Blind Flying*, Chapter Eleven.

10 Lyman Sands, interviewed in Atlin, May 30, 1997.

11 See Corley-Smith, *Barnstorming to Bush Flying*, Chapter Ten.

12 *Ibid.*, Chapter Three.

13 Charlie and Julie Callbraith, interviewed in Prince Rupert, December 4, 1998.

14 R. B. (Bob) Cameron, interviewed in Whitehorse, October 26, 1998.

Bibliography

Ashley, C. A. *A Study of Trans-Canada Air Lines: The First Twenty-Five Years*. Macmillan, New York, NY, 1963.

Bain, D. M. *Canadian Pacific Air Lines: Its History and Aircraft*. Kishorn Publications, Calgary, AB, 1987.

Beatty, Sir Edward W. *Letterbooks*. Canadian Pacific Railway Corporate Archives, Montreal, PQ.

Berton, Pierre. *Just Add Water and Stir*. McClelland & Stewart, Toronto, ON, 1959.

Bothwell, Robert and William Kilbourn. *C. D. Howe: A Biography*. McClelland and Stewart, Toronto, ON, 1979.

Cohen, Stan. *The Trail of '42: A Pictorial History of the Alaska Highway*. Pictorial Histories Publishing, Missoula, MO, 1993.

Collins, David H. *Wings Across Time: The Story of Air Canada*. Griffin House, Toronto, ON, 1978.

Condit, John. *Wings Over the West: Russ Baker and the Rise of Pacific Western Airlines*. Harbour Publishing, Madeira Park, BC, 1984.

Corley-Smith, Peter. *Bush Flying to Blind Flying*. Sono Nis Press, Victoria, BC, 1993.

Corley-Smith, Peter and David N. Parker. *Helicopters: The BC Story*, Sono Nis Press, Victoria, BC, 1998.

Davies, R. E. G. *A History of the World's Airlines*. Oxford University Press, Oxford, UK, 1964.

Duffy, Dennis and Carol Crane, eds., commentary by David N. Parker. *The Magnificent Distances: Early Aviation in British Columbia, 1910-1940*. Sound Heritage Series No. 28, Provincial Archives of British Columbia, Victoria, BC, 1980.

Ellis, Frank H. *Canada's Flying Heritage*. University of Toronto Press, Toronto, ON, 1954.

Ellis, John R. *Canadian Civil Aircraft Register, 1929-1945*. Canadian Aviation Historical Society, Markham, ON, 1972-75.

Gardner, Alison. *Grant McConachie*. Fitzhenry & Whiteside, Toronto, ON, 1979.

Hotson, F. W. *The De Havilland Canada Story*. Canav Books, Toronto, 1983.

Hunt, W. R. *Stef: A Biography of Vilhjalmur Stefansson*. University of British Columbia Press, Vancouver, BC, 1986.

Keith, R. A. *Bush Pilot with a Briefcase*. Doubleday, Toronto, ON, 1972.

Lamb, W. Kaye. *History of the Canadian Pacific Railway*. Macmillan, Toronto, ON, 1977.

Main, J. R. K. *Voyageurs of the Air*. Queen's Printer, Ottawa, ON, 1967.

Matheson, Shirlee Smith. *Flying the Frontiers, Volume II*. Detselig Enterprises, Calgary, AB, 1996.

Minter, Roy. *The White Pass: Gateway to the Klondike*. McClelland and Stewart, Toronto, ON, 1987.

Mitcham, Allison. *Atlin, the Last Utopia*. Lancelot Press, Hantsport, NS, 1992.

Molson, K. M. *Pioneering in Canadian Air Transport*. James Richardson & Sons, Winnipeg, MB, 1974.

Morton, W. L. *The Kingdom of Canada*. McClelland & Stewart, Toronto, ON, 1963.

Munson, Kenneth. *Airliners from 1919 to the Present Day*. Peerage Books, London, UK, 1972.

Ormsby, Margaret A. *British Columbia: A History*. Macmillan, Toronto, ON, 1958.

Patterson, R. M. *Trail to the Interior*. William Sloan, Toronto, ON, 1966.

Pigott, Peter. *Wing Walkers: A History of Canadian Airlines International*. Harbour Publishing, Madeira Park, BC, 1998.

Purdy, John (Jack). *Was Justice Always Served?* Edited by Pat Meehan, Vancouver, BC, 1992.

Render, Shirley. *Double Cross: James A. Richardson and Canadian Airways*. Douglas & McIntyre, Vancouver, BC, 1999.

Roberts, Leslie. *C. D: The Life and Times of Clarence Decatur Howe*. Clarke, Urwin, Toronto, ON, 1957.

Sharp, C. Martin. *DH: A History of de Havilland*. Airlife Publishing, Shrewsbury, UK, 1982.

Stefansson, Vilhjalmur. *The Northward Course of Empire*, 1922.

Stonier-Newman, Lynne. *Policing a Pioneer Province*. Harbour Publishing, Madeira Park, BC, 1991.

Sutherland, Alice Gibson. *Canada's Aviation Pioneers: 50 Years of McKee Trophy Winners*. McGraw-Hill Ryerson, Toronto, ON, 1978.

Taylor, J. W .R., Kenneth Munson and John Stroud, eds. *History of Aviation: Air Transport Before the Second World War*. New England Library, 1975.

Turner, Robert D. *West of the Great Divide: An Illustrated History of the Canadian Pacific Railway in British Columbia 1880-1986*. Sono Nis Press, Victoria, BC, 1987.

Twitchell, Jr. *The Decision to Build the Alaska Highway: How and Why it Was Done*. US Naval War College, April 4, 1977, p. 35.

White, Howard and Jim Spilsbury. *The Accidental Airline: Spilsbury's QCA*. Harbour Publishing, Madeira Park, BC, 1988.

JOURNALS

American Aviation Historical Society Journal
American Helicopter Association Journal
BC Aviator
British Columbia Historical Quarterly
Bulletin: the *Journal of Canadian Airways*
Canadian Aviation
Canadian Aviation Historical Society Journal
Canadian Geographical Society Journal
Cariboo Digest
Northwest Digest
Saturday Night
West Coast Aviator
Western Canada Aviation Museum Digest

NEWSPAPERS

The *Alberton*
The Calgary *Daily Herald*
The *Edmonton Journal*
The Kamloops *Inland Sentinel*
The Lethbridge *Herald*
The Prince George *Citizen*
The Prince Rupert *Evening Empire*

The Stewart *Northern Argonaut*
The Vancouver *Province*
The Vancouver *Sun*
The Victoria *Daily Colonist*
The Victoria *Daily Times*
The *Whitehorse Star*

INTERVIEWS

Baker, Jack
Ballentine, Gordon
Barron, Mansell
Begg, Eleanore
Bridcut, Stan
Cameron, Gordon
Cameron, Robert (Bob)
Cowden, Eric
Estlin, Charles
Fisher, Dick
Luck, Sheldon
McGregor, Maurice

McLeod, Bill and Joan
Morrison, Nina
Nairn, Curly
Noble, Herb
Peterson, Herman and Doris
Petley, Jack
Ross, Bill
Ryder, Lloyd
Sands, Lyman
Smiley, Howard
Spilsbury, Jim
Williamson, George

Index

About the Author

Born in India, educated in England, with degrees as a mature student from the University of Victoria and the University of Montana, Peter Corley-Smith served as an SOE pilot in the Royal Air Force in World War II, became in turn a miner, surveyor, cartographer, commercial helicopter pilot and college instructor before becoming a history curator. Since retirement, he has served as a Research Associate at the Royal British Columbia Museum. His previous books include: *10,000 Hours, A Helicopter Pilot in the North*; *Helicopters: The B.C. Story* (with Dave Parker); *Barnstorming to Bush Flying*; *Helicopters in the High Country* (with Dave Parker); and *Bush Flying to Blind Flying*. His latest book is *Wings Over the Alaska Highway* (with Bruce McAllister).